Grand Opera

Grand Opera

The Story of the World's Leading Opera Houses and Personalities

Edited by
Anthony Gishford

Introduced by
Benjamin Britten

A Studio Book · The Viking Press · New York

Contents

Acknowledgments

I have to acknowledge with gratitude advice, encouragement, and help from the following well-disposed persons: Sir Ove Arup, Dr. Jürgen Balzer, Madame Grete Belfrage, Mr. Terence Benton, Sir Isaiah Berlin, Mr. Marcus Binney, Dr. Roberto Caamaño, Mr. Moran Caplat, The Hon. Kensington Davidson, Dr. Karel Eckstein, Madame Irina Elkonin-Johansson, Mrs. Thorneley Gibson, The Earl of Harewood, Mr. Gordon Harrison, Dr. Gustaf Hilleström, Mr. Irving Kolodin, Dr. Brigitte Lohmeyer, Dr. Walter Mitchell, Mr. Nicholas Nabokov, Mr. G. W. Nash, Mrs. Mary De Witt Pelz, Dr. Hans Pischner, Mr. Derek Sugden.

I appreciate the consideration shown me by my collaborators (amongst whom I would particularly mention Mr. Harold Rosenthal, who placed his wide knowledge constantly at my disposal and was generous with his time through every phase of the book's preparation) and by the editorial and art department of Messrs. George Weidenfeld and Nicolson, with whose members it has been a pleasure to work.

And I am doubly indebted to Sir George Weidenfeld himself – first, for having the idea, and second, for entrusting me with its execution.

A. G.

Acknowledgments

The author and publishers wish to record their gratitude for permission received from owners, agents and photographers to reproduce the following list of illustrations (numbers refer to pictures):

Black and white illustrations

Boosey and Hawkes Ltd; Roller designs for *Der Rosenkavalier* used decoratively throughout the book.

Aldeburgh Festival office, 116 (photo Rosamund Strode), 117; Archiv für Kunst and Geschichte, 39, 44, 51, 62, 143; Australian Information Service, 163 (photo W. Brindle); Bettmann Archive Inc. New York, 140, 150; Rudolf Betz, Munich, 60; Bibliothèque Nationale, Paris, 13; Brogi, 12; Camera Press, 34, 111; Civica Raccolta Stampe Bertarelli, Milan, 98; Covent Garden Opera House, London, Photographic Archives, (photos Werner Forman); 99, 100, 101, 103, 105, 110, 112, 113; Culver Pictures Inc., 86; Die Staatsoper, Berlin, Photographic Archives, 37, 38, 40, 41, 42, 43; Die Deutsche Oper, Berlin, 48, 49 (and photo Jise Buhs), 50 (and Heinz Köster), John Donat, 117; Drottningholm Theatre and Lennart af Petersens, 118, 119, 120, 121, 122, 123; Max Dupain, Sydney, 162; Max Erlanger de Roser: Paris, 23; La Fenice, Venice, Photographic Archives, 7, 8, 9; Foto Lala Aufsberg, 70; Fotospielleitung Bayreuth, 68 and 71 (photos Lauterwasser), 72, 75, 76, 77, 79 (photo, Wilhelm Rauch); Foto Studio Sabine Toepffer, 61; Adi Gerhauser: Munich, 73; Gyndebourne Photographic Archives (photo Guy Gravett) 114, 115; Gjon Mili: New York, 142; Institut für Theaterwissenschaft, University of Cologne, 45, 52, 54; Armas Järnefelt, 128; Die Komische Oper, Berlin, 46 (and Arwid Lagenpusch); Siegrfried Lauterwasser, Bayreuth, 69; Liceo, Barcelona, Photographic Archives, 80, 182; The Lyric Opera: Chicago, 155a; Mansell Collection, 5, 14, 21, 155; M.A.S.: Barcelona, 8, 83; Metropolitan Opera, New York, Photographic Archives, 141, 144, 146, 148 (photo Joseph Costa, courtesy Sylvania Electric Products Inc.), 149, (photo Louis Mélancon), 151, 152, 153, 154; Alberto Montacchini, Parma, 16, 17; Musée de l'Arsenal and J. Colomb-Gerard, 31, 36; Museum of Modern Art, New York, 145; National Portrait Gallery, London, 104; Nuova Editoriale, Venice, 11; Novosti Press Agency, 131, 132, 134, 135; L'Opéra, Paris, Photographic Archives and Photo Pic, 19, 20, 24, 25, 26, 26a; Opera News, New York, 139; Österreichischen National-bibliothek (Bildarchiv), 56, 84, 85, 87, 88, 89, 90, 91, 92, 93, 102; Provincial Tourist Office, Parma and Photo Tosi:, 18; Radio Times Hulton Picture Library, 147; G. Ricordi and Co, Milan, 10; Royal Opera House, Stockholm and Lennart af Petersens, 124, 125, 126, 127, 129; San Francisco Opera House Archives, 156, 156a; Service de Documentation Photographique, 28; La Scala, Milan Photographic Archives, 1, 2, 3, 4, 6 (Courtesy Harold Rosenthal); Die Staatsoper, Hamburg, Information Service, 57 and 58 (photo B. Himmler), 64 (photo Peyer), 65, 66, (photo Elisabeth Speidel), 67, (photo Peyer); Dr. Jaromir Svoboda, Prague, 94, 95, 97; Teatro Colón, Buenos Aires, Photographic Archives, 157, 158, 159, 160, 161; Theatermuseum, Munich, 53, 55, 59; Roger Viollet (and Photo Lernitzki), 27, 29, 30, 32, 33, 35; Richard Wagner Gedenkstätte, Bayreuth, 74, 78.

Colour Illustrations

Izis Bidermanas VII; Civic Museum, Bologna (photos Scala, Florence) II, III; Deutsche Oper: Berlin (photo Uwe Rau) XII; Werner Forman XVI; Josef Keller Verlag, Starnberg VIII; Siegfried Lauterwasser XIV; Magnum (photo Erich Lessing) XV; Mozarteum, Salzburg (photo Werner Forman) V; Roger Pic VI; Phèdon Salou Photographe IX; La Scala, Milan I; Theatermuseum, Munich X, XI, XIII (photo Claus Hansmann); University of Arizona (photo Western Ways) XVIII; Reg Wilson XVII.

Introduction

I was most interested to learn that my friend Anthony Gishford was producing a book on opera, in the context of the great Opera Houses of the world. His knowledge of the subject is wide, for he has been a keen amateur of opera all his life, and for the last twenty years or so he has actively taken part in its administration, encouraging those who perform and create it.

I am interested in the book because for thirty years writing operas has been my main musical occupation. Many complain about this, those who do not like the medium, who distrust it ('impure!'), would rather I wrote more symphonies, quartets, concertos, song cycles and cello suites. Be that as it may, ever since those fruitless struggles with *Paul Bunyan* up to the immediate struggles with the problems of *Death in Venice* I have been fascinated by the most powerful medium of musical communication that I know.

There have always been Cassandras. Before *Peter Grimes* there was no future for an English opera. In spite of its favourable reception in 1945 those responsible for its production were all summarily removed from Sadlers Wells. There was no money (there never is) for opera, so a group of friends and I tried to devise a cheaper form of it – no chorus, tiny cast, an orchestra of twelve. After a successful opening of *The Rape of Lucretia* at Gyndebourne and an encouraging visit abroad, a dismal tour of the English provinces followed – 'casts must be international' – and so we were compelled to start our own opera group, and our own Aldeburgh Festival.

In Germany the destroyed opera houses were going to be rebuilt, and indeed in London at the last minute Boosey and Hawkes had rescued the Royal Opera House from being turned into a Dance Hall, but the outlook was uncertain and Covent Garden was hardly the place for small-scale opera. At Aldeburgh we made do with the Jubilee Hall. The critical Cassandras had again raised their voices – if only another *Peter Grimes* rather than these chamber affairs – *The Times* damned *Albert Herring*. But thank goodness the old piece survived, since many a small struggling opera company has relied on it to keep going, and five years ago Budapest totted up its fiftieth performance.

But art never wants to stand still, even the art of opera was once new and strange: even if all the great popular favourites of today belong to the proscenium-arch theatres, it has to express itself in the framework of an ever changing society. So we tried operas for children and by children, audience participation, operas in churches (usually the best buildings in small towns and villages), and finally opera on the open stage (the Maltings). And so it goes on.

Opera is not dead. The book before you demonstrates this. The view across the centuries is magnificent, revealing much beauty and truth, tragic, every-day – even occasionally funny.

One learns much from the past, but one is living in the present. There are many daunting problems, but there is much that is encouraging: think, in Britain alone, of the success of Covent Garden, the astonishing rise of the Coliseum, the Scottish and Welsh operas and the possibility of a new company for the Midlands. Among the many problems, the financial one daunts us the most, with costs rising everywhere, and experimental works scarcely getting a look in. Opera has always cost a lot of money. But since there are today no princelings to put their hands deep in their pockets and show that the Darmstadt opera is as good as the Kassel one, now all opera houses are in receipt of substantial subsidies from the state, the municipality, from private communities of opera lovers, from great and small charities, from radio and television and even (if we are very lucky) from business firms. Yet not all of these together can dam the rising tide of costs. The answer seems to be that composers, producers, organisers of operas (or 'music-theatre' as some people prefer it to be called) must be flexible, think of different ways of presenting them, ways that suit the all-purpose hall, the factory canteen, the school gym, the college campus, with good lighting, or no lighting, with elaborate costumes, or in every-day dress, full orchestra or piano and drums – they will all work as long as singers can act and actors can sing, the producer can produce, the conductor (if there is one) can conduct, and composers can find the right notes.

For the great repertoire of the last three hundred years the beautiful baroque houses so well described and lavishly illustrated in this book will always be needed. This is what most people still consider to be 'going to the opera', but it isn't the only way.

Benjamin Britten

Foreword

Opera, over the past 450 years, has proved itself a resilient art with an organic life of its own. Except for photography and the cinema, it is the newest art form to have come into existence and persisted. And this despite the fact that it is the most complex of all art forms – more complicated than either the theatre or the cinema – bringing and welding together as it does a number of separate arts and a variety of almost inevitably disparate personalities who must work in a kind of chain-gang, the links of which are rarely all of the same strength. It demands, because of the sung word, a more exacting 'suspension of disbelief' than either the theatre *or* the cinema. It seems disaster prone, both by its nature and gratuitously. It is as irresistible to its addicts as the green baize table to gamblers.

The psychology of opera audiences would really be worth a study in itself – audience acceptance, audience rejection; the reasons why works come into fashion and go out of fashion; why, at some periods, opera should be 'fashionable' in the sense of providing rich people with an opportunity to dress up and show themselves off; how much of the spell derives from the voice itself, as distinct from the personality of the singer; whether singers create their own myth, or whether audiences create it for them because they like the voice and therefore feel a need to like the owner of the voice.

The possibilities are endless, and the fact remains: opera can unite in a collective emotional response more people from every segment of the social spectrum than any other form of organized activity except association football, horse-racing and bullfighting.

In the following pages we shall see some of the settings in which this magic is performed, some of the magicians and their equipment, some of the spectators; something of the differing *ambiance* in different places, at different times. But the thing itself – opera – will still be as much of a mystery on the last page as on the first.

A G

ITALY

Preamble

Bella Italia,
Alfin ti miro, alfin ti miro . . .

Ah! del Ciel e della terra,
Bella Italia sei l'amor[1]

These are the words with which Selim, the eponymous Turk of Rossini's *Il Turco in Italia*, greets Italy as he steps ashore from his ship near Naples. They are the words which all of us who love Italy would certainly re-echo, and they explain why we love to return time and time again to that country of sunshine, warmth and song. When one comes to think of it, Italy is the only country that *could* have given birth to opera, and its opera houses are, without doubt, the most beautiful and atmospheric temples of the art in the world.

It was in Tuscany, the very heart of Italy, that opera was born – in Florence, that most cultivated of cities. There, in 1597, Peri's *Dafne* was produced; it was the result of the establishment of the *Camerata*, a group of poets and musicians including Peri, Caccini, de' Cavalieri and Rinuccini, who met regularly in a room (hence *camerata*) in the houses of two Florentine nobles, Giovanni de' Bardi and Jacopo Corsi. The aim of this group was to restore the dramatic use of music as practised in classical Greek drama; and if the final results were not quite that, it was from their discussions and experiments that the new art form, which eventually was to become known as 'opera', emerged.

Although Florence was the birthplace of opera, and has, since 1656, always possessed a theatre situated at No. 12 Via della Pergola (the Teatro della Pergola), it cannot boast an operatic history comparable to those of Milan, Naples or Venice. Nor are its two opera houses, the Comunale and Pergola, part of the *lingua franca* of the operatic world (professional and amateur), as are the Teatro alla Scala, the San Carlo, La Fenice and even the Regio of Parma. It is as if Florence, having given the world the art form we know as opera, decided to leave to other cities the struggles, the intrigues, the triumphs and the failures – in fact all the fun of Italian opera.

1 'La' Malibran died at Manchester in 1836 at the age of 28, as the delayed result of a fall from her horse. Alfred de Musset mourned her passing in a poem of 27 verses. This portrait of her is by Luigi Pedrazzi.

La Scala
Milan

'There are in Italy two theatres of major importance,' wrote Stendhal in his famous *Life of Rossini*, 'La Scala in Milan and the San Carlo in Naples.' He then continues:

> The Teatro alla Scala can hold three thousand five hundred spectators with the greatest of ease and comfort, and there are, if I remember rightly, two hundred and twenty boxes, each seating three people in front, in a position to watch the stage; but, except at premières, there are never more than two people occupying these seats, the escorted lady and her recognized gallant and servitor, while the remainder of the box, or rather salon, may contain anything up to nine or ten persons, who are perpetually coming and going all the evening. Silence is observed only at premières; or, during subsequent performances, only while one or other of the memorable passages is being performed.

Today the theatre seats 3,600 spectators and has rather fewer boxes – but Stendhal's description is still valid – though I have been conscious of chatter even at premières! How, then, has it happened that Milan, which, unlike Florence and Naples, could not boast a Monteverdi, a Cavalli or a Scarlatti in the days when opera was developing in Italy, was able to build itself a theatre which has become the most famous opera house in the world; a theatre where virtually every performance is an occasion, and where the spirit of dedication is, more often than not, at least in evidence on one side of the footlights?

Opera was rather late in establishing itself in Milan because of the rigid moral code imposed on the city by Carlo Borromeo, who was Archbishop of Milan from 1560 until his death in 1584, and continued by his son, Frederico. Despite an attitude which one might call puritanical, a theatre was opened in the ducal palace in 1598 in honour of Princess Margherita of Austria, who was on her way to Spain to marry Philip III. The theatre's official name was the Regio Ducale, but it was affectionately known to the Milanese as the Salone Margherita. Although occasional operatic performances were given there, Milan's preference was for orchestral works, oratorios and cantatas; only in the mid-eighteenth century did Milan begin to announce performances of new works; first by foreign composers, including the young Gluck, five of whose early operas were staged at the Regio Ducale; and then by Milanese composers, including Lampugnani (1706–81) whose early successes in Milan led to his being summoned to London to succeed Galuppi as composer in residence at the King's Theatre, and who, quite early in La Scala's history, was appointed as *maestro al cembalo*.

On 26 December 1770, Lampugnani played the second *cembalo* at the Ducale on the occasion of the first performance of a new opera, *Mitradate, Re di Ponto*, by a young composer called Mozart; less than a year later the fifteen-year-old Mozart produced his *Ascanio in Alba*, written for the wedding of the Archduke Ferdinand and Princess Maria Ricciarda Beatrice of Modena, and in 1772, his

11 Teatro alla Scala, Milan. Perhaps the most famous opera house in the world. Detail of a painting by Angelo Inganni, 1852.

1 Site of the present Milan Opera House.

Lucio Silla. At last Milan was becoming really opera-minded; then, on the night of 25 February 1776, the Ducale was burned down. The box holders wanted a new theatre, and they appealed to Maria Theresa, Empress of Austria and Duchess of Milan, for permission to build one on the site of the Church of Santa Maria della Scala and the adjoining Scuola Cannobiane. The land cost the box holders 120,000 lire; the building of the new theatre, to the plans of the great architect Giuseppe Piermarini, cost them a further 1,400,000 lire. The box holders retained the private ownership of the boxes and were allowed to display their coats of arms on the front of them; and many famous Milanese families have inherited their boxes down to this day. The completed theatre was named after Regina della Scala, wife of Duke Bernado Visconti (the same Visconti family which today boasts among its members the outstanding producer Luchino Visconti).

Despite its virtually complete destruction during an air raid in 1943, La Scala has altered very little since it opened on 3 August 1778, with Salieri's *Europa Riconosciuta*. The stage is larger and higher, the orchestra pit wider and deeper, the foyer and vestibules much improved; but the decorations of the enormous and traditional horseshoe-shaped auditorium, with the ceiling coming right down to the sixth and top tier of seats, is both beautiful and restrained; and although Piermarini's eighteenth century interior decorations were replaced by those of Sanquirico in neo-classical style in 1830, the interior structure and beautiful proportions of the auditorium remain unaltered. Externally La Scala is not enormously impressive; it has neither the grandeur of the Vienna State Opera nor the classical portico of the National Theatre in Munich; yet its façade of yellow and white blends subtly with the surrounding commercial buildings.

Perhaps modern electric lights may be harder than the Argand lamps[2] first introduced in 1788, or the gas lighting installed in 1860; but nothing can prevent that magic moment in the auditorium when the lights dim. At La Scala the centre chandelier and clusters of lights round the tiers dim first, leaving the lights in the boxes and galleries on a little longer, then these fade slowly. To quote Stendhal again, 'Nothing on earth is better fitted to prime the soul into a state of musical receptivity than the little thrill of pleasure that runs through the audience as the curtain goes up at La Scala, and the magnificence of the set is revealed for the first time.'

Milan, because of its geographical position in Lombardy, on the road to Florence and Rome, has seen many invading armies come and go; it is natural, therefore, that La Scala should have reflected Italian political and social history. There were the festivities to mark the coronation of the Emperor Joseph II in 1793, with free admittance to everyone; there were the ballets *Junius Brutus* and *The Pope's Dances* or *General Colli in Rome* in 1797 to mark the end of the Austrian domination and the dawn of the 'age of reason' under the French, when the huge royal box was divided into six smaller boxes reserved for the 'liberated people'; and there were performances to mark the coronation of Napoleon as Emperor. Then, with the return of the Austrians, La Scala became the scene of demonstrations against the occupying forces. The 'Guerra, guerra' chorus in Bellini's *Norma* and the rousing choruses in Verdi's *Nabucco* and *I*

2 'Confusion here hath made his masterpiece'.

Lombardi became the occasions for patriotic demonstrations – the audiences identifying themselves with oppressed Hebrews on the one hand and the crusaders longing for their distant homeland on the other. The famous cry 'Viva Verdi', which in reality acclaimed *Vittorio Emanuele Re D'Italia*, was soon taken up in the theatre.

In more recent times, after La Scala had become Toscanini's opera house, there followed a series of clashes between the great conductor and Mussolini which centred on the question whether the fascist anthem 'Giovanezza' should be played at first nights and other important occasions. Although the actual physical clashes between Toscanini and the *fascisti* took place in Bologna, it was La Scala and Toscanini that remained for many Italians the symbols of liberty and democracy. Following the destruction of the theatre on the night of 16 August 1943, large notices bearing the words 'Evviva Toscanini' quickly appeared on the walls of the bombed theatre. Toscanini indeed did return to reopen the restored Scala in May 1946.

As far as the social life of Milan was concerned, La Scala was the only place in Milan where gambling was permitted – that was in 1778, when the theatre first opened and funds were needed. In addition to the gaming tables, profits from the sale of pastry and drinks helped swell the theatre's coffers. In 1788 gambling was prohibited; but it was again permitted in 1802 and not finally abolished till 1815. In the immediate post-Second World War period, a 2 per cent amusement tax throughout Lombardy and a proportion of the gate money on football matches helped to rebuild the bombed opera house.

Official rules and regulations governing audience behaviour may seem very strange today; but at La Scala two by-laws were passed in 1793, one forbidding encores, the other prohibiting any displays of disapproval during or at the end of the performance. Another nineteenth-century rule forbade the calling back of a singer onto the stage more than once; and yet another forbade the audience to applaud in a manner 'which did not represent the true worth of the performance'.

The 'no encore' rule still holds, though there have been occasions when the insistent cries of

'*bis, bis*', probably initiated by the official singers' claque, have, in the end, forced a conductor to accede to the audience's wishes. Toscanini would not tolerate this, however; and the audience's insistent demand that an encore be granted to Giovanni Zenatello for his singing of 'E scherzo ed è follia' in Verdi's *Un Ballo in Maschera*, on the closing night of the 1903 season, so enraged him that he threw his baton at the audience and stormed out of the theatre, leaving the performance uncompleted. He refused to return to La Scala until the 1906–7 season.

Yet one must not think that La Scala audiences are not among the most enthusiastic in Italy. They are generally cool and often 'sit on their hands', as

3 This was a moment when the name 'Toscanini' meant everything that was the opposite of the name 'Mussolini'.

the Italians say. A first-night subscription audience at La Scala can be the most dispiriting of all to sing to; and modern works are often played to steadily diminishing numbers in the auditorium; even those who are prepared to sit through a performance of *Wozzeck* or *Troilus and Cressida* may chatter loudly, and rudely and almost continuously.

The smart subscription audiences have, in recent years, run into trouble, and the opening of the 1968–9 season saw student demonstrators pelting the elegantly dressed leaders of Milan society with eggs, fruit and paint – mink-coated ladies being the special targets: all this happened despite La Scala itself waiving the hitherto inflexible insistence on evening dress for opening nights!

Against this historical, political and social background there has unfolded over the years the artistic story of La Scala: a story dominated by composers, singers, impresarios and conductors, for to appear at La Scala, to have one's work produced there for the first time, was, and still is, the fondest wish of most of those engaged in the art of opera. A theatre that has staged the first performances of Rossini's *La Gazza Ladra*, Donizetti's *Lucrezia Borgia*, Bellini's *Norma*, Verdi's *Otello* and *Falstaff*, Puccini's *Madama Butterfly* and *Turandot*, Boito's *Mefistofele* and *Nerone*, Giordano's *Andrea Chénier* and Ponchielli's *La Gioconda*, to mention just a small selection of works that have enjoyed Scala premières, has, by the very nature of things, become the Mecca of opera personalities from the rest of Europe. Not all those premières were successful ones – and the first-night failures of *Norma*, *Nerone* and *Butterfly* seem slightly surprising in the light of their subsequent careers.

How are operas commissioned and singers and conductors engaged? Obviously by the theatre – but that all depends on who the impresario, manager or musical director happens to be at any given time. La Scala's great managers and musical directors reflect the changing patterns of opera during the last 150 or so years. In the days of Rossini, Donizetti and Bellini, the Italian operatic public was avid for new works. Audiences wanted to hear different operas each season performed by their favourite singers; and at that time it was the impresario who was the most important figure in Italian operatic life. He not only controlled the theatres but chose the composers, selected the librettos and engaged the artists. The composer was required to compose to order, generally in quite a hurry; and to turn out music that the singers of the day expected, even demanded should be grateful to the voice.

Domenico Barbaia, who was born in Milan in 1775, and who started life as a waiter (he invented *Schlagobers*[3]), was the highly successful manager of La Scala from 1826 to 1832 (he had previously held the same position at the San Carlo in Naples and at the Theater an der Wien in Vienna). At La Scala he was responsible for the commissioning and production of Bellini's *Il Pirata*, *La Straniera*

and *Norma*, as well as new works by Pacini, Mercadante and Ricci. He had an ear for good singers too – as well as an eye for pretty ones.

Barbaia's immediate predecessor at La Scala was the English-born Joseph Glossop, who had built the Coburg Theatre in London (later known as the Old Vic). Glossop, who married an Italian soprano, was the father of Augustus Glossop Harris, stage manager of the Royal Italian Opera, Covent Garden, during the 1860s, and grandfather of Augustus Harris. The latter not only rose to become Lord Mayor of London, but was one of Covent Carden's most successful managers, from 1888 to 1896. Thus inextricably are linked the destinies of Europe's leading operatic institutions.

One of Barbaia's successors, perhaps the greatest of all La Scala's impresarios, was Bartolomeo Merelli, whose mistress, Giuseppina Strepponi, later Verdi's second wife, was really responsible for introducing Verdi to the Italian operatic stage. Merelli was a poet and musician, born in Bergamo,

a pupil of Simon Mayr and a fellow student of Donizetti. His connections with La Scala began when he acted as agent for Carlo Visconti di Modrone, who became manager of La Scala after Barbaia. Merelli guided La Scala's destinies from 1836 until 1850 and again from 1861 to 1863.

It was Strepponi who persuaded Merelli to stage the young Verdi's first opera, *Oberto, Conte di San Bonifacio*, in November 1839; it was Merelli himself who had faith in the young composer, and who stood by him during the sad and difficult days after the death of Verdi's wife and two children. And so La Scala saw the premières not only of Verdi's second (and unsuccessful) opera, *Un Giorno di Regno* – his only comic opera until *Falstaff* – but also of *Nabucco* and *I Lombardi*, the works which launched him in the world of opera outside Italy. If La Scala was not to see another Verdi première of note until the revised *Simon Boccanegra* in 1881, it was Verdi, nonetheless, who dominated the Scala's programmes each season, until in 1887 and 1893 respectively, came the premières of *Otello* and *Falstaff*.

Verdi, who had meant so much to the Scala, died only a few hundred yards from the theatre where his career had started. On 21 January 1901, the veteran composer was staying at the Grand Hotel when he suffered a stroke. He lingered on until shortly before 3 o'clock in the morning of 27 January. Straw had been put down in the streets to deaden the noise of passing traffic and huge crowds assembled outside the hotel to await news of his condition.

As soon as his approaching end became known, La Scala immediately closed its doors, not opening them again until February, when Toscanini conducted a concert of the dead composer's music, in which Caruso and Tamagno were among the soloists.

Verdi's funeral was, at his own request, simple and quiet; he had asked that it should be 'very modest, either at dawn or at the hour of the *Ave Maria* in the evening'. As his coffin was lowered into the grave, those in the cemetery began to sing the famous chorus from *Nabucco*, 'Va, pensiero'. A month later, as requested in his will, the bodies of Verdi and his wife, Giuseppina,

5 Verdi appearing on stage with the cast of Falstaff, Milan 1893. A London newspaper reported that 'Verdi's appearance before the curtain was the signal for an outburst of applause such as has rarely been equalled . . .'

were moved from the cemetery to be re-buried in the House of Rest (Casa di Riposo) for old musicians that he had been instrumental in building. On this occasion the whole of Milan turned out for the procession. It is recorded that 200,000 people lined the streets and that the rest of the city's population marched in the procession. The spectators sang or hummed his music as the cortège passed by. The coffins were followed by princes, statesmen and musicians, and Toscanini conducted a choir of eight hundred in the *Nabucco* chorus.

When Toscanini himself died in New York, almost exactly fifty-six years later, Milan and La Scala again felt the sense of a very personal loss. His body was brought back to Italy to be buried, as he had wished, in Milan. Once again, thousands assembled in the streets to watch the funeral procession, and as the cortège reached the Piazza della Scala, Victor De Sabata, who had relinquished conducting for reasons of health, took up his baton and, in the empty auditorium of the theatre, con-

ducted the funeral march from Beethoven's *Eroica* symphony, the sounds of which were relayed to the silent crowd outside. At the cemetery, just as Toscanini had led the choir in 'Va, pensiero' when Verdi's and Giuseppina's coffins were taken for re-burial, so Verdi's music was now sung as a tribute to one of his greatest interpreters.

Arturo Toscanini's important rôle in La Scala's fortunes had begun among the cellists at the first performance of *Otello*. In 1898 he was summoned by Duke Guido Visconti di Modrone to what one can only term a 'rescue operation'; he took hold of the theatre's destinies as artistic director, together with Giulio Gatti-Casazza as director-general. Except for the break of three seasons (1904–6), Toscanini and Gatti-Casazza remained at La Scala until the end of the 1907–8 season, when they were both lured to the Metropolitan, New York. Gatti remained in New York until 1935, but Toscanini returned to La Scala in 1921 as virtual

25

6 Franco Zeffirelli's production of *La Traviata* for the
1964–65 season at the Milan Scala was a masterpiece of
imaginative coordinated design. Here is Act II, Scene 2.

dictator. He was everything – the theatre's chief conductor, artistic director and general administrator all rolled into one. By this time La Scala had become an *Ente Autonomo*, i.e. a self-governing corporation. Had Toscanini not quarrelled with Mussolini and the fascists, he would have undoubtedly remained at the helm of La Scala – despite the increased financial losses which were the result of his insistent search for perfection – until well into the 1930s. But this was not to be, and he left La Scala in 1929, though not before he had taken the company to Berlin and Vienna.

Toscanini did, however, return to conduct the opening of the rebuilt Scala in May 1946, but he never conducted another complete opera there. He stood in the orchestral pit for the last time on 10 June 1948, to conduct scenes from Boito's *Mefistofele* and *Nerone*, on the 30th anniversary of the composer's death.

If Toscanini was the greatest of all Italian operatic conductors, there were others before and after him who are worthy to be mentioned in the same breath: Franco Faccio, Luigi Mancinelli, Leopoldo Mugnone, and nearer our own time, Tullio Serafin, Gino Marinuzzi and Victor De Sabata; then came Toscanini's own protégé, Guido Cantelli, who conducted *Così fan tutte* at the Piccola Scala, the small auditorium that adjoins the larger house, in January 1956, and who was tragically killed in an air crash a month later. And there is the unique Carlo Maria Giulini, whom many think the greatest Italian conductor since Toscanini, who had a glorious, if all too brief relationship with the Scala from 1952 to 1956.

That was also the period of Callas and Luchino Visconti; and when they joined with Giulini for Gluck's *Alceste* and Verdi's *La Traviata*, it was opera-making and opera-giving at its very best. That is what is so wonderful about La Scala, for despite its quota of bad performances (which indeed can be very bad), when it mounts a successful production, then it is very, very good, for then, all the expertise founded on years of giving opera with the greatest artists in the world, comes into play. In such instances, a performance becomes an occasion, and La Scala clearly remains the greatest opera house in the world.

7 The water entrance to the Fenice, depicted here in 1821

Il Teatro la Fenice
Venice

In 1961, a magazine, *Opera*, held a competition among its readers to decide which was the most beautiful opera house in the world. The one that received by far the majority of votes was that jewel, La Fenice, in Venice: an opera house which, as Spike Hughes so aptly put it, is 'the most feminine of theatres'. It is graciously aristocratic, worthy of the city which has played so important a part in the development of opera in Italy.

It was in Venice in 1637 that the first public opera house (as opposed to the private court theatres) was opened: the Teatro San Cassiano. It was in Venice, at the Teatro San Giovanni e Paolo, five years later, that Monteverdi's great opera, *L'Incoronatione di Poppea*, had its first performance; and it was in Venice, at the Teatro San Moisè, opened in 1640 (and which gave opera regularly until 1818) that Rossini's first, third, fifth, seventh and eighth operas were first produced.

Venice, too, was the first city in Italy to have a regular 'carnival' season of opera. In the second half of the seventeenth century, about 350 different operas were produced in the various Venetian theatres; and by the end of the eighteenth century another 1,600 had been added. Indeed, there were some eighteen theatres in Venice dedicated to opera and drama; and when Dr Burney visited the city in 1770, he found seven opera houses open – three for *opera seria* and four for *opera buffa*; not to mention four more theatres devoted to the drama, and all playing nightly to capacity. 'In Venice', he

wrote, 'one needs to be all ears for music and all eyes for painting and architecture.'

The Fenice Theatre, or the Phoenix, to give it its English name, was so called because it arose from the ashes of the Teatro San Benedetto, although not, as it happens, on the actual site; for after the fire in 1773 which destroyed the San Benedetto, the Venier family, who owned the land on which the former theatre stood, claimed the right to control the proposed new theatre. The society that had been managing the old theatre went to law over the issue but lost their case and were forced to sell their shares for 31,000 ducats (£15,000). They looked for another site on which to build, and found some property near the Church of Santa Maria Zobenigo, costing 56,000 ducats (£28,000).

The society organized a competition for the design of the new theatre, a design that would 'appeal to the eye as well as the ear of the spectator'. There were twenty-nine entries and the winning one was submitted by a thirty-seven-year-old architect, Gianantonio Selva. Building began in May 1790, and finished in April 1792. On the façade of the theatre, which stands in the Campo San Fantin, over the central window above the portico, is the word SOCIETAS and the date MDCCXCII, which indicate that the theatre was built at the command of a society of noblemen, together with the Council of Ten. Selva had been well schooled in classical architecture, and had learned a lot from the Palladian style. His new

theatre was not without its critics, however, and the clever Venetians made a satirical acrostic from the word SOCIETAS. It ran: Sine-Ordine-Cum-Irregularitate-Erexit-Theatrum-Antonius-Selva.

In 1836 there was the inevitable fire that seems to have destroyed or partly destroyed every great European opera house – it occurred while rehearsals were in progress for the first Venice performance of *Lucia*. This time La Fenice rose again from its own ashes within seven months. Although Selva's ground plan was followed, the new theatre was designed by the brothers Tomaso and Giovanni Battista Meduna. However, the mere seven months spent on rebuilding meant that some things were skimped; and so, in 1853, the theatre's administrators decided to hold a competition to 'restore and retouch – while preserving the present splendour of the decoration and gilding – the purely ornamental parts of the theatre, without incurring serious expense'. The Fenice was accordingly closed for nearly a year, and when it reopened in December 1854, it looked very much as it does today – intimate and refined.

In 1936, a hundred years after the fire, the Fenice was completely modernized and at the same time an important administrative reform was carried out. The box holders, many of them descendants of the original members of the SOCIETAS, handed over their boxes to the municipality, and the Fenice, like La Scala, the San Carlo, the Teatro dell'Opera in Rome, and two or three other Italian opera houses, became an *Ente Autonomo*. This event took place almost exactly three centuries after the Tron family had decided to admit citizens of all ranks to their rebuilt Teatro San Cassiano in 1637.

When the Fenice opened in 1792, it was with an opera by Paisiello, *I Giuochi d'Agrigento*. Between then and the advent of Rossini, many operas by Paisiello, Mayr, Zingarelli and Farinelli were produced, often with such great singers as Grassini and Catalani in the casts. Beginning with Rossini, however, La Fenice began to register more important world premières than possibly any other Italian opera house. The list is most imposing:

Rossini:	*Tancredi* (1813), *Semiramide* (1823)
Bellini:	*I Capuleti e I Montecchi* (1830), *Beatrice di Tenda* (1833)
Donizetti:	*Belisario* (1836), *Maria di Rudenz* (1838)
Verdi:	*Ernani* (1844), *Attila* (1846), *Rigoletto* (1851) *La Traviata* (1853), *Simon Boccanegra* (1857)

There have, of course, been many other premières by such composers as Wolf-Ferrari, Giordano, Mascagni, and Ghedini, culminating in the first

9 The main entrance to the Venice opera house, La Fenice. The facade, like that of many houses is mute as to the charms and splendours that lie behind it.

8 (*Opposite*) The gaiety and intimacy of the Fenice auditorium comes as a surprise made the more delightful by the fact that the foyer and main staircase are architecturally somewhat austere.

performances of Stravinsky's *The Rake's Progress* in 1951, Britten's *The Turn of the Screw* in 1954, and Nono's *Intolleranza* in 1961. The Fenice also pioneered performances of Wagner's operas in Italy: *Rienzi* had its Italian première there in 1874, and the complete *Ring* enjoyed its first Italian performances in 1883.

Venetian audiences have their own characteristics. They are warmer-hearted and more given to enthusiasm than those of Milan; they are certainly not so cruel or critical as those of Parma; nor are they as noisy and as unpunctual as those in Naples. They are more carefree, gay, tolerant, and have their own sense of humour. Since the eighteenth century the gondoliers have enjoyed the privilege of free admission to the Venetian theatres. Burney gave this as one of the reasons why 'the common people of Venice sing in such a cultured, noble manner as compared with the same class elsewhere'.

Tunes from Rossini's *Tancredi*, especially 'Di tanti palpiti', were sung in the streets and squares, on the gondolas, and even in the law courts, where one judge had to reprimand the public · for disturbing the trial. The tune they were singing was almost certainly 'Di tanti palpiti', which became the most popular aria of the day (much as did Verdi's 'La donna è mobile'). In Venice this aria was known as the 'Aria dei risi' (the rice aria), as Rossini was said to have composed it in four minutes one evening, waiting for the rice to boil!

In *Semiramide*, Rossini introduced a military band onto the stage of the Fenice; the audiences were so pleased by this innovation that they hired several military bands and got them to play in gondolas, accompanying Rossini through the canals on his way back from the theatre to his lodgings.

If the Venetians could find an excuse to fête a singer, they did so in a manner we could only call extravagant. But was not Venice the city of carnivals, masquerades and processions, on water as well as on land? So Malibran, Pasta and Grisi, the three most celebrated prima donnas of the first half of the nineteenth century, came, sang and conquered at the Fenice.

In 1835, Malibran was engaged to sing the rôles of Norma, Rosina, Rossini's Desdemona and Cenerentola. 'Hail, sublime angelic butterfly', wrote the Venetians. They struck medals in her honour, showered her with flowers in the Piazza San Marco, and even gambled on her in the casinos – staking their bets on the numbers six, seventeen and twenty-four, the number of performances she was contracted to sing, and dates of her announced and actual début! Despite all this, Malibran herself was depressed by Venice; she refused to ride in the black gondolas, saying that it was as if she was going to her own funeral. She then proceeded to arrange for the decoration of her private gondola: scarlet and gold for the interior, blue curtains, and dove-grey outside; and special costumes for the gondoliers, consisting of blue trousers, scarlet jackets with black velvet sleeves, yellow hats. 'When I go by thus', she wrote, 'everyone knows it is I.' And in this manner her gondola drew up each night at the Fenice. So loved was this great artist by the Venetians that the Teatro San Giovanni Grisostomo was renamed the Teatro Malibran in her honour – today it is a cinema. ·

Composers were fêted in like style, and when Donizetti came to Venice for the première of his *Belisario* at the Fenice, he was carried shoulder high from the theatre, while the crowd sang patriotic songs from the opera. The Venetians, with their republican spirit, bitterly resented the years of Austrian occupation, and Verdi's operas, not surprisingly, were the excuse for patriotic demonstrations in the opera house.

Ernani communicated the restless strength of a subjected people; the music, which sounded rough and vigorous to an audience nurtured on Bellini and Donizetti, aroused great enthusiasm. There were fifty curtain calls, and Verdi was carried in triumph to his hotel. *Attila*, two years later, became the occasion for more patriotic demonstrations, and when *Macbeth* arrived at the Fenice in 1847, pandemonium broke out nightly after the tenor duet in the last act, 'La patria tradita'. At the opera's twenty-second performance a ballerina appeared on the stage with a tricolour, and then, at a prearranged signal, all the women in the audience took out tricolours, and draped them

10 Giuseppe Verdi, one of the twin pillars – but how far apart they were – of opera in the nineteenth century.

over the sides of the boxes, forming huge Italian flags. Troops were summoned, and the following morning the Austrian authorities announced that in future performances of *Macbeth* the last act was to be omitted and that of Donizetti's *Maria di Rudenz* was to be performed in its place.

It was obvious that Verdi's name was by now anathema to the occupying authorities, and so when the Fenice submitted, as it had to, the libretto of the new opera it had commissioned from Verdi, there was a crisis of the first order. The libretto by Piave was entitled *La Maledizione* (later to be known as *Rigoletto*), and it was banned out of hand as 'repulsive *immoralità*' and 'obscene *trivialità*'. Changes were suggested by Martello, director of public order. Verdi refused to alter anything at first, but then when it was proposed that the scene be moved from France to Mantua, and that it be retitled *Rigoletto*, he reluctantly agreed. There are still remnants of the French setting in the opera however; the dance in the first scene is a *Périgourdine*, and Sparafucile comes from Burgundy. The Duke of Mantua, in fact, was a title held by the Holy Roman Emperor, and although the last holder of the title had abdicated in 1806, he had died only fifteen years before the première of *Rigoletto* and so was remembered by quite a few of the Fenice audience at the first night of Verdi's new opera. As Emperor of Austria he had been known as Francis I (François I was the name of the profligate duke in Hugo's *Le Roi s'amuse*, on which Piave based his libretto) – again the Venetian's sense of humour was tickled.

The story of the first night fiasco of *La Traviata* has often been told, but recently it has been discovered that these reports were exaggerated. The Fenice's own archives reveal that the opera was given ten performances during its first season, and there were no such whistles and cat-calls as operatic legend would have us believe. The legend, in fact, was invented some thirty years after the

Fenice première by the Italian critic Capponi, who wrote under the name of Folchetto, and contributed notes to Pougin's early biography of Verdi. Nor was the opera given on the first night in 'modern costume'; from the very first performance it was given as a period piece with Louis XIV costumes and décor, as the poster of the première clearly shows.

After the brief interlude of the Manin Republic (1848–9), the Austrians returned to Venice, and the Fenice was closed for 'political reasons' for the 1853–4 season, and again, from 1858 until 1866. With the unification of Italy, however, the Fenice settled down to a less adventurous life, musically and politically.

During the last war there were a few important Italian premières, including those of Strauss's *Friedenstag* in 1940, sung of course in Italian, with Margherita Grandi and Francesco Valentino (Glyndebourne's 1939 Lady Macbeth and Macbeth), one born in Tasmania, and the other in America. In 1941, there was the first performance in Italy of Janáček's *Jenufa*. On 26 April 1945, during a performance of *Madama Butterfly*, with Toti Dal Monte as Cio-Cio-San, the liberation of Milan was announced from the stage. The season was suspended, to be resumed on 8 May, when La Fenice became the first opera house in North Italy to reopen after the liberation.

In addition to the post-war premières of *The Rake's Progress* and *The Turn of the Screw*, possibly the most important event at the Fenice in the post-war period took place during the 1948–9 season, when Maria Callas, who had just been singing Brünnhilde, was persuaded by the conductor, Tullio Serafin, to take over the role of Elvira in *I Puritani* from the sick Margherita Carosio. Thus Callas's 'second career' began, and with it the *bel canto* revival. It was fitting, therefore, that Joan Sutherland should make her Italian début in Handel's *Alcina* at La Fenice. In 1963, the theatre

III (*Above left*) Vincenzo Bellini; born at Catania in 1801 (where the present opera house is named after him), he died near Paris in 1835. He was a seminal influence in the creation of the '*bel canto*' school of operatic singing. IV (*Above right*) Gaetano Donizetti. A native of Bergamo, where he is buried, he was a slightly older contemporary of Bellini, whom he survived by 13 years. Immensely prolific, he has no fewer than 72 operas to his name. *L'elisir d'amore* and *Don Pasquale* are two of the most popular survivals. V (*Below left*) A miniature of Mozart painted on ivory when he was about nineteen years old and already an established operatic composer. VI (*Below right*) It is curious that perhaps the most penetrating of all the many portraits of Wagner should be by a Frenchman, Auguste Renoir. Renoir was predisposed in Wagner's favour all the more because French national sentiment was so hostile. Yet at Bayreuth he exclaimed 'No one has the right to bore people to that extent!'

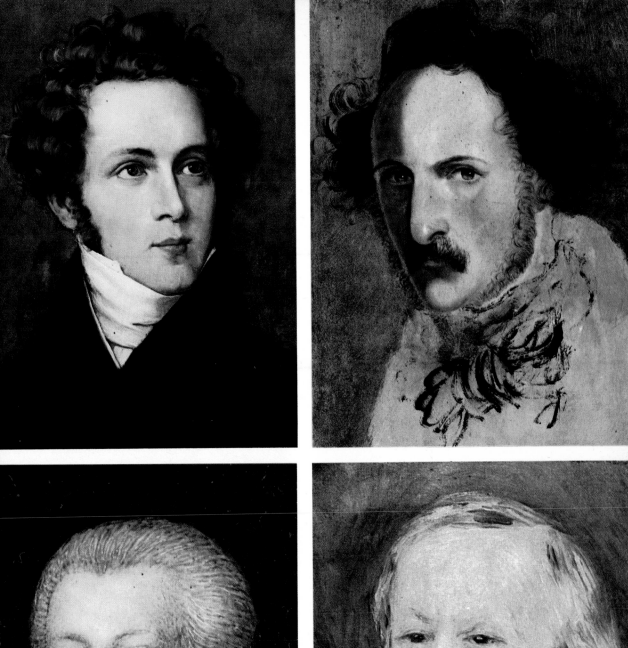

II Nineteenth-century design for *Otello* at the Fenice

gave the first revival this century of Verdi's *Jérusalem* (the 1847 revision for the Paris Opéra of *I Lombardi*); while for the 1970–1 season the first performance this century of Verdi's *Il Corsaro* was staged.

In 1959, Mario Labroca, a pupil of Respighi and Malipiero was appointed the Fenice's artistic director. He had held the same position briefly for the 1946–7 season, and has, in his long career, been the *sovrintendente* of the Teatro Comunale in Florence (and the Maggio Musicale), artistic director of La Scala, Milan (1947–9) and director of Radio Italiana's music programmes from 1949–58. Labroca's work in Venice has also included the organization of the famous international festival, known as the Biennale, in which the Fenice plays

an important part. He is a worthy successor of Alessandro Lanari, who was the theatre's 'impresario' in the 1830s and 1840s, and who earned for himself the title of the 'Napoleon of impresarios'.

Certainly Labroca is a self-effacing rather than a demonstrative theatre administrator; but with the help of a first-rate staff he has successfully rebuilt the prestige of the Fenice. Since 1965, the season, which until then lasted a bare two months, has been lengthened first to three, then to four, and, in 1970, to five months – from some two dozen performances of seven operas to some seventy performances of fifteen operas (and these figures do not include the ballet evenings). Once more, as Burney said, 'In Venice, one needs to be all ears for music'.

VII (*Opposite*) Marc Chagall's ceiling may, by its novelty, seem an incongruous intrusion into Garnier's realized vision. But the achievements of both men have helped to mould the artistic consciousness of their respective eras. It was commissioned by André Malraux, a bold decision in 1963, and took a year to complete. Chagall's iconography is highly personal.

Il Teatro San Carlo Naples

The Fenice in Venice may be the most exquisitely beautiful of the Italian opera houses, the Scala in Milan the grandest and most famous, but it is the San Carlo in Naples that is surely the homeliest and most human of them all. It is the San Carlo, too, that has a place of particular affection in the hearts of many British and American opera-goers, who, when they were in uniform during the Italian campaign and subsequent occupation of Italy in the Second World War, grew to love the theatre. Over one and three-quarter-million members of the Allied Forces attended performances at the San Carlo between 1943 and 1946.

In May 1946 the foyer, which had been badly damaged by bombing, was reopened, and a plaque commemorates the part played by the British Forces in 'keeping alive the flames of its [the San Carlo's] traditions, rising to a new life, and entrusting to the wings of song this message which unites in brotherhood the hearts of the peoples of all nations – Naples, May 1944–May 1946.'

Opera in Naples goes back to the middle of the seventeenth century – to 3 April 1654, to be exact, when the Neapolitans heard their first opera performance, Cirillo's *L'Orontea Regina di Egitto*, at the Teatro di San Bartolemeo. By the end of the century Naples had supplanted Venice as the centre of opera in Italy, and the Neapolitans had built two more theatres: the Teatro dei Fiorentini and the Teatro Nuovo. It was there that Alessandro Scarlatti and his contemporaries Stradella and Rossi flourished. By the middle of the eighteenth century *opera buffa* had developed under Pergolesi and Jommelli and then Galuppi and Paisiello. To these names can be added those of Guglielmi, Cimarosa, Piccinni and Spontini, all of whom, if not Neapolitans by birth, were adopted by that city. As Stendhal admitted, if one were to list the greatest composers, the first thirty would be, almost without exception, Neapolitans; and he found the city itself the 'very fount and birthplace of fine singing'.

In 1737 the Teatro di San Bartolemeo was demolished and replaced by a church (thus reversing the general procedure in operatic history, whereby many opera houses were built on sites previously occupied by a church, convent or monastery). To replace the San Bartolemeo, the Bourbon King Charles III of Naples sanctioned the building of a new Royal Theatre, which was, in his words, to be 'new and grandiose'. The theatre, designed by Giovanni Medrano, was built in 270 days and opened on 4 November 1737 (the Feast of St Charles and so the monarch's name day) with Sarro's *Achille in Sciro*, to a libretto by Metastasio.

The splendid auditorium was lit by oil lamps and some 1,000 candles, which were arranged in groups in front of little mirrors. These produced such a brilliant reflection that the ladies in the audience grumbled that their dresses and even their complexions were made to look dingy! The more candles that were clustered in front of the individual boxes, the higher the rank of the box owner in the local social hierarchy. This custom gave rise to the expression in Naples, 'He's only a one-candle man.'

The splendour of the auditorium was reflected on the stage, if the description of the baroque settings as prescribed by Metastasio in his libretto of *Achille in Sciro* is anything to go by: 'A baroque temple . . . surrounded by porticos, reached by a towering flight of steps. Beyond, an open piazza, sacred wood through a colonnade on one side, with the coast of Scyros.' King Charles added to all this splendour by ordering at least two ballets for every one act of the opera; and *Achille in Sciro* was performed on fourteen consecutive nights.

The building contractor, Angelo Carasale, was the theatre's first impresario. He came to an un-happy end, for according to the Neapolitan historian Pietro Colletta, when asked to produce the accounts of the 100,000 ducats spent on build-ing the San Carlo, he failed to satisfy the royal auditors and was imprisoned in the San Elmo fortress, where he died a year later.

In 1768, to celebrate the marriage of Ferdinand IV to Marie-Caroline, daughter of Maria Theresa, the San Carlo was entirely redecorated and boxes were added to the first four tiers at either end over the stage. Not long after, Mozart and his father were in Naples, and attended the final rehearsals and first night of Jommelli's *Armida abbandonata*, an opera which the fourteen-year-old Wolfgang found 'well composed, beautiful, but too serious and old-fashioned for the theatre'. In a letter to his sister, Nannerl, he went on to describe how the King always stood on a stool at the opera so as to look taller than his consort.

Another important visitor to the San Carlo, before the end of the century, was the British soprano, Elizabeth Billington, whom Reynolds had painted in the character of St Cecilia. Haydn is said to have remarked to the painter, 'You have represented Mrs Billington listening to the angels; you should have made the angels listening to her!'

When Mrs Billington arrived in Naples in 1794, she was travelling incognito, but her presence in the city was disclosed to Lady Hamilton, wife of the British Ambassador (and Nelson's mistress).

13 (*Overleaf*) Built in 1737 and entirely redecorated in 1768, the San Carlo was the scene of many splendid balls during the latter part of the eighteenth century.

12 (*Above*) Status in the social hierarchy was denoted by the number of candles a man could sport before his box. To judge from the number of boxes, this practice must have generated considerable warmth.

Lady Hamilton called on the singer and insisted that she be presented to Queen Caroline. After singing in private to the King and Queen at Caserta, they begged her to sing at the San Carlo, and accordingly, in May 1794, she made her début there in *Inez de Castro*, which had been specially written for her by Bianchi. She was then heard in operas by Paisiello, Paer and Guglielmi. A contemporary writer commented: 'It became the vogue to patronize the beautiful English prima donna, from national pride as well as from personal admiration. The royal example was followed by Lady Templeton, Lady Palmerston, Lady Gertrude Villiers, Lady Grandison, and all the English and Irish nobility then resident in Naples, who either affected or possessed musical taste.'

When 'La' Billington, as the Italians called her, returned to Naples in 1796 for a further engagement, Mount Vesuvius erupted, and the superstitious Neapolitans attributed the latest manifestation of nature to the fact that permission had been granted to the 'heretic Englishwoman' to perform at the San Carlo. Not long afterwards, her husband collapsed and died one night shortly before she was about to leave for the theatre. Again tongues wagged and Naples was full of rumours that he had been poisoned or even stabbed – the lovely soprano having been the object of the devoted attentions of many young noblemen of the city. Mrs Billington did sing at the San Carlo that night, but it is said that Queen Caroline later intervened with the management to prevent her reappearance until she should have fully recovered from the shock.

Billington's great rival was Giuseppina Grassini, who became Napoleon's mistress: Nelson, Lady Hamilton, Grassini, Napoleon – opera certainly made its contribution to world affairs in those days!

The San Carlo was clearly a singer's theatre at this period, and vocal gymnastics and rivalry between the artists were the rule rather than the exception. The behaviour of the audience was said to be the worst in Italy, for as the noise on the stage rose, so did that in the auditorium. An example had already been set years before by the famous castrato Caffarelli (to whom Doctor Bartolo refers in the 'lesson scene' of *Il Barbiere di Siviglia*). When he was appearing at the San Carlo, he was sent a jewelled snuff-box by Louis xv, which he was on the point of refusing because it did not have the King's portrait on it. Told that the King, who was in the audience, only gave his portrait to ambassadors, Caffarelli retorted, 'Very well, then let His Majesty make the ambassadors sing!' During performances, when he was not singing, he would talk loudly to his friends across the footlights, and often shouted out obscenities, which resulted in his being arrested by the authorities.

The San Carlo audiences became famous throughout Europe for their lack of manners. They chattered, ate and visited one another in their boxes. President De Brosses wrote that even the King himself talked through the entire first half of the opera, and fell asleep during the second. The noise must have been enormous, for not only was the auditorium often in an uproar, but the stage was filled to overflowing with humans and, in

14 Mrs. Billington: Born in London (*c.* 1765), she died at her home near Venice in 1818. A brilliant, if tempestuous singing career lay between. Her greatest triumphs were achieved at Covent Garden and the San Carlo. Indeed, during her Neapolitan sojourn she was even held to have provoked an eruption of Vesuvius.

some operas, with livestock. Michael Kelly, the Irish tenor (and the first Basilio in Mozart's *Figaro*) recorded in his memoirs that there were four hundred people and eighty horses on the stage at the production of *Il Disfatto di Dario* in 1779.

Perhaps the most famous period of the San Carlo's history was under the management of Barbaia, who has already been mentioned in connection with La Scala. He came to the San Carlo in 1810, and in his first season introduced Gluck's *Iphigénie en Aulide* and Spontini's *La Vestale* to the Neapolitans. His greatest triumph was undoubtedly his encouragement of Rossini, whom he engaged to write two operas a year for the San Carlo. The results were the premières of *Elisabetta Regina d'Inghilterra*, *Otello*, *Armida*, *La Donna del Lago*, *Mosè in Egitto* and *Maometto* II. It was Barbaia's mistress, Isabella Colbran, who created most of the leading female rôles in these operas. In 1815 she finally deserted the manager, as well as the King of Naples, whose *favorita* she had also become, to live with Rossini, and then in 1822, to marry him.

The Neapolitans adored Rossini and his music; and Stendhal has left us vivid accounts of the first nights of many of his operas, complete with the reactions of the audiences. On the first night of *La Donna del Lago*, for example, the tenor Nozzari sang out of tune, and Stendhal says the audience went mad, becoming 'roaring, ravenous lions . . . Nothing can give the least, the sketchiest idea of a Neapolitan audience insulted by a wrong note!'

It was during the reign of Rossini in Naples that the San Carlo burned down. That was in February 1816, when a spark from a lantern, left alight on the stage after a rehearsal, set the whole theatre ablaze. In less than a year, however, it was rebuilt at the express command of King Ferdinand, at a cost of 200,000 ducats – double the sum of the original theatre. Antonio Niccolini, who had designed the present exterior in 1810, enlarged the size of the stage and auditorium, and furnished the design for the ceiling, which was executed by Giuseppe Cammarano. The San Carlo's ceiling is a splendid affair, showing a procession of the muses and poets, watching, in an engrossed manner, Apollo bearing a lyre, on his way to be crowned in a burst of radiant sunshine.

The new San Carlo (the present theatre) was opened on 12 January 1817, the King's birthday. Stendhal, who was at the reopening, wrote:

> The great day of the San Carlo opening has at last arrived – wild enthusiasm, torrents of people, a dazzling auditorium . . . At first I felt as if I had been transported to the palace of some oriental emperor. My eyes were dazzled, my soul enraptured . . . There is nothing in the whole of Europe that can even give a distant idea of the place, let alone compare with it.

There were more Rossini operas, and Barbaia's reign continued successfully, with two short breaks, for twenty-eight years. He discovered and encouraged Bellini and Donizetti, and the San Carlo saw the premières of the former's *Bianca e Gernando* in 1826, and the latter's *Lucia di Lammermoor* in 1835 and *Roberto d'Evereux* in 1837.

Verdi's relations with the San Carlo were not of the happiest. The failures there of *Oberto* and *Alzira* were followed by censorship troubles which resulted in *La Traviata* having to be staged there as *Violetta*, and *Rigoletto* as *Clara di Pert* and later as *Lionello*. And as if that were not enough, his *Vêpres Siciliennes* was re-christened *Batilde di Turenna* late in 1857. An opera that the theatre had commissioned and which was to be called *Una Vendetta in Domino*, but which the censors wanted to rechristen *Adelia degli Adimari*, was angrily withdrawn by Verdi and given to the Teatro Apollo in Rome where it appeared as *Un Ballo in Maschera*. However, his *Luisa Miller* had a successful San Carlo première in 1849.

Much has been written about Verdi's *King Lear* project. It was for the San Carlo that this work was to have been written, but nothing came of it and Verdi grew disenchanted with the San Carlo and Naples after the *Ballo* episode. In 1870 he refused an invitation to become head of the Conservatoire in succession to Mercadante, but he did accept honorary membership of the Naples Philharmonic Society. When invited by the government to draw up a scheme for the reform of Italy's operatic life, he suggested that there should be three theatres which would serve as models for the rest of the country: La Scala, the Rome Opera

and San Carlo. His scheme envisaged that the salaries of orchestra and chorus should be paid for by the government; that each theatre should establish an opera school, which would be free, and that the successful students should be given contracts at the respective theatres. He also suggested that each opera house should have an over-all musical and artistic director. These reforms were not carried out, but they certainly included much of what Toscanini had in mind, and indeed carried out, at La Scala some fifty years later.

The story of the San Carlo in the post-Verdi period and in the inter-war years was less distinguished. The most famous singer Naples ever produced, Caruso, appeared there in 1901, but, because his own townsfolk did not give him the kind of reception he felt he deserved, he never sang there again. But the yearly *cartellone* shows that nearly every other great singer appeared at the San Carlo, and so did most of the outstanding Italian conductors.

Censorship raised its head again in Naples during the Mussolini period, when the first night of Honegger's and Ibert's *L'Aiglon*, which reached the final dress rehearsal stage, was inexplicably cancelled. This was in 1937. Yet, to its credit, the San Carlo mounted Honegger's *Judith* in the same year, Bloch's *Macbeth* in 1938, and Kodály's *Magic Spinning Wheel* in 1939.

The chapter in the San Carlo's history devoted to the British Army's rescue and restoration of the bomb-damaged theatre, no less than its actually running the opera house for nearly three years, must be one of the most amazing episodes, not only in Italian operatic history, but also in British military history! It was largely owing to the enthusiasm and devotion of such officers as Brigadier Cripps, Commander of 56 (Naples) Area, and Captain Peter Francis, the first British officer to enter the semi-deserted theatre at the end of October 1943, that the San Carlo came back to life.

These two men, together with Pasquale Di Costanzo, the theatre's general administrator, certainly revived the Neapolitans' flagging interest in opera and contemporary music, as well as kindling it for the first time in many members of the

15 The San Carlo Theatre, Naples: a singularly handsome facade.

armed forces. Di Costanzo is recognized as Barbaia's most distinguished successor, and he is aided by the Marchese Lucio Parisi, the theatre's general secretary and one of the San Carlo's most ardent Anglophiles.

It was not only the 'bread and butter' operas like *Bohème*, *Butterfly*, *Rigoletto* and *Aida* that formed the repertory in those early days of the occupation, but works that were then hardly familiar to the average serviceman, like *Lucia di Lammermoor*, *Andrea Chénier*, *La Gioconda*, *L'Amico Fritz* and *Adriana Lecouvreur*. The singers at the San Carlo during this period included such established favourites as Gigli, Maria Caniglia, Ebe Stignani, Margherita Carosio, Francesco Merli, and Toti Dal Monte, as well as several 'new' names – like Tito Gobbi, Paolo Silveri, Ferruccio Tagliavini, Italo Tajo and Luigi Infantino. Then there were the conductors Franco Capuana, Vincenzo Bellezza, Vittorio Gui, Franco Patanè and the very young Giulini. It was fitting that the first opera to be heard at the reopened Royal Opera House, Covent Garden, in September 1946, was given by the company of the San Carlo, who had been invited to London for a two-month season.

During the post-war period the San Carlo may not have staged the premières of so many distinguished operas as it did in the middle of the nineteenth century, but it has certainly done its duty by contemporary works, with productions (many for the first time in Italy) of Berg's *Wozzeck*, Bartók's *Bluebeard's Castle*, Schoenberg's *Von Heute auf Morgen*, Milhaud's *Bolivar*, Hindemith's *Neues vom Tage*, and Shostakovich's *Katerina Ismailova*. To balance these and to make sure the Neapolitans have their share of good old-fashioned Italian singing, there have been the revivals of many Rossini, Bellini, Donizetti and early Verdi works.

Indeed, Neapolitans love good singing and so the San Carlo audiences unashamedly display their pleasure (and displeasure) during performances, taking deep and audible breaths, hissing at everything that is bad, and welcoming a beautifully turned phrase or note with 'Ah, che bella voce'. At one performance of *La Fanciulla del West*, for example, a Neapolitan matron was greatly disturbed when the hero, Dick Johnson, in the person of Franco Corelli, struggled up a ladder to escape capture by the sheriff, Jack Rance. 'Poverino,' she kept repeating, 'he can't make it! He can't!'

In this atmosphere everybody is quite ready to forgive the San Carlo's wonderful unpunctuality – six o'clock performances often begin thirty minutes late, while one I attended a few years back started nearly an hour late – the prolonged intervals, the late arrivals and the exchanging of the latest gossip between the Neapolitan ladies.

Attached to the San Carlo, or rather to the Royal Palace which adjoins the San Carlo, is the charming Teatro di Corte. Originally the *Sala Grande* of the Palace and used for royal entertainments in the days of the Bourbons, it became a court theatre in May 1768, when it opened with a performance of a Serenata, specially composed by Paisiello in celebration of Ferdinand's marriage to Marie-Caroline.

The early life of this little theatre was chequered and short. In 1799 it became the official seat of government of the Parthenopaean republic. Even when the Bourbons returned to Naples, the Teatro di Corte remained closed, and during the Fascist period it was occasionally used for special functions.

Following the allied occupation of Naples, however, it took on a new aspect. It was turned into a cinema, with drastic structural alterations, but fortunately without damage to the original auditorium. The Neapolitans resented this act of sacrilege – much as the people of Bayreuth protested when a variety show was staged in Wagner's Festspielhaus. However, restoration work began in 1951, and by late 1954 the restored Teatro di Corte was ready to resume life. Far cosier and more elegant than Milan's Piccola Scala, the auditorium, which is decorated in red, white and gold, seats some 600 spectators. The opening performance in November 1954 was Paisiello's *Don Chisciotte della Mancia*. This was followed by *Il Turco in Italia* the following spring, and since then, under the same management as its big sister the San Carlo, it presents regular autumn seasons of classical comic operas, mostly by Neapolitan composers.

Il Teatro Regio Parma

What does the name Parma conjure up? ham, cheese, cuisine; or Verdi, Toscanini, Renata Tebaldi? All answers would be correct, for Parma is as famous gastronomically as it is operatically. It is a city of strange contrasts, with a communist mayor at its head and its Royal (Regio) Theatre; with its most efficiently run town council and its knowledgeable opera audiences who can be the scourge of singers and conductors; with its art treasures and historical monuments on the one hand, and modern hotels and sports stadiums on the other.

In addition to having one of the most famous musical conservatoires in Italy, which has produced such outstanding musicians as Cleofonte Campanini, Toscanini, Pizzetti, Carlo Bergonzi and Renata Tebaldi, Parma possesses the second oldest theatre in modern Italy, the Teatro Farnese (preceded in age only by the Teatro Olimpico at Vicenza, designed by Palladio and opened in 1555).

The city of Parma was given to the Farnese family in 1545 by Pope Paul III; and under the Farnese and then the Bourbon princes, always great patrons of the arts, it became one of the most famous musical centres in Italy. It was Ranuccio Farnese who gave instructions, in 1618, for a theatre seating some 3,000 (though some sources give the figure as 4,500) to be built by Aleotti of Argenta. Constructed entirely of wood, near to the Pilotta Palace, it opened in December 1628 with works specially composed by Monteverdi for the celebrations attendant on the marriage of Oduardo, Duke of Parma, and Margherita de' Medici. These consisted of a prologue and five intermezzi to Tasso's L'Aminta, and a torneo, entitled Mercurio e Marte. While in Parma, Monteverdi also provided another opera, Gli Amori di Diana e di Endimione.

The Farnese theatre continued to be used for court functions until 1732. It was partly destroyed during the Second World War. Rebuilding began in 1957, and it was fully restored by the end of 1965. No one, however, has yet (1972) decided what its future use will be.

Parma was always rich in theatres and as well as the Farnese, Ranuccio founded the Teatro Collegio de' Nobili – actually two theatres. His heir, Ranuccio II, was responsible for the construction of the Teatro Rochetta, the Teatrino di Corte, and the Teatro Ducale, which was the immediate predecessor of the present Teatro Regio.

The Ducale was designed by the architect Stefano Lolli and became one of the most important operatic centres of its day. It opened in 1688 and its artistic life continued until 1832 – today the site is occupied by the main Parma post office. During its almost one-and-a-half centuries of existence it enjoyed a very high reputation among musicians – first under the Farnese dynasty and then under the Bourbons. The Ducale opened with Teseo in Atene by Giannettini, with settings by the famous Bibiena. Operas by Jommelli, Traetta and Gabrieli were succeeded by those of Pergolesi, Paisiello, Sacchini, Paer

16 The most critical audience in the world, leaning over to watch.

(a native of Parma), Cimarosa and Gluck. All the great singers of the day graced the stage of the Ducale, including the rival prima donnas, Cuzzoni and Bordoni, and the castrato Farinelli.

By the time of Rossini, the Parma audience was displaying that peculiar independence of judgment for which it has long been famous, and his *L'Italiana in Algeri* and *Il Turco in Italia* were fiascos; even *Il Barbiere di Siviglia*, which had quite a successful Parma first night, failed to attract the public during the rest of its initial season. It is at about this time that the first reports appear of open hostility being displayed to singers. There was the tenor Alberico Curioni, whose appearances in Federici's *Zaira* were greeted with boos and cat-calls; the tenor, nothing daunted, shouted obscenities at the audience and there was uproar. The police were called into the theatre, and calm was only restored when the police chief appeared on the stage and announced that the tenor had been arrested and that the opera would be replaced by a ballet. Later in the season Curioni decided to have his revenge, and advancing to the footlights whistled at the audience; another riot broke out, and again the police had to be summoned. After eight days in prison, he was escorted to the frontier and expelled from Parma.

More recently at the Teatro Regio, a tenor who had sung the Duke in *Rigoletto* not at all to the audience's liking, was booed and received cat-calls in the true Parma style. Next morning, he packed his bags and made his way to the station. Alighting from his taxi, he hailed a porter to take his luggage to the Milan train. The porter picked up his bags, then suddenly turned to the tenor and asked, 'Was it not you who sang last night?'

'Yes, it was I.'

'Then carry your own bags!' retorted the porter, and stalked away.

Two years after the Curioni episode, the first night of the season failed, and this time it was the impresario who was sent to prison for 'offending the public's sensibilities' – an action by the authorities that opens up wide possibilities to dissatisfied opera-goers the world over!

On the fall of Napoleon, his second wife, the Empress Marie Louise, daughter of Francis I of Austria, refused to accompany him into exile and was granted a divorce. She was then created Duchess of Parma and 'reigned' there until her death in 1847. In 1828 she decided to build a new opera house at her own expense. This was not her only contribution to the arts, for she also established the ducal chapel and ducal orchestra, as well as the conservatoire of music which is now world famous. She chose Nicola Bettoli to design the theatre's exterior, and Paolo Toschi and Gian Battista Borghese its interior. In a curious way she seems to have transmitted something of her own Austrian and French Empire taste to the project. The building took eight years to complete and was designed with 'classic simplicity and severity'. The exterior, in cream stucco, is that familiar soft yellow colour of so many fine public buildings in Italy. The row of ten ionic columns make an impressive façade. The auditorium, modelled on that of the Scala, is decorated in white and gold, with the inevitable red velvet seats and draperies. The seating capacity is small – only some 1,500; there are 112 boxes, in addition to the royal box, each with its own ante-room, furnished and decorated individually according to the taste of the original box holder. The magnificent ceiling, depicting groups of nymphs intent on musical allegories, and the drop curtain with its allegory of the Triumph of Paris, were both painted by Borghese.

The opening night, 16 May 1829, seems to have been typical of Parma's operatic history – a fiasco. The opera was specially commissioned from Bellini who was, in fact, the director's second choice (Rossini was the first, but he was too busy in Paris). Bellini was sent a libretto written by one of the theatre's board of directors, entitled *Cesare in Egitto*, which the composer refused to set, as he found it 'old as Noah'. The people of Parma felt insulted and this, added to the fact that Bellini was the second rather than the first choice, did not augur well for the first night of *Zaira*, Bellini's new piece. Although there were no whistles or cat-calls, the audience sat through the evening in stony silence and the opera was never given again. What is even stranger is that although Rossini had refused the new theatre's invitation to compose the opening opera, the first season included his *Mosè*, *Semiramide* and *Il Barbiere di Siviglia*, all of which were received rapturously. And what happened to the ill-fated *Zaira*? Well, Bellini incorporated much of the music in his *I Capuleti ed i Montecchi*.

Although Verdi was not actually born in Parma, he has always been regarded as belonging to Parma – his birthplace being in the duchy, at Le Roncole, near Busseto and not thirty miles from Parma itself. Parma audiences have always claimed to know every note and every word of all Verdi's works; and woe betide any singer who does not sing the correct note or word; every Verdi opera, except *Un Giorno di Regno*, has been staged at the Regio, and the theatre's official history sums up each production and revival in a word: it was either *ottimo*, *buono*, *mediocre*, *discreto* or *cattivo*; and the cast lists, which may show perhaps five Violettas or three different Dukes of Mantua for one season's production, indicate all too clearly what happened at the individual performances!

The story of the succession of Radameses in 1929 is still told with relish by old (and young) opera-goers in Parma. On the first night, the unfortunate tenor, who was known to own a bicycle shop in Milan, successfully massacred Verdi's music. During the final tomb scene, when the orchestra was at its very quietest, a voice from the upper gallery shouted in Parmesan dialect, 'You, little man, when you have finished, will you mend my bicycle?', While many has been the occasion when someone has shouted out 'Hey, So-and-so, listen! This is how it goes.'

It was at Parma that Verdi's *Les Vêpres Siciliennes* had its first performance in Italy, but, because the censor felt it to be too dangerous to show the Sicilians in a successful revolt, the locale was changed to Portugal and the title to *Giovanna di Guzman*. Although Parma did not enjoy the distinction of being the first Italian city to stage *Aida*, the Parma production had the advantage of being rehearsed by Verdi. The event was commemorated by the city granting the composer its

17 Parma, Teatro Regio. The auditorium is charmingly embellished but there is nonetheless an air of rusticity about the proceedings.

18 Teatro Regio. From the adjacent Piazza Verdi, the Strada Garibaldi leads straight to the
railway station, for the greater convenience of singers who may have to leave in a hurry.

freedom, and presenting him with a gold medal.
It was more than appropriate when the Institute of
Verdi Studies was founded in 1959, that the opera-
loving city of Parma should have been chosen
for its home.

This body, which has the official blessing of both
the Italian Government and UNESCO, had as its first
president Ildebrando Pizzetti, and a council and
committee of the most distinguished musicians and
musicologists. Under the admirable administration
of Maestro Medici the Institute publishes what it
chooses to call an annual 'bulletin'. This bulletin is,
in fact, a very large book (sometimes running to
over a thousand pages), printed in Italian, English
and German. So far these bulletins have included
studies 'in depth' of *Un Ballo in Maschera*, *Rigoletto*
and *La Forza del Destino*, with smaller selections
of essays and documents on *Stiffelio*, *Il Corsaro* and
Jérusalem. In addition, the Institute has organized
three international conferences: one in Venice in

1966, devoted to 'the Present State and Prospects
of Verdi Studies throughout the World'; the
second in 1969, which took place in Verona,
Parma and Busseto, and was devoted to *Don
Carlos*. A third with *Macbeth* as its subject, took
place in 1971.

After Verdi, the name of which the Parmigiani
are most proud is Toscanini; he played the cello
in the Regio's orchestra as a youth, but never conducted opera there, though he did direct a few concerts. Another conductor born in Parma was
Cleofonte Campanini, younger brother of the
tenor Italo Campanini, and husband of the soprano
Eva Tetrazzini, the elder sister of the more famous
Luisa. Campanini conducted a great deal in Parma,
and was responsible for bringing the Parma
orchestra to a very high standard; it was Campanini, too, who was one of the prime movers in
organizing an annual singing competition in
Parma. The 1914 competition discovered Gigli –

'At last we found *the* tenor!' wrote one of the jury on his report.

Continuing the story of the unfortunate singers who have met their Waterloo in Parma, one reads in the memoirs of the famous baritone, Giuseppe Kaschmann, how he was whistled in Parma at his début, and how some of the audience, apparently not satisfied, appeared in front of the hotel in which he was staying, brandishing clubs and scythes! Emma Carelli, a much-loved soprano, appeared in what must have been a horrific performance of *La Gioconda* in 1903. According to her brother, Augusto, who wrote her biography, the whole cast had been 'protested', as the Italians rejoice in saying: first the tenor, then the baritone, then the contralto and mezzo. The jeering next began at the soprano in her second-act duet with the mezzo. Carelli returned insult for insult, left the stage and the theatre and went to the railway station, still in her costume and make-up, to return to Rome. Conchita Supervia, the Spanish mezzo-soprano, failed miserably as Carmen in 1924, and the opera was only given once that season.

Composers no less than singers can also crash in Parma. The Regio would have none of Mascagni's *L'Amico Fritz*, which was laughed off the stage both in 1892 and 1908; and the first Parma *Manon Lescaut*, *Bohème* and *Tosca* hardly fared well. However, the Parmigiani are not so stubborn as to refuse a second chance to composers and even singers. Puccini's operas were eventually accepted; but it is more difficult to persuade a singer to return to Parma after an initial fiasco.

One of the greatest of contemporary singers, Tito Gobbi, has told in an interview that was published in a Chicago newspaper of the ordeals of a young singer making his Regio début:

It was 1946; I arrived in Parma to make my first opera appearance there, driving a new car – a special job – a custom-built Alfa Romeo. I am quite a motor enthusiast, and I recall that this car is what you would call 'cool'. As I pulled into the square and parked my car in front of the hotel, word spread that the new baritone had arrived. A crowd gathered, ostensibly to admire the car, but they had really come to look over the new baritone, of whom, it seems, there had been good reports.

But one could clearly see in their sullen demeanor, their real feelings in the matter, which were: 'We haven't given judgment on him yet!' Later that day, as I strolled through the street, I passed a butcher shop, and the proprietor – a huge, surly man – was lounging out in front (it was just after the war, and there being practically no meat to sell, he had little work to do). 'Are you the new baritone who is doing Figaro in the *Barber of Seville* here tomorrow night?' I politely replied: 'Yes, why?' He then said threateningly: 'You should have come here with a special voice instead of a special car.' I protested: 'You haven't heard me yet!' He ignored this, saying ominously, 'We'll see tomorrow,' and thus dismissed me.

The following night, with trepidation, I began my performance in the title rôle of the *Barber of Seville* before an audience that sat with folded arms like judges in a criminal court. Notwithstanding this pressure, or perhaps because of it, I sang quite well. However, there was practically no applause at the end of the individual arias and in the places where such audience response normally comes during a performance. I was making my greatest efforts and still I thought my goose was cooked. However, at the very end of the performance I received a tremendous ovation, lasting many minutes. Afterwards, practically the entire audience, it seemed, numbering many hundreds of people, followed me to the restaurant where I was to have my supper. All of their former intransigence seemed to have disappeared. They acted as if they loved me. I knew that I had passed the acid test, and this gave me the courage to ask them why they had applauded so sparingly up until the conclusion of the performance. They answered to the effect that they were not sure I could keep on being as good as I was through the whole thing, and until they were sure, that is, until the very end, they were not going to give me the satisfaction of a big hand. One of the spokesmen shrugged his shoulders and said by way of explanation, 'That's the way we are'.

And that is Parma.   HAROLD ROSENTHAL

FRANCE

L'Opéra
Paris

'What on earth is this?' cried the Empress Eugénie, when Garnier – who had just been commissioned to design a new Opéra in Paris – came to show her and the Emperor the plans of the future building. 'It is neither Greek, nor Louis XV nor even Louis XVI. Pray tell me, Monsieur Garnier, what *is* it?' Garnier was no master of etiquette; and besides, he was very cross. 'Madam,' he said, 'those styles are finished with. This is altogether new. This is Napoleon the Third!' As for the Emperor, he pulled his beard, which he was wont to do when annoyed, and intervened: 'Please don't be upset, Monsieur Garnier. She doesn't know what she's talking about.'

The Empress had in fact hoped that Viollet-le-Duc, the most famous French architect of the time and a great friend of hers, would get the job. She did not like her wishes to be thwarted. However, neither the Emperor, on whose command the building of a new opera house had been determined, nor the Empress, who later apologized to Garnier for her rudeness, ever saw the greatest monument erected to their glory. When eventually the Opéra was opened, the Emperor had been dead for two years and the Empress was living in exile at Chislehurst, England. In France, just recovering from her defeat in the Franco-Prussian war, the Second Empire had been superseded by the Third Republic, and so it was not the Emperor but the newly-elected president, the Maréchal de Mac-Mahon, who, at precisely 7.45 p.m., on 5 January 1875, stepped out of a State coach drawn by four black horses and flanked by 200 cuirassiers bearing flaming torches and, with Garnier at his side, slowly ascended the brilliantly illuminated marble staircase of the Opéra.

The building was, in fact, not yet finished. Neither the Pavillon du Chef de l'Etat, which was to have been the Pavillon de l'Empereur, nor the Pavillon du Glacier (refreshment room) or smoking-room were ready. Indeed, the whole building reeked of varnish and paint. But nobody minded. For the Parisians who, scarcely four years earlier had been besieged by the German army and literally dying of hunger, such a celebration was more than a solace. It was the unmistakable symbol of rebirth. It is not surprising therefore that the opening caused such excitement. On the black market, stalls were sold for 1,000 francs (official price: 30 francs), while one box changed hands for the then astronomical price of 15,000 gold francs. Not only was the whole government there but everyone who was anyone in Paris and – in addition – the young King Alfonso of Spain with his mother, the former Queen Isabella. Most glamorous of all was the Lord Mayor of London, ceremonially robed and wearing his chain of office. He had arrived in his gilt coach, preceded by mounted trumpeters in the livery of the City, and was attended by his sheriffs, his swordbearer, his halberdiers and his Master of the Poultry (that impressed the Parisians most of all), all brightly clad in their various uniforms. His party in itself said the press, matched up to this 'dazzlingly

19 The President of the Republic, M. le Maréchal de MacMahon, and Madame la Maréchale, arriving for the opening on 5th January, 1875.

resplendent setting of marble and onyx', to this great, massive building 'bristling with groups in metal, laden with statues and busts, fluted with innumerable columns, crowned by a girdle of antique masks, raised from the ground by eagles spread in flight. . . .'

Garnier was sitting with his wife in a second-tier box. For them it had been a day of strong emotions, from the moment when a messenger delivered to the bewildered Madame Garnier a letter from the Minister of the Interior saying that His Excellency 'would be pleased to put a box seating six for the Opening Ceremony at the disposition of Monsieur Garnier for the sum of 120 francs'. Madame Garnier's reply must have been pretty sharp, because apologies and free tickets followed promptly. In any case, Garnier

had been in his opera house since dawn. Now, at last, the former blacksmith's apprentice with 'such a gift for setting wheels' watched his dream come true as the director of the Opéra – Monsieur Halansier – in front of a packed and glittering house, knocked the boards three times with a heavy wooden pole and announced: *'Place au Théâtre!'*. On that memorable evening, the programme consisted of the Prelude to Auber's *La Muette de Portici*, the first and second acts of Halévy's *La Juive*, the Prelude to *Guillaume Tell*, the 'Bénédiction des Poignards' from Meyerbeer's *Les Huguenots*, sung by Pedro Gailhard, who was to be the second director of the Opéra, and finally Léo Delibes's ballet *La Source*. Originally it had been planned to present an act of *Faust* and an act of Thomas's *Hamlet*, but for reasons of precedence

55

(already!) Christine Nilsson – the Callas of her time – had refused to appear. Another demonstration of wounded feelings nearly spoiled that first night. Considering themselves insulted at being 'buried in a hole' (the orchestral pit), the musicians played *pianissimo* the entire time. From the auditorium they were virtually inaudible. After the performance, as indeed during it, the guests went on inspecting the building and mixing backstage with the performers, forming a strange medley of medieval knights, ballerinas straight out of Degas, starched shirts and *grands décolletés*.

The press was delirious about the new building:

The main façade is brilliant. It cannot fail to surprise. The side on the Rue Auber is majestic: it commands respect. The back, where the offices are, is stern: it means work. The front on the Rue Halévy is ample; in a few minutes 300 carriages can drop under its arcades the whole crowd of its patrons. . . . Ten bronze street-lamps form a girdle of nude women around the building. . . . It dazzles. It resplends. It is worthy of the Thousand-and-one nights. . . .

And so, in a blaze of gaslight, torches, diamonds, gold braid, fanfares, *entrechats*, high Cs and self-praise, the great night had come, happened, was gone and passed into history.

But to realize why the magic word '*l'Opéra*' means so much to the French, one must go back seventeen years, to an equally cold evening and another gala performance on 14 January 1858.

The front of the Opéra, then in the Rue Le Peletier, was brilliantly lit. 'Hundreds of gaslights emphasize the main lines of the building and contours of the windows. Their tiny blue and yellow flames dance merrily in the breeze and their flickering is reflected like so many will-o'-the-wisps in the helmets of the mounted guard. The street is strewn with sand. . . .'

That evening, the famous singer Massol (of whom a contemporary critic wrote that 'the roaring of the bull was his normal pitch', while another spoke of his 'threatening voice') was giving his farewell performance. Rachel and La Grisi were going to appear, the Emperor and Empress were both to be present, and Rue Le Peletier was overcrowded. As, at 8.30 p.m. precisely, the Imperial

20 and 22 (*Above and far right*) Some of the appurtenances of the opera in a contemporary engraving.

21 (*Right*) Charles Garnier's masterpiece: the Paris Opéra.

carriage, coming from the Boulevards, nears the entrance of the narrow street a violent explosion, closely followed by two others, rends the air. At the same time, all the lights go out. In the sudden darkness, cries of anguish are heard. Over 150 people are injured, some of them horribly. The Imperial carriage is blown to pieces, the coachman killed. A piece of metal tears the Emperor's hat, a bit of glass grazes his nose. Otherwise, the occupants are unhurt. The bombs had been thrown by an Italian called Orsini, who wanted to establish a Republic in France and in his own country. The Emperor and Empress remained perfectly calm. But, says an eyewitness, when he extricated himself from the debris, the Emperor 'looked like some macabre and profoundly sad clown, like a Pierrot haunted by a ghost'. In spite of the shock, the Emperor decided that he would attend the performance. And when he and the Empress – who, by then, had completely regained her composure – appeared in their box, a thunder of cheers and applause greeted them.

However calm the Emperor seemed outwardly, he had been enormously shaken by the incident –

and understandably so. Indeed, after he and the Empress had given the Préfêt de Police a piece of their mind, the Emperor decided that a new opera house should be built as soon as possible to replace the one in the Rue Le Peletier. After various consultations a decree was pronounced ordering a competition for the construction of the new Opéra. This was to be the thirteenth since, on 28 June 1669, Pierre Perrin, in association with the Marquis de Sourdeac, received the first privilege, confirmed by letters patent, 'to present and have sung in public operas and spectacles with music and in French verse'. Incidentally, by 1858 Paris possessed no fewer than four opera houses: the Théâtre Italien, the Théâtre Lyrique, the Opéra-Comique and, finally, the Opéra. But so great was the vogue for opera that the four could profitably co-exist.

From then on, things moved speedily. The site which, according to the Emperor's wishes, should be properly isolated in order to avoid the risk of another attempt on his life, had to be in the district north of the Place de la Concorde which Haussman was then reconstructing. A monu-

mental avenue (which never materialized) was to lead to it. One hundred and seventy-one entries were received, some quite crazy – for instance, the building should be shaped like a violin or a lyre. From the original total, six were selected for a second round. Garnier was then in fourth position and received a prize of 1,500 francs. However, when it came to the final decision, his plan was chosen unanimously.

Aged thirty-five, this man, whose name has since become world famous, was still practically unknown. Of very modest origins, he was unsure of himself and had a slight stutter. He had been admitted eleventh out of eighty-nine candidates at the École des Beaux-Arts, had worked for the famous architect Viollet-le-Duc (for a wage of 75 centimes an hour) and was subsequently awarded the Prix de Rome, the highest academic distinction for French artists (it has recently been abolished). It was in Rome that he fell in love with the theatre, writing plays and songs, going to fancy-dress balls, and acting. Back in Paris, he became Inspector of Architecture, an apparently rather dull position for someone with such revolutionary ideas.

On 1 August 1861, the plans having been duly completed and the contractors chosen, work on the new building started with a flourish of fanfares, speeches and demonstrations. But problems soon appeared. It was discovered that deep under the site was a swamp formed by a small river called ruisseau de Ménilmontant; it took the workmen from 2 March to 13 October 1862 to dry it out and to build two tanks capable of storing two-and-a-half million litres of water, for use against possible fire. They were, in fact, used only once. However, while the drainage was going on, the other work progressed and, on 21 July 1862, Count Walewski minister of state, laid the foundation stone. Then, on 15 August 1867, on the occasion of the Exposition Universelle and of the National Holiday, the façade was solemnly unveiled. Yet it was to take sixteen more years before the building was far enough advanced to be put into use, sixteen years which were to see the Franco-Prussian War, the fall of the Second Empire, the Siege of Paris (and the use of the Opéra as a gigantic store house), the

establishment of the Third Republic, a stoppage of work due to the rival claims of the Hôtel de Ville, and finally the fire which completely destroyed the Opéra in the Rue Le Peletier, thanks to which the estimates were at long last voted and the work eventually resumed and completed.

Paris could now proudly proclaim itself the owner of the largest, most glamorous and most modern opera house in the world. A few figures may help one to realize the vastness of the Palais Garnier, as it soon came to be called: 172 metres long and 101 metres wide, it rises 71 metres above the ground and goes down 19 metres below. The stage is 15.60 metres wide, 32 metres deep, and the drop curtain measures 14.50 by 17.55 and (although in aluminium) weighs 7 tons. The Opéra prides itself on 1,606 doors, 6,319 steps, 450 chimneys, 7,593 keys, 334 dressing-rooms amongst which – untouched since her marriage to the industrial tycoon Marcel Boussac and her retirement – is that of the soprano Fanny Heldy, complete with its precious Louis XVI furniture, its Persian carpets and gilt mirrors. She never entered it after she left the Opéra thirty years ago, but occasionally lent it to stars of great brilliance such as Callas, Nilsson or Nureyev. The interior volume of the building measures 430,000 cubic metres (more than twice that of the Panthéon) and has a surface area of 11,975 square metres. There are seventeen floors from the lower ground floor to the roof and 365 steps lead from the former to the latter. It takes the firemen over two hours to make their round. Originally, 9,000 gas lights connected by 15 kilometres of pipes (electricity being considered too dangerous) burnt in 'dazzling splendour'. Underground there are workshops and storerooms for costumes, scenery and stage properties, while on the stage itself – which is large enough to contain the whole building of the Comédie-Française – and below it, row upon row and roll upon roll of sets sleep their last sleep. At the back, and separated from the stage by a small drop curtain, lies the famous Foyer de la Danse with its gilt sculptures, plush settees and its huge mirror in front of which generations of dancers have stretched their weary limbs. Also below are stables large enough to accommodate twenty horses. 'These noble animals ("the most noble conquest of man," according to Buffon) reach the stage by means of a gentle slope', wrote a contemporary, 'to appear in the procession of *La Juive*, or take part in the triumph of Masdaniello in *La Muette de Portici*'. The marble columns of the façade come from the same quarries as those which Michelangelo used for the columns of St Peter's. A Frenchman, M Hureaux – the owner of the quarry – chose to lose money on them 'rather than miss the opportunity of making available such exceptional marble to his country'. Similarly, the firm of Blunière only charged 32,000 francs for the casting of the statue of Apollo which crowns the building, thus losing 14,000 francs on the job.

Despite its size, its vast proportions, all its marble, bronze, gold, precious wood, mirrors, sculptures, paintings, velvet and brocade, the Opéra could not pride itself on any pictorial masterpiece until Chagall painted his famous ceiling, and had only one notable sculpture: Carpeaux's *La Danse*, now transferred to the Louvre, a copy having taken its place on the façade of the Opéra. The only reason, in fact, why the rather eccentric Carpeaux should have been given the commission was that he was a personal friend of Garnier. He worked on the group in a state of mad frenzy, but when it was finally un-veiled, the reactions of public, press and officialdom were equally disastrous. 'Is the Opéra meant to become a brothel?' inquired a journalist. 'When the dancer on the right is arrested for drunkenness the whole group will collapse' wrote another. 'Sir,' wrote a father, 'I have a wife. I have two daughters. I will never agree to take them into a building whose signboard is that of an evil haunt!' In 1869, in fact, it was officially decreed that the group should be removed and replaced by another group to be commissioned from a Monsieur Gumery, which would be more in keeping with the aesthetic standards of the building. However, M Gumery died shortly after and the change never took place.

And how much did all this cost? The sum originally allocated by the National Assembly for the building itself amounted to 35,400,000 francs.

23 In the 1850s there were four opera houses in Paris. This one, the Opéra Comique (seen here in 1840) was formerly known as the 'Salle Favart'. It was burnt down in 1887, but rebuilt on the same site.

24 Laying the foundation stone of the Opéra in 1861.

But to this must be added the cost of the site, the compensation of the expropriated landowners and tenants . . . in all, roughly 100 million gold francs. In spite of this, Garnier maintained that, of all the momuments erected in Paris during the nineteenth century, the Opéra was the cheapest per cubic metre 'with the possible exception of the Punch and Judy show in the Champs-Elysées'.

This was indeed something to be proud of. Nor was it the only thing. When people met M Garnier, either in the Opéra or in the street, they often greeted him with a respectful 'Bonjour Monsieur Garnier, Bravo pour l'Opéra!' or simply 'Congratulations, Monsieur Garnier!'. This meant much to him. But what moved him most was the gift he received in 1874 from his workmen: a medal commemorating the building of the Opéra and recalling the happy relationship which had always existed between him and all those who had worked for him. The letter of thanks which he sent them, a simple letter from a simple man, read: 'Gentlemen, I am profoundly moved by the expression of sympathy which you have just given me. Nothing could have touched me more and I can assure you that I will keep this medal which will be a most precious reminder to me that I am surrounded by good people who wish to honour me with their friendship. So, Gentlemen, I thank you all for your affectionate thought. I am still too moved to be able to express as I would like the pleasure which you have given me. Allow me to shake hands with you and to send you the expression of my cordial friendship. And thank you. Charles Garnier.'

On 3 March 1898, Charles Garnier died and his students asked the Government to arrange an official funeral. The Minister refused to see them. As his secretary left his room, he sighed to them: 'If only he had been a painter . . . but an architect!'.

And now, what judgment should one pass on that gigantic marzipan cake topped with the largest and greenest onion in the world, on that gold and crimson auditorium, those marble halls, that scintillating building where every surface, corner, nook and cranny is covered with a painting, filled with sculpture, adorned with the most ornate and intricate decoration?

'To the uninformed passer-by', wrote Claude Debussy, '[the Opéra] looks like a railway station; inside, one might be forgiven for thinking it was the central lounge of a turkish bath.' The French architect, Charles Marrast, was more restrained. 'If for his time', he says, 'Charles Garnier was a master of design, he was a slave in matters of decoration.' However lavish the ornamentation, however rich the building material, Garnier never allowed it to obstruct his general scheme and purpose. And what was this? To present great shows to splendidly dressed audiences, to enable beautiful, bejewelled women to see and be seen, to allow the less privileged classes to watch the arrival and departure of the rich, to admire the façade, the windows blazing with light, the walls behind which mysterious events happened, to provide separate entrances for pedestrians, for carriages, for the Head of State, to enable the valets to sit and wait, the carriages to be called for; and at the same time to present a glamorous image of France and its emperor, of Paris, its capital city. The Opéra was the palace of the people where everyone could, at least in theory, come and see the rich display their wealth in an equally rich setting. Garnier's Opéra was the triumph of convention in an era of unashamed plutocracy. But it was more than that. It was also a considerable architectural achievement, the first and perhaps the only monument to be built in an entirely new style, owing nothing – as the Empress Eugénie had sharply pointed out – to its predecessors and yet able to hold its own with them. A century has elapsed and still we find it striking. It is easy to imagine the shock which the Opéra must have given Parisians at the time and what a feat its conception and construction must have represented to them.

An opera house is not just a theatre. The word itself has connotations of glamour, lavishness, magic. But in the last analysis, an opera house is a place where lyric works can be performed, seen and heard under the best possible conditions. How does the Paris Opéra respond to these requirements? During the nineteenth century, it seemed to do so perfectly. Its very vastness, which, later, was to contribute in making it so difficult to

25 The Grand Staircase; an engraving of the 1860s.

manage, was in keeping with the times. Performances took place, sometimes cheered, occasionally
booed; people arrived in the middle of an aria;
ladies settled themselves in their boxes with a
great rustle of silks, glanced absent-mindedly at
their programmes, waved to their friends and
passed round chocolates; men in full evening dress
surveyed the house through their opera glasses,
wandered in and out of the boxes and stalls, went
to the smoking-room, drifted backstage.

Amongst them, a small but powerful group
made its presence and its influence constantly felt.
These were the *abonnés*, the subscribers. Most of
them had one or two seats in the stalls (men only –
full evening dress to be worn up to the date of the
'Grand Prix'). But the more important subscribers
– and the richest – owned a box in the back of
which they entertained friends or clients or played
whist, emerging only to listen to some new singer,
hear an aria, or watch the ballet. However, their
main privilege was to be allowed backstage and
on the stage even when the curtain was up, and
to be admitted to that holiest of sanctuaries, the
Foyer de la Danse. Their activities were not
limited to giving *boules de Boissier* (the fashionable
sweet) to the *petits rats* – the child dancers – or
jewellery to their mistresses; they also made their
weight felt in matters of musical policy and even
of composition. Every new opera had to include
a ballet, and not earlier than the second act. In
fact, nothing important was allowed to happen
before then. Revivals were no problem: if the
work contained no ballet, one was commissioned
and added. Influential lovers also interfered with
the casting. Foreign works were blacklisted,
German ones prohibited. If a director was fool-
hardy enough to try and break the rule, the
offending production was likely to be howled
down by the *abonnés*, and by the members of the
reactionary Jockey Club in particular, whose box,
number one, was nicknamed *La Loge Infernale*. It
was the *abonnés* who were responsible for the fact
that France was the last major country to perform
Wagner: the downfall of *Tannhäuser*, the monstrous booing that greeted *Lohengrin*, were two of
their greatest triumphs. When Berlioz wrote that
the Opéra had 'fallen in love with mediocrity',

26 Marthe Chenal, appropriately draped, leading a
huge crowd from the steps of the Opéra in singing the
Marseillaise.

it is really the influence of the *abonnés* he was
referring to. The wishes of the *abonnés* were
indeed treated as orders by Halansier, the first
director 'since Lully' to show a profit. During his
reign not one note of foreign music was played –
with the exception of Verdi's *Aida*, tolerated for
political reasons, and of Rossini, who was considered a Parisian by adoption if not by birth. Thus
the artistic standards hardly matched the financial
results. Hackneyed favourites were given a new
look. And that was that. Yet so successful was
Halansier that the Government threatened to
withdraw his subsidy or to take part of the profits.
It took all his resourcefulness to keep both.

Vaucorbeil, who succeeded him, was scarcely

more enterprising. And, as the building lost its 'tourist value', receipts fell and profits vanished. One evening, Vaucorbeil asked a few journalists and *abonnés* to come with him two floors below the stage. There, to their utter amazement, they heard the second act of *Les Huguenots* through earphones connected with the stage far above. One month later, four Ader microphones placed in the prompter's box enabled a few distinguished guests to hear the performance from the Opéra's store house half-a-mile away. The 'theatrophone' was born. It was to enable hundreds of subscribers to hear all performances on the telephone.

In 1884, Pedro Gailhard, a cobbler turned bass, became director. This meant, of course, that he had to give up his singing career, but he did resume it once, when, sitting in the prompter's chair, he sang 'Masetto' while a voiceless singer mimed the part on the stage. Gailhard relied mainly on *Roméo* and *Faust* to bring in the money. Apart from those favourites, the repertory consisted of *Guillaume Tell*, *Robert le Diable*, *La Juive*, *Les Huguenots*, *La Favorite*, *Hamlet*, *Aïda*, *Le Cid*, *Rigoletto*, *Sigurd*, *Patrie*, all of which – *Rigoletto* and *Aïda* excepted – are largely forgotten today. Nonetheless, Pedro Gailhard was enterprising enough to present *Lohengrin* in 1891. Stink bombs were thrown and even outside the theatre, such was the anger of the demonstrators – motivated more, no doubt by patriotic than by musical motives – that troops had to be called to re-establish order. It was to take another ten years of heated controversy before Wagner found final acceptance in France. By then *l'affaire Wagner* had been at the centre of the French musical and emotional life for nearly half a century. Several other incidents marked the long, and on the whole successful, directorship of Pedro Gailhard. In 1889, the Shah of Persia visited the Opéra. The orchestra tunes up. The Shah starts clapping, then falls asleep, only waking up for the ballet and startling everyone by picking out a few ballerinas and asking them to join him in his private suite. 27 October 1893; the Russian Fleet visit Toulon, the first foreign navy to give the vanquished French the 'Great Power' treatment. Russian sailors attend a performance at the Opéra and to the accompaniment of Bizet's Overture 'Patrie' and the chiming of the Opéra's sixteen bells (the heaviest weighs 650 kilos) the two-headed Eagle carrying the Chariot of Peace, rises from below stage, the audience shouting *'Vive la Russie!'*

1896. While Rose Caron sings the great aria in the first act of *Thétis et Pelée* a terrible noise is heard. One of the counterweights holding the Opéra's gigantic crystal chandelier suddenly breaks loose and falls on a woman sitting in the gallery, killing her on the spot.

1905. Gailhard takes a step which seems no less than revolutionary. He decides that the conductor's name shall henceforth be printed on the posters. Before that, there were just two *batteurs*: the chief *batteur*, whose name everyone was supposed to know and who conducted on first nights, at galas, the ballet, and occasionally an act or two of a routine performance ... and his assistant, who did the ordinary work and took over, sometimes in the middle of a performance, when his chief had a more urgent – or attractive – engagement. But it was not until 1 February 1907 that a committee of musicians fixed a place for the conductor's stand. Before that, the *batteur* led the performance sitting beside the prompter's box, turning his back to the musicians and only facing them for the overture or the orchestral interludes.

The following year, in 1908, Messager took over. It was he who put on the first performance of *Parsifal* in Paris, 4 January, 1914. By then the *abonnés* had practically disappeared. The impact of the performance was tremendous. It was also during his directorship that an age-old institution, the *claque*, officially disappeared from the Opéra although, unofficially, it remained till 1939. Before then, the *chef de claque* would start the applause for any artist prepared to pay his fee of 150 francs. The *claqueurs* were recruited at the Café du Passage de l'Opéra, Rue Le Peletier, and the job was much sought after because it carried a free seat with it.

1914. The First World War. Marthe Chenal sings the *Marseillaise* on the steps of the Opéra; the crowds join in. Jacques Rouché had just taken over the directorial chair which he was to occupy so brilliantly and without interruption for the next thirty years. His directorship was not only the longest but also the happiest in the chequered history of the Opéra. Rouché enjoyed a considerable income (he was head of the *Parfumerie Pinat*) and considered it absolutely normal – indeed his privilege – to pay the deficit of the Opéra out of his own pocket. He was *le Patron* and every year the Opéra quietly accomplished its season of nine months. *Alceste, Boris Godunov, Der Rosenkavalier, Falstaff, Fidelio, Die Zauberflöte, Hérodiade, La Traviata, Les Troyens, Turandot*, all received their first performances at the Opéra during his directorship. France could then pride itself on some of the greatest singers in the world. In thirty years, Rouché presented 71 lyrical works and 73 ballets. The Paris Opéra was the undisputed leader of the operatic world. One did not need to say 'the Paris Opéra'. 'L'Opéra' *was* Paris.

Maximilien was the first of Milhaud's operas to be performed at the Opéra in 1932. Eight years later, on 8 May 1940, his *Médée* was the last new work to be presented before the German occupation. Six weeks later – on 22 June – a lonely visitor knocked at the door of the closed, silent building. Under the guidance of a fireman, Hitler walked on to the stage, looked at the vast auditorium covered in its grey dustsheets, went slowly up the great white, marble staircase, strode through the Grand Foyer and finally, having cast a quick look out onto the empty Avenue de l'Opéra, departed as sullenly as he had come. Gradually, the Opéra resumed normal activity,

26a A set designed by Fernand Léger for *Simon Bolivar* at the Paris Opéra in 1950. The producer was Max de Rieux.

though for the French some events there seemed far from normal, for example the sole production of *Die Fledermaus* ever given there – for occupation troops only.

Jacques Rouché was the last independent director of an independent theatre. In 1939 the Government set up an amorphous body called Réunion des Théâtres Lyriques Nationaux, grouping together the Opéra and the Opéra-Comique, placing them under State supervision, pooling their repertories and artists, appointing a host of advisors, controllers, supervisers and directors whose task was in principle to assist the general administrator but who in fact often made his work more difficult. The participation of the State in the management of the Opéra not unnaturally brought with it an increasing amount of red tape. Singers, dancers, orchestral players and technicians became civil servants and union members who all too often defended their privileges at the expense of their duties. Administration had superseded artistic direction. The general administrator was the slave of 'the system'.

Yet when, by a stroke of luck – or a clever piece of diplomacy – a great work is presented in the Opéra's unique 'grand manner', then the house comes into its own again and it is possible to see performances there which outshine all others.

Such, for example, were Rameau's *Les Indes Galantes* presented for the first time by Lehmann in 1952, since performed 266 times, almost always to full houses. Lehmann was responsible, too, for an admirable production of Milhaud's *Bolivar*, even though it was only to have a run of twenty-six performances. Those who, during Georges Auric's administration, were privileged to see one of the five performances of the production of *Turandot* by Marguerite Walmann, with sets by Jacques Dupont and Birgit Nilsson in the title rôle, will never forget the experience. The same is true of the 1963 production of *Don Carlos* with Boris Christoff, (the *auto-da-fé* scene in particular

was unforgettable), as well as *Wozzeck* under the musical direction of Boulez. One of the rare visits of General de Gaulle to the Opéra – apart from State occasions – was to see the revival of *Carmen* transferred from the Opéra-Comique with Rhodes, Guiot, Lance and Massard in the principal rôles, and conducted by the twenty-two-year-old Roberto Benzi. The producer was Raymond Rouleau and the sets were by Lila de Nobili. But the greatest triumph of the Opéra, the work that always sells out, whatever the cast, whatever the day, whatever the season, is Gounod's *Faust*. Surprisingly enough, it was not the Opéra but the Théâtre Lyrique which first did *Faust* (in 1859), the Opéra (of the Rue Le Peletier) only taking it up ten years later. By the end of 1970, *Faust* had been given 2,383 times at the Opéra, the most memorable performances being the 2000th on 1 February 1944, and the centenary productions, with three Marguerites, four Fausts and five Mephistopheles. Perhaps the strangest performance was one for charity (the third act only) in 1875, using the sets for *Guillaume Tell*. The runners up are *Rigoletto* (985 performances), *Samson et Dalila* (852), *Thaïs* (672), *Lohengrin* (602) – Wagner eventually got his revenge – *Roméo et Juliette* (588) and *Les Huguenots* (511). Of the many works presented at the Opéra during the past century, only thirty reached one hundred performances.

And now, what about the future? Lifts have been installed to enable orchestra and singers to reach the rehearsal rooms quickly and easily (it took them over an hour before), a new lighting console has been set up – and Chagall's *Bouquet de rêves* has replaced the original ceiling by Lenepveux. The subsidy of the Opéra is the highest in the world. Rolf Liebermann, the wizard of the Hamburg Opera, has been appointed General Administrator. Georg Solti will assist him. No effort is being spared to make the Opéra worthy of the City of Paris and of its own glorious past.

L'Opéra Louis XV
Versailles

You have been directed towards a small, crowded stone lobby at the far end of the Cour d'Honneur. There, sitting behind a series of little windows, ladies of forbidding aspect gingerly deliver admission tickets to the various parts of the palace. After a few unsuccessful attempts, you find the right lady and get the right ticket. Splendid! A group of people is just assembling for the visit to the theatre. But no! Only twenty-five are admitted at a time. All right! You will go and have a walk in the gardens. But no! Admission takes place in order of arrival. So, rather disgruntled, you decide to sit and rest. But no! The few benches are already occupied. So you just stand and get cross. Also there are queues everywhere. Are you in the right one? Luck may have it that you are. The *gardien* arrives with his bunch of keys. One, two, three, four, five ... You are in. Off you go; through various empty rooms and doors which have to be unlocked, along a marble corridor lined with staring busts, through another door into a narrow, semi-circular stone corridor. You are locked in. Then you pass through yet another narrow door. And suddenly you forget it all as you find yourself standing in a medium-sized theatre of incredible beauty. A ring of rock-crystal chandeliers reflected in large mirrors of the purest quality sheds a soft, glittering light on the scene. High, fluted columns enframe three tiers of small boxes. From the cream and gold circle decorated with delicate golden bas-reliefs a royal loggia advances in a graceful curve.

Golden carved trophies hang on either side of the proscenium while a deep blue curtain magnificently embroidered with the royal Arms and a scattering of golden fleurs-de-lis hides the wide and deep stage. All the seats are covered with stamped blue velvet. 'The shape of this theatre is perfectly noble and graceful,' writes Paul Valéry. 'It calls to mind all that the most distinguished, the most sensitive company can wish for when it gathers together for entertainment. The architect has – to perfection – succeeded in making each viewer enjoy the view of his fellows set in an admirably balanced structure of interior spacing.'

The Versailles Opera is indeed a miracle of balance, sensitivity and taste; a work of genius which, like genius itself, is the fruit of long patience, a patience which lasted over one hundred years.

Louis XIV loved the theatre. Most of Molière's and Racine's plays were first performed at Versailles. Lully wrote operas and ballets for him and yet – during the King's lifetime – there was no permanent theatre at Versailles. Temporary theatres were built either in the gardens or in various rooms or courtyards of the Palace, or even in the stables, and then pulled down. Since the indoor theatres were always too small for operas, outdoor performances were given in the *bosquets*. These could only take place in the summer. Plans for a permanent theatre were made and given up. The wars were costly. Money was scarce. At long

27 Jean Cocteau supervises The Dance of the Unicorn at Versailles, 1957. This uniquely beautiful setting has been host to many other brilliant occasions as well as opera.

28 (*Above*) The beautifully
restored auditorium of the
Louis XV Opera House at
Versailles. The stage can be so
adapted as to transform the
whole interior into one large
ballroom or banqueting hall.

29 (*Left*) The Opera House at
Versailles, seen from across the
lake.

last, in 1748 – thirty-three years after the *Roi Soleil* had died – Gabriel was commissioned to prepare the plans for a permanent theatre. At the same time, M de Marigny, brother of Madame de Pompadour, and *Directeur des Bâtiments du Roy*, was sent to view the new theatres in Italy. He was accompanied by Cochin and Soufflot. Their experiences and findings no doubt greatly influenced Gabriel. His plans having been approved, work started at last. But progress was slow. By the end of 1753 only the actors' dressing-rooms have been completed. Work is then stopped because of lack of money due to the Seven Years' War. In 1763 changes are made to the original plans. Gabriel Dumont has just published his *Parallèle des plus belles Salles de Spectacles de France et d'Italie*. The design is simplified. So is the decoration. 1764. New lack of money. New stoppage. Meanwhile, the theoreticians keep busy. Chaumont publishes '*La Véritable Construction d'un Théâtre d'Opéra à l'usage de France*', and Maginot, '*l'Exposition des Principes qu'on doit suivre dans l'Ordonnance des Théâtres Modernes*'. Well and good. But the person most directly concerned – Gabriel – is about to give it all up. Happily the coming marriage of the Dauphin (the future Louis XVI) with Marie-Antoinette is announced. All of a sudden the matter becomes urgent – and funds miraculously materialize. After some understandable hesitation Gabriel agrees to go on with the work. He chooses his assistants: Pajou for the sculptures, Rousseau for the trophies, Dropsy for the marble work, Vernet for the garlands, Durameau for the ceiling. The hall can be transformed into a ballroom by laying a floor to raise the pit level with the boxes. It is indeed a banquet – given in honour of the Dauphin and his young and beautiful Austrian bride – which at long last marks the opening of the Opéra (as it was henceforth to be called). 'Nothing equals the beauty of the theatre when it is converted into a banqueting hall,' writes the Duc de Croy. 'It is no doubt the most beautiful hall ever seen in Europe. ... As one looks at it, one is tempted not to disapprove the two-and-a-half million francs that it has cost, especially in view of the fact that thus one will not have to build a new one for every celebration'.

Twenty-one years later, after three other royal marriages had been fêted there, and now and then an opera or a play performed, Louis XVI – as he had become – and Marie-Antoinette, paid what was to be their last visit to the theatre and indeed the last celebration to take place there before the Revolution. The time is October, 1789. Three months had already elapsed since the fall of the Bastille. Nerves were on edge. Madame de Lafayette describes the occasion:

> The King's Garde du Corps wished to give a dinner for the Officers of the *Régiment de Flandre* and of the *Garde Nationale*. For this occasion they asked to borrow the great theatre of the Château. ... The theatre was brilliantly lit. Suddenly, it was announced that the King and Queen were to appear at the Banquet. The Sovereigns did indeed appear in the Centre Box accompanied by the Dauphin who was nearly five years old. ... A Swiss Officer asked the Queen's permission to take the Dauphin round the Banqueting Room. ... The officer put him on the table and he walked boldly round it, smiling, quite undismayed by the shouting all about him. The Queen was less confident and when he was brought back to her she embraced him tenderly.

This celebration was badly interpreted in Paris. Four days later Versailles was invaded and the King left the palace for ever.

From then on, the Opéra suffered all sorts of humiliations. During the Revolution – its furniture and decorations having been plundered – it became the meeting place of the *Club des Jacobins*. Napoleon and Louis XVIII simply forgot about it. Louis-Philippe, who was to dedicate the Château 'to the glory of France' redecorated it – and most horribly. In 1837, the Overture of *Iphigénie en Aulide* and fragments of *Robert le Diable* were performed there, a play being presented in the middle. In 1848, Berlioz conducts a concert. The choir and orchestra are 450 strong. The enthusiasm is enormous. Seven years later, Napoleon III and the Empress Eugénie give a State Banquet there on the occasion of the visit to France of

30 Much detailed craftsmanship of the highest quality came to light when the building was restored.

Queen Victoria and the Prince Consort. In 1864 it is the King of Spain who is entertained there and watches a performance of *Psyché*. After the fall of the Second Empire, it becomes the seat of the National Assembly. The Third Republic is proclaimed there on 30 January 1875. After which it is abandoned. Meanwhile, monstrous alterations have been made both to decoration and structure. The white and gold jewel case with its delicate, pale-blue lining has become a dark, gloomy undistinguished hall. Things were going from bad to worse for the theatre when at last, in 1952, private and public funds made it possible to start the work of restoration. About one thousand million francs were spent, mainly on the stonework, masonry and timber. The royal box has now reclaimed its original size; ravishing pictures and delicate colours have been discovered under layers of dark brown paint; sculptures have been cleared of plaster and glue. A seat covered with its original blue stamped velvet has been found in the prompter's box and, thanks to this, the very firm which had supplied the original fabric two centuries ago was able to weave the same material – on the original loom. Other pieces of material and gold braid were found under the flooring. The royal-blue drop curtain with its pure gold embroideries is a faithful replica of the original. And backstage the whole complicated seventeenth century machinery is now in working order, with complete electrical equipment thrown in for good measure.

The opening of the renovated Opéra Louis XV took place on the occasion of a particularly moving event: the first State visit of Elizabeth II, Queen of England. One century after her august great-grandmother, she was entertained at Versailles and, following a banquet in the Galerie des Glaces, attended a performance at the Theatre. That day the glittering hall was bedecked with flowers, the ladies wore (by request) light coloured print dresses with matching hats, the Queen looked dazzlingly beautiful in a pale blue ensemble. The Opéra and the Comédie-Française presented a 'Royal' programme. A few performances have been given there since, but on that day only, the Opéra Louis XV really came into its own again.

L'Opéra Monte Carlo

On 25 January 1879, the Monte Carlo Opéra's inaugural performance was nearing its end. Artists from the Paris Opéra and from the Comédie-Française had been singing their most entrancing arias, reciting tear-jerking verse. Sarah Bernhardt, with a voice whose golden timbre matched the gold leaf on the walls, had declaimed a poem by the young Mediterranean writer Jean Aicard, specially written for the occasion. Flowers had been showered, the curtain dropped and raised innumerable times. . . . Then a few members of the audience spotted a little man with a big nose, in one of the official boxes, wiping his eyes. The cheers started again, perhaps even louder than before. Charles Garnier was living another of his great hours.

He had been commissioned to build the Monte Carlo Opéra immediately after his Parisian triumph. And the golden decoration, the profusion of mouldings, sculptures, paintings, hangings, pelmets, fringes, garlands, caryatids, marble columns, masks and nudes bore witness to the unashamed pride he took in his Parisian *magnum opus*, by then world famous, as well as to the Prince's determination to give his people as splendid an opera house as that of Paris. But whereas in Paris the imperial pomp for which it was conceived was never to be displayed, in Monaco the Opéra was – and still is – the Prince's own theatre, with its gold and crimson state box, and private suite, and its four large boxes for members of the cabinet, the princely household

and the municipality, while the six hundred privileged guests admitted to the stalls feel that they are not in a theatre at all, but in the large drawing-room of some fairy-tale palace. Two days after the opening, Garnier and his family left Monte Carlo from the little station under the Casino. Crowds had assembled to cheer him for the last time. From the Tir aux Pigeons just outside, the Prince's guns fired a sovereign's salute.

If, as in Henry James's phrase, the Piazza San Marco in Venice was 'the drawing-room of Europe', so *à la Belle Époque*, the gingerbread villas and hotels of Monte Carlo might have been termed its *petits appartements*. There, year after year, during autumn, winter and early spring, but *never in the summer*, came kings, princes, grand dukes and archdukes, tycoons and adventurers and last but not least, ladies of varying degrees of virtue, flashing their jewels, showing off their ospreys, rustling in silks. There they all were to make love, to gamble, to meet and to be seen at the Casino, at the Café de Paris, the Tir aux Pigeons – and at the Opéra.

Garnier's house was the perfect setting for such an audience, but for him glamour was never allowed to supersede either design or functional requirements. The Monte Carlo stage is vast, its equipment up-to-date, the rehearsal and dressing-rooms are easily accessible and comfortable. It was indeed fortunate that within eleven years the ideal impresario should have appeared on the scene and been put in charge of it. He was Raoul

31 There is a florid grandeur about the heavily gilded
ceiling of the Monte Carlo Opera which seems exactly
to fulfil Garnier's intentions.

Gunsbourg, a Romanian, born in 1859, who had
previously worked in Russia and at Nice. His
first important Monte Carlo production was the
first performance anywhere of Berlioz's *Le Damna-
tion de Faust*, in his own stage version. Thereafter
followed a whole series of notable premières of
new works by Bizet, Franck, Messager and –
above all – Massenet: *Le Jongleur de Notre Dame*,
Chérubin, *Thérèse*, *Don Quichote*, *Roma*, *Cléopâtre*
and *Amadis*. Puccini's *Le Rondine* had its première
there in 1917, and Ravel's *L'Enfant et les Sortilèges*
in 1925. It was there, too, that Nijinsky first
danced *Le Spectre de la Rose*, and after the First
World War Monte Carlo became the home from
home of the exiled Russian Ballet.

But it is Massenet's frail shadow that lingers
most evocatively from the past, even though
during his lifetime he never commanded the
universal voice of the great. He did, however,
possess above all the gift of pleasing, and the
'soft arms' of his harmonies, the 'undulating
spine' of his tunes and, more generally, 'the
quivers, the outbursts, the embraces' of his music
(to quote Debussy) were in perfect harmony with
the mood of 'those charming beauties' who, at
Monte Carlo, 'only see in music a discreet but
helpful accompaniment to their smiles'. Massenet
loved women and he loved Monte Carlo. And
this love was duly requited.

32 The Opera at Monte Carlo, next to the Casino
buildings.

Le Capitole
Toulouse

Coming to the footlights the singer – Louis Tharaud – beckoned to the conductor, saying, 'Would you mind starting again from the beginning of the aria? My top C was quite awful.' The bewildered conductor did as he was bid, the top C came out triumphantly, was sustained magnificently, and the audience responded with deafening cheers.

This, of course, could only have happened in Toulouse, and at its Opéra, Le Capitole.

Where else, too, could a singer – it was Cavandoit – after having been painfully out of form during the whole last scene of an opera, address the public when taking his curtain call and say: 'I do apologize for what happened just now. I know I was awful. But then, I had had a terrible row with Modeste (the *régisseur*), so it affected my voice. . . .'

The special relationship between public and singers is indeed one of the strongest and oldest features of the Toulouse Opéra where the proverb, 'He loves thee well who makes thee weep', is particularly true. Already a century-and-a-half ago a local newspaper could write: 'The whistling craze has reached a frightening degree.' The more deafening the noise, the better. In 1829, the boos are so loud that the singer – Madame Saint Clair – has a fainting fit on the stage. Again, in 1829 a singer, Mlle Pouilley, leaves the stage in protest at a chorus of boos. The public wants her to apologize. She refuses. When the noise gets really deafening the police are called in. Nine youngsters

are arrested, brought to court . . . and released. 'Leniency will bring appeasement', says the judge. When another singer refuses to apologize for conduct considered 'irreverent', the public decides that no more performers shall appear until amends are made. The *Préfet* addresses them. No good. The police have to clear the hall, fighting breaks out in the streets. No wonder that – in spite of her reputation – Madame Garcia Vestris, described as the *Première Chanteuse du Théâtre Italien de Paris* on the poster announcing her performance, should 'crave the indulgence of the public because, being a foreigner, her pronunciation might not be perfect'. Even when a singer is 'admitted', the public remains restless. At the slightest lapse, it shouts, it stamps. Police, soldiers even, are called in. People are arrested . . . only to start shouting again next day.

A few years ago, a well-known French broadcaster, Pierre Crenesse, speaking of an evening at the Met., said: 'If this had happened at Toulouse, the artists would not have escaped alive'.

Things of course are quieter now. And how could passions break loose in the streamlined modernistic aquarium that is now the Capitole? Gone are the garlands, the stuccoes of Guillaume Cammas – who also built the beautifully baroque town hall of which the theatre is part. Gone is the work of Cellerier and Gisors which replaced it when, in 1807, it was declared unsafe. Gone too is the theatre of Dirulafoy which was burnt down in 1917 and the delightfully Edwardian

33 (*Above*) 'Le Capitole', or town hall of Toulouse, of which the opera house forms part.

34 (*Right*) Teresa Berganza, the brightest singing star to emerge from the Toulouse music festival.

theatre of the octogenarian Paul Pujol which took its place. 'Like the old Faust rejuvenated by Mephisto, the antique Capitole rolls on towards a new life, in the bloom of its radiant youth, at the service of art and of the people of Toulouse.' Thus speaks the handbook issued on the occasion of the opening of the new hall. Which proves at least that those who planned the new building truly meant well.

However, it requires more than a change of setting to alter the feelings of the Toulousains towards music. In the very year that the new hall was opened Flagstad appeared for the first time at the Capitole to sing Isolde's 'Liebestod', 'Du bist der Lenz' from *Die Walküre*, and the final scene of *Götterdämmerung*: quite a feat – even from such a tower of vocal strength. The conductor was George Sebastian. A few years later, Régine Crespin sang Fauré's *Pénélope*. Her triumph there was the beginning of her international career. The year 1958 saw the Bayreuth production of Wagner's *Ring* with Birgit Nilsson in *Die Walküre*, singing in France for the first time. From then on a Wagner season has taken place in Toulouse every year. 1962: *Parsifal*, again in the Bayreuth production. From 1966 onwards, all the productions have been given in the original language. New works, mainly by French composers, are presented regularly and at the same time revivals are staged of the great operas which made the fortune of the Paris

Opéra in the last century and are now being sadly – and no doubt unjustly – neglected: 1962 saw *Guillaume Tell* with Tony Poncet and Izard – the director – in the prompter's box to fill in a few gaps; and in the same year *Sigurd*, *La Juive*, *Il Trovatore* and *Fra Diavolo* were presented. In 1963 *Les Huguenots* was revived, in 1966 *I Puritani*, in 1967 *La Reine de Saba* and, for the Berlioz bicentenary, *Benvenuto Cellini*; while 1970 saw the Glyndebourne production of *La Pietra del Paragone*. Also, since 1954 an annual international singing competition takes place at Toulouse. Teresa Berganza is no doubt its most illustrious 'find'. Every year promising singers are rewarded not only with the *Vase de Sèvres* offered by the President of the French Republic, but with many important engagements, so that the two words, Toulouse and singing, remain as closely linked as ever.

Thus, although the Toulousains may have lost some of their rough ebullience of many years ago, and although they may, when they enter their own *Capitole*, have a sinking feeling at the view of so much light, so little warmth, when they see from outside the beautiful Place du Capitole with their theatre shining at the far end and listen to the great works which are performed inside, they have no reason to feel depressed. Toulouse is still, and will always be, one of the living centres of opera in the world.

Le Grand Théâtre Bordeaux

April 8, 1880. Bordeaux is commemorating the centenary of its Opera House, Le Grand Théâtre. The Mayor, rather surprisingly called Brandenburg, wishes the celebration to be worthy of the event. A subsidy of 12,000 francs has been voted. A face lift has been given to the hall. Charles Garnier is among the many celebrities attending the performance. Already, before the interval, the emotion of the audience has reached a high pitch, on the three orchestras of Bordeaux joining forces to give a rousing performance of the 'Hungarian March' by Berlioz. But the ecstasy reaches its climax when a character impersonating Posterity appears on the flower-bedecked stage and crowns a plaster replica of the statue of Victor Louis[4] – the architect of the building (and later of the Palais-Royal, in Paris) – by the sculptor Jouandet (it is now in the entrance hall) whilst an actress from the Comédie-Française declaims an *ad hoc* poem ending with the following lines:

Ta merveille, ton nom, ton image elle-même,
O Louis,
Bordeaux avec orgueil les salue à la fois.[5]

And well could Bordeaux pay homage – and amends – to the man of genius who gave this beautiful city what is without doubt its finest monument, a monument of which the Bordelais have always been inordinately – and understandably – proud, and which since its inception they seem always to have endeavoured to spoil. True enough, the outside of the theatre has now been cleaned and has recaptured its pristine splendour. True enough, there are hopes of restoring the auditorium to its original white, turtle-grey and blue – as has been done at Versailles, and in the exquisite theatres of Nantes and Dôle – and of getting rid of all the unfortunate changes, the so-called improvements that nearly two centuries of changing taste have imposed on the theatre. But who will ever restore the delightful oval concert hall which was destroyed in 1837 – now the Second Empire foyer – the charming lounges on the ground and first floors, or the theatre's original approach?

From the very start, the story of Bordeaux's opera has been a succession of quarrels, strife, intrigues, delays and bankruptcies. Even the initial bill could eventually only be settled thanks to the generosity of two Bordeaux citizens, Monsieur Dubergier, alderman, and Monsieur Streikheisen, consul of the King of Prussia. Louis, for his part, gave up his fee, and the decorators even volunteered to work on Sundays (although they were stopped from doing so) so that the excited Bordelais could witness on the given date the solemn opening of their Grand Théâtre – at the time no doubt one of the most beautiful and largest of its kind in Europe. With bated breath they watched the curtain rise on *Le Triomphe d'Apollon*, by Blincourt, 'prompter and rehearser' of the theatre, and on Racine's *Athalie*, glorified with resounding choruses specially composed for the occasion. They came, they

35 Le Grand Théâtre, Bordeaux, built between 1753 and 1780, at the head of the Allées du Grand Tourney – named after the Marquis de Tourney who was Governor of the city from 1743 to 1757, and to whom it owes its finest buildings and streets.

listened, they saw and were conquered. And so the chequered existence of the Grand Théâtre – as it was to be called – started.

And from then on it has been the scene, not only of the changing trends of artistic and musical taste, but of many political demonstrations. Royalists and republicans confronted one another there during the French Revolution. The Empire was never popular. When Napoleon paid a state visit to the theatre he was driven by mistake to the front door while the officials were all waiting for him at a special entrance on the side. Furious at not seeing anybody to receive him, Napoleon ordered his bewildered coachman to drive him home immediately. However, he agreed to attend a performance the following day. Bordeaux's subconscious had had its fling. In 1814 'God Save the King' was played for the British occupiers. The Restoration, the Revolutions of 1830 and of 1848 found their echo there – mainly by way of bitter, and often noisy, opposition between the management, the *abonnés* and the *parterre*, the promenaders of the day. Order reigned during the Second Empire, the white tulle dress and the diamonds and emeralds worn by the Empress at the gala performance in Their Majesties' honour feeding the local gossip for weeks. At the end of the Franco-Prussian War, the theatre was briefly the seat of Parliament. During the First World War it remained closed, whilst during the Second World War the German occupying forces were its most frequent visitors. Since then the Opéra has led the quiet life becoming to such a grand old lady.

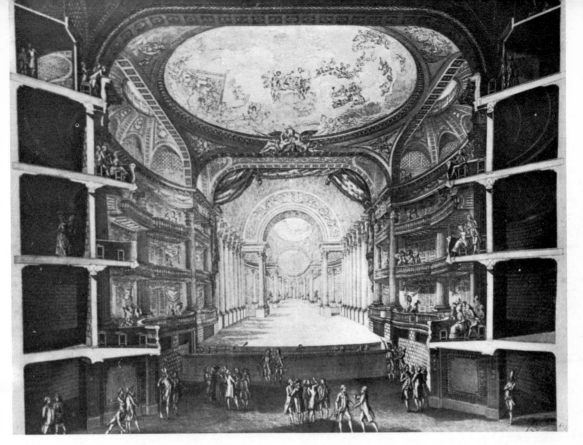

36 The stage and part of the auditorium. It was in this theatre that the National Assembly sat in 1871.

In Bordeaux, the nineteenth century has seen the same amount of nonsense talked about the same works as anywhere else. *La Traviata* could 'not be compared to any of Meyerbeer's works' and Bizet's *Carmen* 'reeked of the effort to avoid triteness'. *Manon* was an 'incoherent muddle', *Tosca* 'too ruthless' and anyway the performance should have included a ballet. *Samson et Dalilah* 'had no arias', but, surprisingly enough, *Tannhauser* got a good reception and gradually there, too, Wagner made his mark although, before the first performance of *Rheingold*, a journalist – no doubt echoing popular feeling – wrote: 'Instead of taking that gold out of the Rhine, you would have done better to throw it into the Garonne'.

For the last twenty years, Bordeaux has been the seat of a major festival of the arts in which opera has naturally enough had an important part to play. Contemporary works have been commissioned and presented for the first time and many gala performances with world-famous artists have taken place there. Since the war Vanni-Marcoux (another singer turned director), Roger Lalande and, at the time of writing, Gérard Boireau have managed the theatre in perhaps less exciting circumstances but with no doubt a greater sense of their responsibility to the public than most of their predecessors. Above all they strive to present productions worthy of the *Nouvelle Salle de Spectacle par Monsieur Louis* and of the noble city whose proper pride it still is.

TONY MAYER

GERMANY

Die Staatsoper; Die Komische Oper; Die Deutsche Oper Berlin

Opera in Germany derives from a variety of sources: civic wealth and pride in the case of Hamburg; an aristocratic tradition of courtly festivities such as was cultivated by the Electors of Saxony in Dresden; the sudden achievement of political power and prominence that King Frederick II of Prussia found himself confronted with at his Berlin *Residenz*; or the almost sensual delight in theatrical manifestations that the Bavarians have shown at Munich for centuries. There is, however, one point in history when nearly all the German opera houses, built on these various foundations, suffered a common fate: between 1943 and 1945 they were reduced to rubble. After the Second World War they had to start anew – to plot a fresh course, not only architecturally, but in respect of repertory and ensemble as well.

In Berlin the building of an opera house became a political declaration of independence when Frederick the Great ascended the throne in 1740. Though no less a soldier-king and strategist than his father, and involved in lifelong warfare against Maria-Theresa, Empress of Austria, he was also a man devoted to the Muses; an accomplished flautist and a composer. Thus one of his very first commands was to Baron von Knobelsdorff, supervisor of all royal buildings, for an opera house to be erected on the grounds of the former fortifications, along what is now Unter den Linden, East Berlin's main – indeed only – boulevard. And though Prussia was engaged at that time in a bloody war in Silesia, and money was lacking in every department, the King constantly admonished his architect to hurry up. So urgent was his desire to have an opera house of his own, that the opening performance on 7 December 1742, for which Karl Heinrich Graun's *Cleopatra e Cesare* had been chosen, took place amidst scaffolding and sheets covering the half-painted ceiling. It was almost a miracle that the house, brightly lit by thousands of candles, did not collapse in all its incomplete splendour.

Just how splendid the Lindenoper really was, in its Prussian sobriety overlaid with Frederician rococo elegance, only became obvious some few weeks later, when everything was finished, and a court ball was held in all the three main sections of the building; the banqueting hall, the theatre and the 'Corinthian' hall (which was really the stage). That the architect provided space outside for no less than a thousand carriages has earned him the eternal gratitude of generations of opera-goers, for this must be one of the very few opera houses in the world with absolutely no parking problems.

It was, however, a building dedicated to Italian opera – and to be attended by special invitation only. Not until 1806 were the Berlin citizens admitted and appropriately charged for their curiosity. This made some rebuilding neces-

37 Paul Dessau's *Puntila* (1966) is one of three operas by this contemporary composer that have found their way from the Staatsoper on to other stages.

38 Mozart, hurrying back from Leipzig to Berlin in May 1789, went straight to a performance of *Die Entführung aus dem Serail*. He was quickly recognized from his more than half audible comments on the orchestra, and subsequently made much of.

sary. After a proper stage had been installed, the body of the house, which provided only standing-room and boxes, was converted into an auditorium with seats and tiers. Yet for years to come opera in the vernacular was confined to the nearby National theatre, as the home of drama, operetta and opera in German. While the Italians reigned supreme at the Lindenoper, even Mozart had to make do with the modest Nationaltheater am Gendarmenmarkt. It was here that he paid a surprise visit in 1789 to a performance of his *Belmonte und Costanze* (as *Die Entführung aus dem Serail* was known in Berlin), here that Berlin heard its first operas by Gluck, here that E. T. A. Hoffmann's only opera *Undine* received its world première in 1816, after which the house burnt down. It was rebuilt on a much nobler scale by

one of Germany's greatest architects, Karl Friedrich Schinkel, and in 1821 the new house, the 'Hofoper', witnessed the birth of Carl Maria von Weber's *Der Freischütz*, the work which gave such a tremendous impetus to German operatic morale.

The entire operatic life of nineteenth century Berlin was characterized by a continuous fight between cosmopolitan and nationalist forces. Under Gasparo Spontini and Giacomo Meyerbeer as chief musical directors, the international policy was emphasized, while the authorities showed little concern to establish closer ties with composer-conductors like Weber, Lortzing or Wagner, whose works – apart from *Der Freischütz*, of course – had to be tried out at other houses before being allowed to grace the boards of the Berlin Hofoper. Thus the record of first performances consists only of long forgotten titles, the sole noteworthy exceptions being Heinrich Marschner's *Hans Heiling* in 1833 and Otto Nicolai's *Die lustigen Weiber von Windsor* in 1849. This last had already been performed at the new Lindenoper, opened in 1844, after the Knobels-dorff building had been burnt down. Though the façades were reconstructed according to their original design, the interior underwent drastic changes – a fourth gallery was added, the seating capacity was enlarged to 1,800 and the stage was considerably widened. What had still remained of aristocratic feudalism in the old house gave way to rather more bourgeois ideas of comfort and good sight-lines.

This was the house that survived the revolutions of 1848 and 1918 as well as the so-called 'power seizure' of 1933, by which time the Hofoper had become the Staatsoper. Of course there were occasional constructional alterations, some to improve safety precautions, others to increase the efficiency of the stage facilities. At times the house had to be closed for repairs, the ensemble being evacuated to the Kroll-Oper in the Tiergarten, originally a pleasure garden devoted to middle-class relaxation and entertainment, with a regular summer season of opera on a private basis. The State eventually took the Kroll-Oper over in 1895, and there were constant plans to build an

39 Unter den Linden, Berlin, in 1842. The first house
of Opera in Berlin, and now the Deutsche Staatsoper:
Painted by Wilhelm Brücke the younger.

affiliated opera house on its site. These eventually
materialized in 1927, when Otto Klemperer
became the director of the Staatsoper, attracting
world-wide attention with his avant-garde productions.

For all the changes the Staatsoper had under-
gone architecturally, and· whatever political
régime its general administrators had to bow to –
Hohenzollern imperialists, Prussian republicans or
Nazi maniacs – it was this house which represented
the summit of opera in Germany – though
Munich and Dresden may boast of a prouder
record of first performances through their close
liaison with composers of the stature of Wagner
and Strauss. Here Weingartner, Muck and Strauss
controlled the operatic destiny of the nation, to
be succeeded in turn by Kleiber (who not only
presented to the world Berg's *Wozzeck* and

Milhaud's *Christophe Colomb*, but was instrumental in securing recognition of Janáček's *Jenufa*
for the masterpiece it is), Blech, Furtwängler,
Clemens Krauss, Karajan, Heger and Schüler. As
a devoted Wagnerian, Heinz Tietjen – general
administrator, producer and conductor from 1927
to 1945 – made up amply not only for the sins of
omission of his predecessors, but strengthened
considerably the ties of the institute with the
Bayreuth Festival. And if the house did not
produce a single memorable opera during the
fortunately brief span of the Nazi millennium (its
sole surviving specimen is Werner Egk's now
decidedly dated *Peer Gynt*), even those wretched
dictators valued the Staatsoper so highly as the
national symbol of German art, that they immediately rebuilt it on an even more splendid
scale after it had first been bombed in April

40–43 (*Overleaf*) In rehearsal Felsenstein gives
everything of himself and demands everything of his
singers. Here he is working on *La Traviata*.

44 Leoncavallo's high regard for William II was one of the less well publicized *ententes cordiales* of the early twentieth century. A caricature of 1914.

45 The 1925 production of Alban Berg's *Wozzeck* at the Berlin Staatsoper was one of the most important musical events of the twentieth century (so far). This is the design for Act III, scene 2 in which Wozzeck cuts Marie's throat.

1941 – and defied the world with a new production of *Die Meistersinger* in December 1942. It throws a macabre light on the strangeness of the time when one notes that the supreme chief of the Prussian State Theatres was General Field Marshal Hermann Göring and that the conductor was Wilhelm Furtwängler.

Yet it was a very short-lived splendour; late in the summer of 1944 all German theatres were closed due to the exigencies of total war, and early in February 1945 the Staatsoper was once again razed to the ground. In the years immediately after the war, the Deutsche Staatsoper, as it was now called, found temporary refuge in the Admiralspalast, a former revue theatre near the Friedrichstrasse station. The new start of the house, as one of the representative theatres in the capital of the German Democratic Republic, set up in 1949, was characterized by a good deal of internal political manoeuvring, but still more by the determination to build up a strong ensemble and to renew relations with the rest of the world. All this was made the more difficult by the growing political estrangement between the eastern and western parts of the city, culminating in a complete split between them. The company returned in 1955 to the house Unter den Linden, which had been rebuilt yet again.

And there it stands, rather small by today's standards, a careful reconstruction of all that could reasonably be conserved of Knobelsdorff's original design, while the necessary alterations were made in complete harmony with his architectural style. The best proof of this is the marvellous Apollosaal, which serves not only as the main foyer, but is regularly used for chamber-music concerts and performances of chamber-operas; and in the warm, festive, yet astonishingly intimate auditorium, with a seating capacity of almost fifteen hundred.

The repertory now performed there before a somewhat uniform public is concentrated on Handel, Gluck, Mozart, Wagner and Strauss, but offers also the customary Italian pieces and a careful choice of Russian and Czech works. Since 1945 the Deutsche Staatsoper has been conscious of an obligation to foster contemporary opera as well. So far it has succeeded best with Paul Dessau, whose *Das Verhör des Lucullus*, *Puntila* and *Lanzelot* have found their way from here to other stages. International currency regulations make appearances by Western singers of renown rare in East Berlin, but there can be no doubt that the Staatsoper offers today opera performances of a sound and competent, if not always very inspired, let alone exciting, ensemble standard, which obviously has its own attraction for many a West German, English or American opera-lover visiting the city, although interested West Berliners by reason of the almost total lack of intercourse between the two sectors, are effectively prevented from going into the Eastern one.

What attracts visiting opera lovers today even more to East Berlin, despite the often very troublesome and humiliating controls on the east side of that unnatural Wall, is Walter Felsenstein's Komische Oper. It is a completely new type of opera house – unique in the world, though its name refers to the French genre of *opéra comique*. Actually there was already a Komische Oper in Berlin prior to the First World War, run by private enterprise and thus doomed from its very beginnings in 1905. It was the first attempt in Germany to reform opera by way of a more modern approach to staging – to make it dramatically and theatrically more telling – with *Les Contes d'Hoffmann* and *Carmen* as the most successful productions.

It was from this point of departure that Felsenstein embarked on his big scheme of reform, which has made him one of the most talked about and controversial opera producers in the second half of the twentieth century, comparable only to such people as Giorgio Strehler, Peter Brook, Roger Planchon and Wieland Wagner in his influence on the contemporary theatre scene. Felsenstein's ideas found favour and the Soviet authorities in East Berlin handed over to him the former Metropol-Theater, which had been the city's leading operetta and revue theatre before the war – situated in a street running parallel to Unter den Linden. After substantial alterations and a formidable extension of the area occupied

46 Foyer of the Komische Oper, East Berlin. Under Walter Felsenstein this house, in the post-war era, has seen some of the most exciting productions in the world.

to accommodate new storage rooms, rehearsal studios and offices, the whole complex now extends right up to the main boulevard. With its late nineteenth century rococo-style auditorium, surrounded by the staircases, foyers and corridors of mid-twentieth century functionalism, the house does not compare architecturally with the much more noble Staatsoper, but it has an inviting openness, a distinctly classless atmosphere favourable to a feeling of homogeneity in the audience, which makes opera-going much less formal than in other houses.

With Felsenstein's unending quest for the dramatic truth of the works performed, with emphasis on every factor contributing to the theatrical validity of their messages, and the closely integrated ensemble-style of performance, brushed up and polished by constant rehearsal, the Komische Oper provides equally well for the naïve visitor out for an evening of thrilling theatre, as for the intellectual élite, bored stiff by the usual type of opera performance. It does *not* provide for the *bel canto* specialists and the people who prefer closing their eyes and submerging themselves in lush sounds, emanating from the

47 Anthropomorphism nowhere presents deeper pitfalls than on the stage, but Felsenstein successfully avoided them all in his production of Janáček's *The Cunning Little Vixen*.

48 An engraving of the Deutsches Opernhaus, built in 1912, when the Berlin suburb of Charlottenburg was still an independent city. It was destroyed by bombs in 1943.

throats of leading international stars or the instruments of a divine orchestra. The musical side of the performances, though rarely falling beneath the standard of solid decency, is seldom something to rave about. The theatrical aspects, however, never fail to engage one's mind.

With his young crew of brilliantly gifted producers like Götz Friedrich and Joachim Hertz, Felsenstein has built up a discriminating and superbly realized repertory which has become the epitome of modern music-theatre, stretching from Monteverdi's *Il Ritorno d'Ulisse in Patria*, by way of Mozart's *Die Zauberflöte*, Wagner's *Der fliegende Holländer*, Offenbach's *Contes d'Hoffmann*, Strauss's *Fledermaus*, Bizet's *Carmen*, Verdi's *Falstaff*, Richard Strauss's *Die schweigsame Frau*, Puccini's *Turandot*, Janáček's *The Cunning Little Vixen* and Gershwin's *Porgy and Bess* to Britten's *A Midsummer Night's Dream* and Henze's *Der junge Lord* – to mention only some of the milestone productions of this company. Among the great opera houses of the world, Felsenstein's East Berlin Komische Oper, opened only in 1947, has surely earned a position for itself that is *hors concours*.

While the accent at the Staatsoper is on tradition, with an open mind towards the more conventional developments of modernism, and at the Komische Oper on a distinctly modern approach, the Deutsche Oper, Berlin, situated in the Western part of the city, on the Bismarckstrasse, tries to combine both aspects. Since 1961 it has been housed in a strictly functional, brand new, gigantic opera factory, which shows no signs at all of the former house that was opened on the same site in 1912 as the Deutsches Opernhaus of the independent (as it then was) city of Charlottenburg. In the early 1920s, when Charlottenburg became part of Greater Berlin, the opera house was rechristened the Städtische Oper, Berlin, only to return to its somewhat more grandiose original name when Hitler came to power. Alas, not all its pomposity could prevent the Allies from bombing it in 1943, after which the company moved to the same Admiralspalast that was later to become the make-do quarters of the Staatsoper. After 1945, once more named the Städtische Oper,

Berlin, it opened at the former Theater des Westens, near the Zoo Station – where Caruso had first appeared in Berlin and where the Nazis had installed Berlin's third regular opera house, the Volksoper. It was at this house, along the Kantrasse, that the Städtische Oper laid the foundations of the international reputation it enjoys today, before moving back to its new building on the Bismarckstrasse to become the Deutsche Oper, Berlin.

Little remains to be reported about the early years of the huge Deutsches Opernhaus with its seating capacity of 2,098 (today it seats 1,900 people) and marvellous stage equipment. It was constantly in financial trouble and was always considered a rather cold and anonymous house, though it warmed up considerably under Tietjen's and Carl Ebert's reign during the later twenties and early thirties, when first Bruno Walter and then Fritz Stiedry became its chief conductors, with Furtwängler a frequent guest, and an ensemble of singers that included Maria Ivogün, Maria Müller, Lotte Lehmann and Sigrid Onegin. Competition with the Staatsoper's two houses on Unter den Linden and at the Kroll ran high at that time – as can well be imagined if one considers that on some nights it was a question of deciding between Walter at the Bismarckstrasse, Kleiber at Unter den Linden or Klemperer at the Kroll.

There was always some commuting of artists and executives between the various houses in Berlin, but it was strictly limited and not at all encouraged by the authorities. During the Nazi years the slightly modernized Deutsches Opernhaus steered a rather conventional course, with good singers in mostly rather empty-headed productions, culminating in the new *Ring*, specially staged for the 1936 Olympic Games. But after the war, again with Tietjen and Ebert as general administrators, and then under Gustav Rudolf Sellner in the new house, the Städtische Oper – Deutsche Oper Berlin embarked on an operatic course of its own, assisted at first by many experienced former Staatsoper artists who preferred to work in the West. Later on, after the Wall had been built, it came to rely more and

49 Hans Werner Henze's *Der junge Lord* is a bitter, sardonic, and at the same time a genuinely musical and highly entertaining work. This beautiful production was at the Deutsche Oper, Berlin. (See also XII)

50 Dietrich Fischer-Dieskau as Falstaff and Pilar Lorengar
as Alice Ford in the 1962 production of Verdi's final
masterpiece at the Deutsche Oper. It proved a triumph for both artists.

more on the unending stream of talented young-sters mostly coming from abroad. This lent to the house an international flavour, which is a true reflection of the city's present international out-look.

Today the repertory is grouped around the established Mozart, Wagner, Verdi and Strauss classics, with Schoenberg's *Moses und Aron* as one of the most frequently performed modern works. Henze figures prominently among the contem-poraries, while a number of operas have been specially commissioned from such composers as Boris Blacher, Luigi Dallapiccola, Roger Sessions, Giselher Klebe and Aribert Reimann. Nor has the house shied away from such demanding pieces as Pfitzner's *Palestrina*, Janáček's *The Excursions of Mr Brouček* or Berg's *Lulu*. With its regular guest-appearances of international singers

and conductors, from Nilsson to Böhm, with Dietrich Fischer-Dieskau, Evelyn Lear, Pilar Lorengar, Giacomo Aragall, Thomas Stewart and Martti Talvela among its resident singers and Lorin Maazel as its musical director until 1971, the Deutsche Oper, Berlin, is today firmly established in the international opera circuit – thanks not least to its splendidly situated airport, only fifteen minutes away.

Clearly, however, the running is not always smooth, for there is a more than usual share of booing and protest at premières from a strong minority of young people. This reflects the element of unrest which can be observed in all sectors of West Berlin's social scene today, and it sets one wondering what is going to become of the city and its brilliantly efficient operatic amenities in a few years' time.

VIII (*Opposite*) The Cuvilliés Theatre, Munich, designed by Francois de Cuvilliés, and built between 1751 and 1753. By timely dismantling and dispersal the marvellous rococo interior was preserved from bomb destruction in World War Two. IX (*Overleaf*) L'Opéra Louis XV at Versailles. The auditorium seen from the stage. The proportions of this theatre are beyond praise.

Die Staatsoper Dresden

Though occasionally we come across the same names, opera in Dresden always took a rather different course from opera in Berlin. It started, long before anybody was thinking of opera or *dramma per musica*, with the foundation of the Musikalische Kapelle, in 1548, at the nearby Torgau Castle, where the same orchestra was responsible for the first known performance of an opera outside of Italy – the German-language *Dafne* by Heinrich Schütz (1627). Since that time the orchestra has been the backbone of Dresden's operatic life – in an unbroken tradition up to its present existence as the Dresdner Staatskapelle. Under this name it still ranks among Germany's foremost orchestras, though its tradition of having great conductors at its helm came to an end for the time being when Rudolf Kempe left Dresden in 1952.

Dresden's operatic culture grew from a soil which had been deeply impregnated with all the multifarious forms of renaissance and baroque festivity, most of them imported from Italy. In fact, the gradual emergence of German opera in Dresden owed its success only to the long and continuous fight against Italian predominance favoured by the Electors of Saxony and kings of Poland at their Dresden court – a situation of which Carl Maria von Weber was only too well aware when he became musical director in 1817 and thus had to compete directly with the senior *Kapellmeister*, Francesco Morlacchi.

After individual opera performances had been given at the Riesensaal of the castle, Dresden got its first solid opera house in 1667 – an enormous building, seating 2,000, at the Taschenberg. It suffered what must be one of the strangest fates of all opera houses, for in 1708, after August the Strong had been converted to Roman Catholicism, it became the official Catholic court chapel. From that spiritual eminence it was turned into a ballroom, and it ended its days as the State Archives. From 1719 on, however, Dresden possessed a beautiful new opera house in Pöppelmann's luxurious Zwinger ensemble of baroque fantasies. Here Italian opera enjoyed its greatest triumph under Johann Adolf Hasse, 'il divino Sassone', as he was called in international operatic circles. But soon other theatres sprang up, partly used for dramatic performances, partly for opera. In 1726 the Theater auf dem Linckeschen Bade was founded (where E.T.A. Hoffmann later reigned as chief conductor and Dresden saw its first *Fidelio*); in 1746 Mingotti's private theatre in the Zwinger (the first Dresden theatre open to the public); and in 1755 another entrepreneur, Moretti, built a theatre of his own which later on – after several alterations – became the Königliches Hoftheater. Here Weber thoroughly reformed the Dresden operatic and concert scene between 1817 and 1826. Under him, Dresden gradually became the capital of the progressive German opera movement, a change of course which was wholeheartedly supported by its intensely opera-loving citizens.

x (*Above*) Galli di Bibiena was the greatest designer of 'spectacles' of the baroque era, and his talents were in demand at most of the Courts of Europe, including that of the Elector of Saxony. Here is his Dresden setting for Dido's farewell to Aeneas. xi (*Below*) This first 'Semper House' was built by Manfred Semper, the Zurich based architect whose work was to serve as prototype for many important opera houses.

51 The world première of Richard Strauss's *Der Rosenkavalier* in 1911. Margarete Siems created the rôle of the Marschallin and the Octavian was Eva van der Osten. Ernst von Schuch conducted. Sketch in oils by Robert Sterl (1867–1932).

Here, too, the very young Richard Wagner admired Weber as 'the greatest man alive'. But when Wagner returned to Dresden for the first performance of his *Rienzi* in 1842, he found a new building which had been opened only the year before, designed by Gottfried Semper – a house not dedicated to the vagaries of aristocratic taste, but aiming solely to serve the art of drama and opera and its public. In its noble and sober neo-renaissance elegance it became the model for many theatres throughout the world, and after it burnt down Semper's son rebuilt it on an even grander and more monumental scale than before. During the interregnum a curious wooden building, looking like a cross between an enormous barn and a Russian country church, served as a temporary theatre. The new Semper Opera House, opened in 1878, became the dominating architectural feature of Dresden's 'klingende Platz' (ringing square) – a house with marvellous acoustics, which was to become the scene of many inextinguishably memorable performances; some

of them the greatest in operatic history. Alas, it, too, shared the fate of the whole beautiful city when it was utterly destroyed early in 1945, three months before the end of the war. And though an empty shell still proclaims its former greatness, rebuilding only started in the late 1960s, to be completed, it is hoped, by the mid-1970s.

With Wilhelmine Schröder-Devrient, Johanna Wagner and Joseph Tichatscheck as his faithful interpreters, Wagner went on from where Weber, through his untimely death, had been interrupted. The first performances of his *Der fliegende Holländer* (1834) and *Tannhäuser* (1845), are only two (alas, not very successful) examples of his enormous activity as chief conductor. Equally notable were his sensitive productions of Gluck's operas, his revolutionary concert programmes (culminating in a triumphant vindication of Beethoven's Ninth Symphony), and his memorandum calling for a complete reorganization of the court theatres. In all, he was a shade too active for the leisurely pace of the Dresden court

52 The Taschenburg, Dresden's first real opera house built in 1667, with a seating capacity of 2000. It was the scene of many baroque splendours.

53 The interim theatre which served between the destruction of Semper's first opera house and its rebuilding.

54 (*Above*) Moretti's Theatre, built by
private enterprise in 1755, was later to
become the first Royal Court Theatre
– much transformed to accord with
its enhanced status.

55 (*Left*) The world première of
Wagner's *Cola di Rienzi, der Letzte der
Tribunen* (he based his own libretto
on Bulwer Lytton's novel) was given
at Dresden in 1842: Watercolour by
Baron von Leyser.

officials, and when, to cap it all, he joined in the revolutionary uprising of 1849, he was proclaimed a traitor and had to flee overnight.

After Wagner, the Dresden opera suffered a temporary decline until Ernst von Schuch became musical director in 1872. Thanks to him and his inexhaustible initiative, Dresden not only got to know Wagner's latest output, but became familiar with Verdi and Puccini, while undoubtedly his greatest contribution was to start the Dresden tradition of first performances of Richard Strauss, which he personally supervised, from *Feuersnot* (1901) to *Der Rosenkavalier* (1911). He was succeeded after his death in 1914, first by Fritz Busch and Karl Böhm, and after 1945 by Joseph Keilberth and Rudolf Kempe. But it was not only the operas of Strauss that were given their premières in Dresden. There were also, to name only a few, d'Albert's *Die toten Augen* (1916), Busoni's *Doktor Faust* (1925), Weill's *Der Protagonist* (1926), Hindemith's *Cardillac* (1926) and Schoeck's *Penthesilea* (1927). It is easy to see why Dresden was called the 'Eldorado of premières'. Yet it might equally well have been called the Eldorado of repertory performances: certainly its performances, not only of Verdi and Puccini, but also of Mussorgsky, let alone of Mozart, Weber and Wagner, offered ample proof of the high standard the Dresden opera maintained throughout its very rich and varied repertory.

During Hitler's 'millennium', the institute's firmly rooted tradition was its salvation, too tough and resistent to allow the Nazis to graft on to it their narrow, nationalist ideas. Growth was inevitably retarded in the lean post-war years of makeshift theatres, until the former Schauspielhaus had been restored in 1948. The Dresdner Staatsoper now shares this with the drama company, until such time as it returns to its legitimate Semper home. There is also, incidentally, a 'Kleines Haus' for smaller-scale operas and plays. While the management works very hard to live up to and to re-shape the traditions of the past, and while the people of Dresden are still as opera-minded (not to say opera-mad) as before, there can be no doubt that the Dresden opera is currently going

56 Wanted by the police! One of the temporary embarrassments of Wagner's turbulent career.

through a period of stagnation. In the German Democratic Republic it has been clearly surpassed by Leipzig. But as we have seen, this has happened before, and yet has never prevented the Dresden opera from coming splendidly into flower again. It may well do so now, under the recently appointed Siegfried Kurz.

Das Nationaltheater; Das Cuvilliés Theater Munich

Though Dresden beat Munich by a quarter of a century in the first performance of opera on German soil, the Bavarian capital of the Wittelsbachs was the first German city to erect a special building for opera, till then staged in the Herculeshall of the Residenz. The new opera house on the Salvatorplatz, a former granary, opened in 1657. It became the exclusive home of Italian baroque opera – and it was, of course, a house reserved exclusively for the members of the court. German opera seems to have had an even more strenuous fight in Munich to emerge and survive than in Dresden or Berlin, and just as in both these cities, the cultivation of Italian and German opera was the concern of two different companies. It was not until well into the nineteenth century that Munich's Italian opera ensemble was disbanded, after which there was only one company for the German and Italian wings of the repertory.

By that time, however, Munich's operatic centre had long since shifted elsewhere. In 1753, *opera seria* was transferred to the Residenztheater, today the Cuvilliés-Theater, named after its architect, François Cuvilliés, who built within the complex of the royal palace the world's most exquisite rococo theatre, an architectural capriccio of unsurpassed grace, harmony and musicality. Here Mozart's *Idomeneo* had its first performance in 1781; his earlier *La finta giardiniera* (1775) had been first performed at the Redoutensaal, the Munich home of *opera buffa*. At that time Munich could easily have captured Mozart, for as he said in terms of enthusiasm to be shared by many a later opera-visitor to the city: 'hier bin ich gern' (I like it here). Alas, Mozart had to travel on, but his operas have always held a secure place in the Munich repertory – a fact often overlooked in the light of the city's more recent Wagner and Strauss tradition. Munich's Mozart performances during the nineties of the last century under Levi, Strauss, and with Possart as producer, were of world-wide renown – and the same held true throughout Bruno Walter's term as musical director from 1913 to 1922.

What we today primarily associate with opera in Munich, the Nationaltheater, was inaugurated in 1818. It was the work of Karl von Fischer, modelled upon the Paris Odéon, and in its noble and lively classicism it is a fine adjunct to the city's buildings of that period. Though the actual process of construction had been accompanied by the usual complications and set-backs, making life occasionally very hard for Herr von Fischer (who was married to an opera singer), the people of Munich were in the end so pleased with it that when it burnt down five years later they insisted on it being promptly rebuilt in the same style. To finance this, an extra penny was added to the beer tax: an appropriate enough gesture by the capital city of German brewing. And the whole

57 and 58 On 21 June 1868 the world première of *Die Meistersinger von Nürnberg* was staged at the Bavarian State Opera House. On 4 October 1943 the same opera was billed but the theatre was gutted by fire the previous night, following four successive air-raids. On 23 November 1963 it reopened with a brand new production of *Die Meistersinger*.

59 Stage design by Quaglio (son) for the Munich
production of *Die Zauberflöte* in 1816.

thing was accomplished within the space of two
years.

Soon there dawned the era of Franz Lachner,
who raised the standard of orchestral playing
considerably and who was the first to introduce
Wagner's operas to Munich, though he resigned
when faced with the master's later output. But
it was, of course, just that particular series of
Wagner first performances, starting with *Tristan
und Isolde* in 1865 and continuing by way of *Die
Meistersinger* and *Das Rheingold* to *Die Walküre*
of 1870, which is now recognized as Munich's
proudest contribution to opera history. Without
the added fuel of Ludwig II's passion for Wagner
and his work, this golden age might never have
come about. Even as it was, relations between
the king and the municipal authorities were
subject to not inconsiderable strain while it was
in progress. What Lachner had so conscientiously
begun was continued by conductors of the status
of Hans von Bülow, Hermann Levi, Felix Mottl
and Richard Strauss; and these were followed
later on by Bruno Walter, Hans Knappertsbusch
and Clemens Krauss. Now the name of Richard
Strauss came to be added to those of Mozart and
Wagner as Munich favourites: *Friedenstag* and
Capriccio both had their first performances there.
Finally, Hans Pfitzner must be mentioned because
of the premières of *Palestrina* in 1917 and *Das
Herz* in 1931 (simultaneously with the Berlin
première).

Though Ludwig II planned a magnificent

Wagner-Festspielhaus, to be situated above the Isar, nothing came of the design prepared by Dresden's Gottfried Semper. So Munich had to wait until 1901, when the Prinzregententheater opened its doors – a building modelled upon Wagner's Bayreuth Festspielhaus and intended at first only for the Wagner Festival to be held during the summer months. Out of this grew the much bigger opera festival, which is now a magnet for disciples of opera commuting between Bayreuth and Salzburg. That Ludwig II indulged the most luxurious operatic taste of any sovereign is demonstrated by the extraordinary fact that during the course of his reign he commanded no fewer than 209 private performances – mostly of operas by Wagner, of course – for his own enjoyment alone.

The entire basis of Munich's operatic life, shared between the Nationaltheater, the Cuvilliés-Theater, the Prinzregententheater and the Theater am Gärtnerplatz was completely shattered during the Second World War. But at least the interior decoration of the Cuvilliés-Theater had been carefully removed and stored away in a safe place before the house itself was destroyed. For long years after 1945 the Prinzregententheater had to do as Munich's main opera house. First under Georg Hartmann and then under Rudolf Hartmann as general administrators, and with Ferdinand Leitner, Georg Solti, Rudolf Kempe, Ferenc Fricsay and Joseph Keilberth as musical directors the traditions of the past were cautiously revived – with special emphasis on the Richard Strauss *oeuvre*, while Werner Egk and Carl Orff

60 The interior of the Cuvilliés opera house in Munich, with Rhine maidens.

were given what many Bavarians considered their due. In and out, resigning and coming back, the figure of Knappertsbusch loomed large over the Munich opera scene.

Meanwhile, the rebuilding of the opera houses started, becoming for years one of the main planks in municipal policies, for the mere raising of a *Bierpfennig* would no longer do: much larger sums were involved now, so that occasionally one had the feeling that the city was facing bankruptcy because of the ever mounting building costs. However, in 1958 the Cuvilliés-Theater, which had been re-installed in the inner complex of the Residenz, was ready once again to receive its delighted patrons. It is the city's architectural jewel among theatres – an ideal house for small-scale opera, which bestows on its visitors a festive expectancy all its own. Five years later the Nationaltheater was finished, more beautiful, noble and elegant than ever before – certainly Germany's most civilized post-war theatre building, which under Günther Rennert's prudent guidance has embarked on a more contemporary approach to opera, without in the least severing its traditional bonds.

Today, with Wolfgang Sawallisch having just taken up the post of musical director, the Bavarian State Opera once again enjoys a considerable international reputation. Its first performances are of a high quality, so is the standard of its repertory. Yet, for all its preoccupation with modern methods of opera production, Munich has never neglected that native taste for luxury which I mentioned in my first paragraph: an unashamedly sensual love for sumptuous and beautiful voices. Whoever has been to the opera in Munich must have come to feel that the city is orientated culturally much more towards Vienna and Milan than towards Berlin or, say, Hamburg.

It would be unfair to leave the subject of opera in Munich without at least mentioning the most burning topic of the hour: the future of the Prinzregententheater – if it has a future. There it stands, empty and dismantled. Is it relaxing after the stress of the post-war period? Or is it just decaying?

61 It is a far cry from the exquisite Baroque elegance of the Cuvilliés Theater to the extreme architectural Teutonism of the National Theatre. Yet both are equally valid expressions of Bavarian operatic history.

Die Staatsoper Hamburg

While opera in Berlin, Dresden and Munich started its life as a court entertainment, Hamburg, a wealthy independent city, a member of the Hanseatic League which had been spared the demands and destruction of the Thirty Years' War, built its first opera house at the Gänsemarkt in 1678 as a sort of object lesson in civic pride. At that time Hamburg was not only the biggest German city, but it had a very mixed population of war refugees within its walls from all over the Continent. If one adds to this Hamburg's close sea-faring connections with Venice, the city with half a dozen public opera houses, and Hamburg's ambition to be acknowledged as the 'Venice of the North', the foundations of opera there seem to be fairly defined. To these sources, however, has to be added one further influence, which sets Hamburg apart from every other competing city – the strong influence of the local Protestant clergy, who carefully watched over the moral decency of the spectacles performed. Appropriately, the first opera shown in the rather primitive wooden building had a biblical subject: *Adam und Eva* by Johann Theile.

This lecturing and moralising tendency – which was a genuine need considering the rather rude character of much that was performed – became a marked trait of the emerging German operas, which were really mostly *Singspiele* with spoken dialogue and interspersed songs. The Hamburg burghers loved the many topical and local references of these early specimens, and they frequented the performances in great numbers. They achieved real artistic distinction at the turn of the eighteenth century, when Sigismund Kusser and Reinhard Keiser shared the repertory with Johann Mattheson, while Handel played in the orchestra and enjoyed no mean success with *Almira*, one of his four operas performed by the young company. Later on, Georg Philipp Telemann became Hamburg's foremost opera composer, but even he was not able to halt the quick decline of the institution, suffering as it did from a lack of qualified librettists and composers, while giving more and more space to crude stage-effects (like the spilling of gallons of calves' blood) and gross indecency. And so after sixty years this first attempt at German opera in Hamburg came inevitably to a halt.

Later on, touring companies, performing both plays and operas, catered for the Hamburgers at the Comödienhaus, from which there grew the Deutsches Nationaltheater and in 1809 the Hamburgisches Stadttheater. But this was a period during which Hamburg's operatic history closely resembled that of other second-string cities – as it did virtually throughout the nineteenth century, when it moved to a new building at the Dammtor-strasse, the site which is still the home of the Hamburg State Opera today. Though designed

62 (*Above*) The old Hamburg Opera House on the Gänsemarkt, built in 1765.

63 (*Opposite*) A prospect of Hamburg, from operatic text book *Mistevojus*.

by one of Germany's best architects, Karl Friedrich Schinkel, little remained of his original magnificent plans when the Neues Stadttheater opened its doors in 1827. There was the same repertory of operas that could be encountered everywhere, there were the same guest singers who could be heard anywhere, and there were the same conductor-composers from Wagner to Tchaikovsky (though in the last case the young Gustav Mahler had to step in to conduct the German first performance of *Eugene Onegin*), who paid their fleeting visits as they did to the other cities. There was, however, not a single opera creation from Hamburg which went into the general

German repertory. The usual routine was suspended during Mahler's invigorating term as chief conductor between 1891 and 1897, but afterwards Hamburg again returned to its mediocrity, brightened every now and then by the appearance of a guest star.

During the Nazi era, with such men as Oscar Fritz Schuh and Caspar Neher at its helm, later on joined by Eugen Jochum and Hans Schmitt-Isserstedt, the Hamburg State Opera gained new artistic respect, though more for its general standards than for any special spirit of enterprise. In 1943 the auditorium was completely destroyed and the ensemble had to move to improvised

MISTEVOJUS,

In einem
Sing = Spiele
Auf dem
Hamburgischen Schau-Platze
vorgestellet
Im Jahr 1726.

Gedruckt mit Stromerischen Schrifften.

64 (*Overleaf left*) In 1967 the chief conductor at the Hamburg State Opera gave Alexander Goehr's *Arden muss sterben*. This was a world première. 65 (*Overleaf above right*) Joan Sutherland and Huguette Tourangeau in the 1969 production of Handel's *Julius Caesar*. Richard Bonynge conducted. 66 (*Overleaf below right*) Dietrich Fischer-Dieskau and Gwyneth Jones in the 1970 *Salome*. Design was by Toni Businger and Karl Böhm conducted.

67 In recent years Hamburg has staged a whole series of spectacular productions. This one in the 1970/71 season, is Ravel's *L'Heure espagnole*, directed by Arno Assmann, with scenery and costumes by Hermann Scherr.

quarters, where it continued with its makeshift performances well into April 1945, though officially all German theatres had been closed in the autumn of 1944. However, through the energetic efforts of the stage personnel the whole stage area of the house survived the blitz, and it was on this very stage that an interim theatre was constructed with 606 seats, which opened early in 1946, becoming the springboard of Hamburg's post-war operatic activities. Gradually the temporary auditorium was extended to a seating capacity of 1,232, while the new opera house went up all around it; a curious phenomenon. For one season, that of 1954–5, the State Opera had to move to the Theater am Besenbinderhof while the work of reconstruction was being completed, but in the autumn of 1955 it was ready and was hailed as Germany's most original large-scale theatre of the new era, with room for 1,649 spectators in its sober, but not uncheerful, auditorium. The architect had clearly derived some of his inspiration from London's Royal Festival Hall.

Günther Rennert was its general administrator for the first ten years. Then followed Berlin's Heinz Tietjen, until Rolf Liebermann took over in 1959 with Leopold Ludwig, who was musical director from 1951 to 1971. The Hamburg State Opera now entered what must undoubtedly be termed the most glorious era of its three hundred years' history. If Rennert made the house famous by his ambitious repertory, stretching from Purcell and Handel, by way of the classics to Schoenberg, Berg and Hindemith, Dallapiccola, Britten and Křenek, as well as through his marvellously integrated productions, Liebermann has not only continued on these lines (with Rennert often returning as guest-producer), but has managed even to extend the contemporary side of its activities by commissioning a number of new works from established as well as untried, young composers. And even if Liebermann's practice has lately come under attack by people

who think that his liberalism has resulted in too much dross, while some of the really important works like Bernd Alois Zimmermann's *Die Soldaten* or Roman Haubenstock-Ramati's *Amerika* have been ignored, he has undoubtedly created a sense of operatic curiosity among his audiences such as is not to be found anywhere else in Germany today. His departure for Paris will be long regretted.

If Hamburgers decide to whistle or boo their premières, either because they are too daring or too conventional, it is nevertheless obvious that they have been in complete agreement with Liebermann's policies. And why not, for, in addition, they get the normal repertory, in productions that are mostly of high quality, with some of the best international singers available? It is true that not every commissioned work proves the hoped-for success, but probably more new works have gone on from Hamburg to other theatres than from any other opera house in the world. Consider just part of the record: Giselher Klebe's *Jacobowsky und der Oberst*, Gunther Schuller's *The Visitation*, Humphrey Searle's *Hamlet* (though, alas, not Alexander Goehr's very entertaining *Arden Must Die*); Gian Carlo Menotti's *Help, Help, the Globolinks!* and Krzysztof Penderecki's *The Devils of Loudun*. Now that the Liebermann era draws towards its end (Ludwig resigned in 1971, Liebermann himself in 1972), Hamburg's operatic future is again open – but it does not seem likely that it will follow a very different course when August Everding and Horst Stein take over as general administrator and musical director in 1972 and 1973 respectively. In any case, Hamburgers have now lived too long with *Wozzeck* and *Lulu* to be likely to fall back on an outmoded bread and butter diet. Anyway, they have covered quite a distance from *Adam and Eve* to *Lulu*, which has now been in the repertory since 1957 and has become Hamburg's chief exhibition piece when the company makes guest appearances abroad.

HORST KOEGLER

Das Festspielhaus Bayreuth

The idea of an opera house in a modest Franconian town devoted exclusively to performances of works by a single composer is no less incredible today than it was in Wagner's own time. It is the more so when one remembers that the Bayreuth Festival lasts only five summer weeks (in July and August) and that Wagner himself thought of his theatre as only a provisional structure. Today it stands as solidly as ever on the green hill above the town, its essential features unchanged since it was first built. Nothing is allowed to come between the listener and the experience of that blend of music, words and stage picture which is the Wagnerian music-drama. Virtually every seat in the large amphitheatre enjoys an excellent view of the stage. Conductor and orchestra are out of sight in the sunken orchestra pit. When the house lights go down the auditorium is quite dark and the expectant silence is the more complete in that there is no knowing when the prelude will begin. When it does, it is not at all apparent that the music's source is the 'mystic chasm', for it seems to hover in the air all around. Some argue that the sound seems too distant and that instrumental bloom is missing, but few would disagree that the Bayreuth acoustic (its reverberation time of 1.6 seconds at middle frequencies is probably longer than that of any other major opera house) has a quality all its own which is instantly recognizeable even in recordings and broadcasts. When the cool, plain grey curtains part and the singing begins, one is immediately aware of how superbly Wagner calculated the vocal and orchestral balance. The auditorium itself is an integral part of the acoustic design – the floor is made of bare wooden planks, the seats are moulded plywood (installed in 1969 to replace the original cane and wood constructions). At the rear there are some boxes and a gallery. The entrances to the amphitheatre itself are through doors along each side. Although there are no gangways, the most centrally placed spectator can be out in the open air or the various restaurants (all detached from the main building) within minutes of the end of an act.

All this came into being because Wagner, exasperated by inadequate performances in small court opera houses, decided that he would be satisfied with nothing less than his own theatre. To Wagner, opera was not a fashionable entertainment for the prosperous bourgeoisie, but the highest form of art (because it drew on all the arts). It demanded the maximum concentration and seriousness from performers and audience alike. Operas were not written to provide show pieces for star singers, nor to furnish ballets to display the charms of the patrons' mistresses, but because the composer wished to present a musical and dramatic entity to an audience who were prepared to take it as seriously as he himself did. 'Art as religion and the theatre as temple', was how Stravinsky, with irreverent intent, not inaccurately described it. Bayreuth was probably the first opera house designed not so that the audience could spend the evening surveying each other, but rather that all eyes should be constrained to take note of the stage. It used to be customary for opera house lights to be left up during performances and we owe it largely to Wagner that they eventually came to be extinguished.

Wagner's original idea can be traced to a letter to Theodor Uhlig dating from 1850. Frustrated by requests for cuts in *Lohengrin* (whose first performance took place that year under Liszt in Weimar), he said that he longed for a wooden theatre built to plans of his own in a beautiful meadow near Zürich. It would be furnished merely with what was necessary to produce *Siegfrieds Tod* (the first title for *Götterdämmerung*). The best possible singers and orchestra would be 'invited' to Zürich for six weeks. There would be three performances, free to friends of the musical drama, after which 'the theatre would be pulled down, and the score burnt'. If people liked the idea and asked for something new, his reply would be 'You raise the money!'

As there was no likelihood whatever of such an experiment, the plan was patently absurd – a fantasy provoked by the frustrations of the moment. Yet it must have taken root in Wagner's mind. Fourteen years later it looked as though the idea would blossom overnight and into rather more than a disposable wooden theatre, for on his accession in 1864 the young King Ludwig II of Bavaria quickly rescued his favourite composer from a tightening net of creditors.

A lavish spender, Wagner was always in monetary straits and his financial ethics were something quite his own. The projected Festival Theatre was to be in Munich, but Wagner quickly lost interest, knowing that such a theatre would never be more than partly his. Only his very own theatre and total dedication to his own requirements would serve. Thus he also rejected many later offers to build him a theatre, from such places as Berlin, Darmstadt, Baden-Baden, Reichenhall, London and even Chicago.

Bayreuth first suggested itself because the baroque court theatre in that town (completed in 1748) had the largest stage of any German theatre. It was there that Wagner had thought of produc-

68 The sunken orchestra pit in the Bayreuth Opera House, part of Wagner's bold new design aimed at increasing acoustics and dramatic effect and reducing the fashionable indifference of contemporary opera audiences.

70 (*Above*) The stage of the old Bayreuth house.

69 (*Opposite*) The ceremonial box of the Margrave and
Margravine in the old opera house of Bayreuth,
designed by Carlo Galli di Bibiena.

ing his complete *Ring*. In April 1871 Wagner and his wife Cosima travelled to inspect this theatre, which they swiftly rejected (its design, as courtly as the rest, was anything but Hellenic). But they liked the town, and its officials were warmly co-operative. Early next year a suitable site had been found and the Leipzig architect Otto Brückwald was commissioned to draw up a plan. The cost of the building and preparations for the festival was estimated at 300,000 thalers, to be raised by selling 1,000 (later 1,300) *Patronatscheine* (subscriptions) of 300 thalers each. Land was bought (with Ludwig's money) for Wagner's last home, which he named Wahnfried, and on his birthday (22 May), in the pouring rain, the foundation stone of the Festspielhaus was laid. The ceremony was followed by a celebratory performance of Beethoven's Ninth Symphony in the old opera house. The King, who had for some time been embittered by Wagner's independence – the Bayreuth plan was itself a flagrant infringement of the King's own rights in the *Ring*, which he had acquired and paid for at an earlier point in their friendship – nevertheless brought himself to send a telegram of 'sincerest congratulations on this day that is so significant for all Germany'. It was duly buried in a casket in the foundation stone.

71 Drawing of Wagner's projected new opera house at Bayreuth.

In the summer of 1873, when the theatre was substantially complete, work had to be halted for lack of money. Only 130,000 thalers had been raised by concerts and the sale of *Patronatscheine*. Appeals to the King, now obsessed with his castle-building mania, and to nearly three thousand German book and music dealers, met with rebuffs. In desperation Wagner asked the Grand Duke of Baden to intercede with the Kaiser, but in the end it was Ludwig who baled Wagner out once again – he could not allow their old joint venture for the regeneration of German culture to flounder so near its goal.

The first festival was to be in 1876 and Wagner's

plans took final shape in 1874. Most indispensible of all was the completion, in November, of *Götterdämmerung*. The stage machinery was to be designed by Carl Brandt of Darmstadt, the scenery by the Viennese painter Joseph Hoffmann, and executed by the brothers Max and Gotthold Brückner from the Coburg Court Theatre. The costumes were commissioned from Carl Emil Doepler of Berlin (they were *not*, said Wagner, to be on semi-classical, pseudo-Germanic lines – the right ideas might well be obtained from archaeologists who had specialized in the Teutonic Middle Ages). Richard Fricke, ballet master in Dessau, was invited to choreograph everyone and everything from Fafner (who he shrewdly though unsuccessfully advised should be kept out of sight) to the swimming machines ingeniously devised by Brandt for the intrepid daughters of the Rhine. Orders for pantomime props and 'stage fauna' were placed in England; they included Fafner (who cost £500), 'a car with a yoke of rams for Fricka in *Die Walküre*, a bear, a magpie and an ousel for *Siegfried*, and sacrificial beasts and a pair of ravens for the *Götterdämmerung*'. It was settled that performances should begin at 4 o'clock (as they do to this day), the spectators refreshing themselves during the intervals in the gardens and adjacent countryside and being summoned back by trombones from the terrace of the theatre.

Wagner assembled his orchestra, singers and helpers (about 140 in all, most of whom agreed to forego fees) for rehearsals in the summer of 1875. It was then and in the immediate pre-festival rehearsals of the following year that the Bayreuth performing tradition was founded. Never before had a whole company submitted to being drilled so intensively and for so long. This was in an age when prima donnas sent their maids along to declare where they would stand, and when 'arias' (which Wagner had tried to eliminate from his operas) were treated as show pieces for the individual singer rather than as contributions to a whole.

The first music to be heard in the theatre (on 24 July) was the Rhinemaidens' trio, sung unaccompanied by Lilli Lehmann, her sister Marie,

72 The original Rhine-maidens at play.

and Fräulein Lammert, with contributions from Alberich (Karl Hill), who remained in the wings. The orchestra was heard for the first time on 2 August. As Wagner entered the theatre that day he received an ovation and Franz Betz sang Wotan's opening monologue, 'Vollendet das ewige Werk!' ('The eternal work completed!').

Solo rehearsals were held in Wahnfried. In the theatre Wagner concentrated on the stage while Hans Richter conducted. Several of the soloists agreed to swell the Gibichung chorus to twenty-six.

The final year of preparation was not without difficulty – Wagner lost his Sieglinde, who had inconsiderately allowed herself to become pregnant, and there were other troubles too – but at last everything was ready for the opening, or rather nearly everything. For even the skilled London craftsmen had met their match with Fafner and friends. Desperate telegrams arrived in London: 'For heaven's sake have the bear sent off before the last part of the dragon; *Siegfried* is to be rehearsed again next week. The King will be here, and Wagner will be in despair if the bear is wanting. Car has arrived. Rams still missing, body of Fafner ditto.' The poor beast's neck never did arrive perhaps because, as speculation has it, it had been directed to Beirut, now capital of the Lebanon.

Ludwig, who disliked public performances no less than meeting blue-blooded aristocracy (who were to be present in some force) came to the dress rehearsals. The first of these was a private performance, but for the other three Wagner persuaded him, for acoustic reasons, to be joined by a privileged audience of *Patronatscheine* holders and others. The King was deeply impressed, so much so in fact that he returned for the third of the three cycles. Less involved was the Kaiser; after *Rheingold* on 13 August and *Walküre* on the following day, he left for the military manoeuvres at Babelsberg.

The festival was an enormous success, although Wagner told the audience in a short speech of thanks after the final *Götterdämmerung* that he did not know whether it would be repeated – which was surely but another way of saying 'Now you raise the money!' He had unreserved praise for Betz's Wotan, Albert Niemann's Siegmund, Hill's Alberich and Gustav Siehr's Hagen – he was delighted with Amalie Materna's Immolation scene with the Rhine-maidens.

Two years later, in 1878, when Wagner was writing *Parsifal*, the King made a further financial arrangement which wiped out the remaining unpaid loan and secured not only a second festival in 1882, which was devoted to the first performances of *Parsifal*, but also the future of the festival after Wagner's death (in 1883). Although Wagner had theoretically already signed away to the King the Munich rights in his work, future royalties were promised to Wagner and to his heirs for twenty years after his death.

The 1882 *Parsifal* performances (conducted by Hermann Levi) were probably the most completely satisfactory of those given at Bayreuth in Wagner's lifetime. The opera itself had been composed with the Festspielhaus acoustic in mind and the stage designs were by the young Russian painter Paul von Joukowsky. His settings remained undisturbed until 1912, and his Gralstempel (based on the Cathedral at Sienna) survived until 1934 (when it was replaced by a design of Alfred Roller, Mahler's former collaborator at the Vienna Opera).

But even with Joukowsky's aid, Wagner left many scenic problems unsolved: he complained to Ludwig, apropos the Blumenmädchen costumes, that 'having invented the invisible orchestra, he now wished he could invent the invisible stage'. Nearly seventy years later his grandsons Wieland and Wolfgang were to show that there was something in this.

It seemed to many that Wagner's death would mean the end of the festivals. He probably hoped that he would live long enough to produce all his works at Bayreuth and that after his death his son Siegfried would take over. Apparently it did not occur to him that Cosima would be either willing to or capable of continuing the festivals herself, although she had been more closely identified with his intentions than anyone else. Yet that was what happened. On Wagner's death she went into permanent mourning and at first shut herself up in Wahnfried with her children: the 1883 and 1884 *Parsifal* performances took place without her. A hint that standards were lapsing made plain to her the rôle she now assumed. She began to supervise rehearsals from a discreetly curtained box at the side of the stage. By 1906, when she relinquished control to Siegfried, she had presented all Wagner's major operas at Bayreuth and established the festival as an institution rather than an experiment. She recreated the original Munich productions of *Tristan* (1886, under Felix Mottl) and of *Die Meistersinger* (1888, Hans Richter), herself produced *Tannhäuser* (1891, Mottl) and *Lohengrin* (1894, Mottl), and put the *Ring* back in circulation in 1896 with Mottl, Richter and Siegfried Wagner, and with new scenery by Max Brückner.

Cosima established the 'Bayreuth tradition' whose validity is still the subject of vehement discussion. The principle of that tradition was absolute faithfulness to Wagner's intentions. She remembered precisely how everything had been done (as twenty years elapsed between the 1876 *Ring* and its restoration to the repertory in 1896 her memory must have been no less formidable than her person). She soon graduated from dispatching tart little notes of correction to conductor and singers from behind her curtained box to teaching singers their parts. She put the musical line first, then the words, and the acting instructions last of all. Some instructions they were, too! According to Karl Kittel, who became chief musical coach from 1912 to 1939, Mime's despair following his failure to forge Siegfried's sword had to be expressed thus:

After the cry '*Könnt' ichs dem Kühnen schmieden, meiner Schmach erlangt' ich da Lohn*' he lowers his head reflectively and (at the first entry of the two bassoons) places the finger-tips of both hands pressed together on his forehead; then (on the repeat of the phrase) he raises his head

121

thoughtfully, so that the stiffly held hands touch the pursed mouth and (at the entry of the tubas) turn into clenched fists.

At rehearsals Cosima proved herself scarcely less resourceful at demonstrating this sort of thing than Wagner himself.

For her stagings of *Tannhäuser*, *Lohengrin* and *Holländer* she had no definitive models to fall back on and so turned to detailed study of the historical periods in which they were supposedly set. These operas – *Tannhäuser* in particular – were already popular and were being produced far and wide in stagings which undoubtedly had more in common with those of the bad old days than with the high ideals of the music-drama. Cosima's model productions emphasized the common ground which these early operas shared with the later works: *Holländer*, for instance, was given in Wagner's original single-act version.

Cosima's zealously imposed 'tradition' was not always as well founded as she imagined. Wagner had always been concerned not only to mould a singer's performance to some preconceived pattern but to bring out his individual contribution. He had even wondered whether his own staging notions were quite so free from nineteenth century convention as he had imagined. Perhaps he sensed the very real clash between the mythological, timeless world of the *Ring* and the romantic naturalism of his stage directions – which were literally interpreted by his scenic artists. At any rate, Wagner's staging ideas were clearly in a state of flux; he was delighted to seize on and incorporate anything which suggested itself at rehearsals. Cosima's path was much more strait-laced. She was a born adjutant, probably secretly disapproving of the more boisterous, practical-joke-loving side of Wagner's nature. After the composer's death, many people were repelled by the sanctimonious aura with which Cosima and her disciples infused the place.

Cosima's pious conservatism ensured that the innovatory ideas of the one man who quickly perceived what kind of stagings were truly complementary to the music, were swept under the carpet. The designs of the Swiss artist Adolphe Appia were recommended to her by Houston Stewart Chamberlain, her son-in-law, who contemptuously spoke of Brückner's 'familiar stuff, without a trace of invention or imagination'. But Cosima dismissed Appia's ideas as those of a madman and compared his sketches to Nansen's pictures of the North Pole expedition. Appia's ideas, with their emphasis on lighting and on settings of extreme simplicity, were not to have their day until Wieland Wagner's Bayreuth. Wieland himself came near to the truth when he suggested that 'Cosima Wagner's ban and curse on Appia's book *Music and Production* was responsible for stuffing Bayreuth with moth-ridden conceptions for decades, so that its original revolutionary function changed into its opposite.'

In his excellent book *Wagner at Bayreuth* (a study to which I am much indebted), Geoffrey Skelton has perceptively pointed to the fact that it took Appia some twenty-five years to get his stagings realized anywhere, as powerful evidence of the widespread influence and respect commanded by Bayreuth wherever Wagner was staged.

The thirty-eight-year-old Siegfried Wagner who took over from his mother in 1907 was not as simple a soul as his photographs and the stories of his naïveté might suggest. Although his original ambition had been architecture, he assumed command of the family business quite naturally and was equal to its exceptional demands. He was already an experienced conductor and producer and an established composer – four of his operas (he was to write thirteen) having been performed with some success in leading German opera houses. In 1896 he had conducted the *Ring* and in 1901 he was responsible for the first ever Festspielhaus production of *Holländer*.

At least until 1914, when the war was to disrupt the festivals for ten years, he must have been very much aware of Cosima's presence, however strenuously he might have denied that she attempted to influence him. But under his direction, and particularly after the reopening in 1924, Bayreuth began to move away from the tradition of classical museum performances at which audiences could congratulate themselves that they were seeing what Wagner himself had seen in 1876 and 1882. Siegfried's innovations were introduced slowly and their path was the easier in that he, after all, was Wagner's son, a homely, likeable man who could be trusted not to do anything too foolish.

Siegfried gradually replaced the painted scenery of the Brückner brothers with three-dimensional equivalents. He modernized the lighting equipment so that, together with the new solid scenery, it could be used to create atmosphere and depth, rather than merely illuminate whatever it was that had been painted on the old canvas flats.

In the winter of 1925–6 Siegfried's principal scenic assistants, Kurt Söhnlein and Friedrich Kranich, gave much thought to the increasingly pressing problem of the hallowed *Parsifal* scenery which was now looking very shabby. Some critics were demanding renewal, others, retention of the old decorations. Kranich and Söhnlein scrapped their preliminary sketches for renewal and it was eventually Siegfried himself who took the initiative when, early in 1927, he suddenly decided that something must at least be done about the second act. Thus there were new 'white gauze drapes with sewn-on transparent flower petals in changing light' (presumably for the *Blumenmädchen*) and the garden was transformed to 'a wasteland as drapes with withered branches'. The new *Klingsorturm* was more stylized; 'half rock, half building'.

In 1927 the 'destruction of Valhalla' on stage was achieved for the first time by optical projection, and in the following year projections were used to suggest waves in the opening scene of *Rheingold*. Söhnlein and Kranich also worked on

73 Wagner, Cosima von Bülow and Hans von Bülow in the Maximilienstrasse: a Munich newspaper cartoon of 1864. Although the ménage could scarcely be described as 'à trois', almost three years more were to pass before the unfortunate conductor started divorce proceedings.

74 Stage design for the first production of *Parsifal*,
given at Bayreuth in 1882.

a new model for the *Ring* whose basic idea was
'three large iron conveyances, each built over
with solid rock forms, which could be put
together in many different ways to form the
basis for all the rocky scenes in the *Ring*'. Here in
embryo was the notion, later to become so
influential, that all the *Ring* settings should be
constructed from one matrix, thus keeping the
tetralogy's underlying unity ever present before
the eye.

Siegfried's Bayreuth was certainly on the rocks.
The copyright of the Wagner operas expired in
1913 and Bayreuth's exclusive right to *Parsifal*
(first violated by the New York Met. in 1903)
was no longer legally enforceable. At the best of
times an opera house with a five-week season is
a financial liability, and never more so than when

it doesn't have a season at all for nine years.
Siegfried, whose own main source of income was
his operas, was only able to reopen the festival
again in 1924 after going round to gather subscriptions for a new foundation. Five thousand
contributions of 1,000 marks each were received,
the donors including such names as the ex-Kaiser,
the former King of Bavaria (Ludwig III), King
Ferdinand of Bulgaria, Gerhart Hauptmann and
Arthur Nikisch. The conductor Felix Weingartner
proposed that the world's opera houses should
come to Bayreuth's rescue by voluntarily paying
a small royalty on all Wagner performances, but
although he set the example in his own house,
the Vienna Volksoper, there was no rush to follow
it.

The festival *was* rescued, although pre-1914

sets were used for all productions until 1927, when Siegfried put on a new *Tristan* (under Karl Elmendorff). A new, and as it turned out, prophetically severe *Tannhäuser* did not reach the stage until 1930 under Toscanini, by which time Siegfried himself lay dying in hospital after collapsing on the stage at a *Götterdämmerung* rehearsal only a month or two after Cosima's death at the age of ninety-three.

Toscanini was the first non-German conductor to have been invited to Bayreuth, and although all are agreed that his performances of *Tristan* and *Tannhäuser* in 1930, to which he added *Parsifal* the following year, were quite outstanding, Siegfried incurred no little criticism for having introduced an internationally acclaimed star. It has always been, and to an extent still is, Bayreuth's preference to seek out young artists who will make their names there, rather than to import established stars – who are expensive and tend to be set in their ways. Siegfried's widow, Winifred, was to bring many more stars to Bayreuth, and thereby earn Sir Henry Wood's sad reproach:

> Everything is commercialized. There must always be a 'star' conductor – Toscanini or Furtwängler – and this famous soprano or that famous tenor. In the old days we never knew who was singing and certainly we never knew who was conducting. The names were not advertised and we had to find out as best we could.

The singers who made their names in the twenties included Friedrich Schorr, who sang Wotan until 1931, and Lauritz Melchior, who began with Siegmund and Parsifal in 1924 and went on to Siegfried in 1927, the same year that Nanny Larsen-Todsen made her début as Brünnhilde. Melchior, whom Frieda Leider regarded as the ideal Wagnerian 'Heldentenor', also sang Tristan in 1930 and 1931. Frieda Leider made her own début in 1928 as Kundry and, alternating with Larsén-Todsen, as Brünnhilde. According to Frieda Leider, the proper rehearsal of productions and singers was still regarded as very much an optional extra by most other opera houses. But

75 Cosima in old age, with her son Siegfried.

the fact of Bayreuth's existence, its continuing tradition and unrivalled training work, were at least an example, an ideal which was carried far and wide by those who had taken part in or seen performances there.

Some idea of the extent of a typical pre-war rehearsal schedule may be gathered from the record of the 1925 season made by Karl Kittel, chief musical coach from 1912 to 1932. The repertory was the *Ring*, *Parsifal* and *Meistersinger*, none of them new productions. In the ten weeks from the start of rehearsals in mid-June to the end of the festival there were:

24 stage rehearsals with orchestra
23 scenery and lighting rehearsals
47 positioning and acting rehearsals on stage

76 A performance of *Das Rheingold* at Bayreuth in 1876.

79 acting rehearsals with individual artists
76 piano rehearsals with groups (Mastersingers, Blumenmädchen, etc.)
439 musical coachings of soloists
159 coachings of soloists in style and presentation
23 separate orchestra rehearsals
16 rehearsals of stage music
26 rehearsals of the *Parsifal* bells and *Rheingold* anvils
an unspecified number of chorus rehearsals
15 rehearsals of the children's chorus.

Siegfried Wagner's death left the festival for the first time in the hands of someone too young to have known Wagner personally, namely Siegfried's widow, the thirty-three-year-old Winifred. She inherited a task scarcely less daunting than the one Cosima had assumed. She was neither a musician, nor a producer, nor even a German. It is hardly surprising that she should have encountered immediate opposition from Siegfried's sisters, Daniela and Eva. The sisters retired to Triebschen, Wagner's home of exile on the shores of Lake Lucerne, which now became the headquarters of the old-guard opposition to the new régime.

Events, though, were moving swiftly to Winifred's advantage, for within three years her close friend Adolf Hitler had seized power. Hitler, unlike Bayreuth's first generous patron, King Ludwig, required Wagner not merely for his private pleasure, but for the public demonstration of an unholy alliance of German *Macht* and German *Kultur*. Wagner's operas do have a nationalistic content, most obviously in *Lohengrin* ('*das deutsche Schwert*') and in *Meistersinger* with Sachs's '*Was deutsch und echt. . . .*', but to emphasize this is to belittle their better part, the universal content.

Winifred had supported Hitler, taking him seriously when few others did, and had welcomed him to Wahnfried in the early 1920s. According to her daughter Friedelind, it was on paper supplied by her that the imprisoned Hitler wrote the first volume of *Mein Kampf*. Now it was his turn to come to her aid and for once Bayreuth

was not short of money. The festival was declared tax-exempt and Hitler allotted it 50,000 marks a year from his own funds.

Productions were largely taken over by Heinz Tietjen, general administrator of the Prussian State Theatres, and his designer Emil Preetorius. They were on a grander scale than any seen before or since. Tietjen mustered a chorus of more than a hundred – in 1897 Wagner's Gibichungs only numbered twenty-six, Siegfried Wagner ran to sixty-four and post-war Bayreuth has usually had between seventy and eighty. A suggestion that the Gibichung shields be emblazoned with the swastika was strenuously resisted, however. Whatever may have gone on at the Führer receptions, and in the coarse camaraderie of the intervals and post-performance, the evidence points to an unusually high artistic standard. Of Tietjen's first season (1933), Frieda Leider wrote that the music-drama had here reached its consummation. She also drew attention to the fact that 'At this time the public still streamed to Bayreuth from all corners of the earth: art had not yet become the servant of politics'. For a few years Winifred was able to secure safe conducts for Jewish singers (no mean tribute to her influence with Hitler), but when things became too difficult, other singers left in sympathy with them. And when singers from abroad found their participation construed as political rather than artistic they too stayed away. Kirsten Flagstad, who sang at Bayreuth in 1933 and 1934, reported that this earned her considerable ill-will, particularly in the United States.

With its international aspect no longer to the fore, Bayreuth became more closely identified than at any other time with Wagner's original vision of his art as a national religion. The programme notes drew attention to the 'Germanness' of Hans Sachs, to Siegfried as liberator, to the *Ring* as a demonstration of the 'terrible seriousness of the racial problem' and to *Parsifal* as being about the 'only religion that a German can embrace, namely, that of struggle towards a life made divine'. There was no mention of crimes of greed and violence being redeemable only through love, of Siegfried's vulnerable heroics, or of Wotan's 'rising to the tragic height of willing his own destruction'.

Between 1933 and 1939 Tietjen mounted new productions of *Holländer*, *Lohengrin*, *Tristan*, *Meistersinger*, the *Ring* and *Parsifal*. Except for the *Parsifal* (1934, by Alfred Roller) they were designed by Preetorius. Together the two men evolved a new, less realistic production style. They were not prepared to go for all-out symbolism, but they did believe that the sense of the timeless whole was strengthened by playing down realism of time and place. Siegfried Wagner's innovations were now taken further along the 'Appian way' as Tietjen and Preetorius relied more and more on lighting to suggest depth, solidarity and atmosphere. Tietjen said that both he and Preetorius 'saw light as the basic element in the visual realization of all Wagner's works, and we sought to evolve a stage setting which restricted the use of objects to essentials and gave the main rôle to the adaptable and highly effective visual instrument of lighting'.

Tietjen retained his position as general administrator of the Prussian Theatres, and although some disapproved of the close alliance which now linked Berlin, Dresden and Bayreuth, it was to Bayreuth's benefit. The festivals enjoyed privileged access to Tietjen's great singers from the Berlin State Opera, among them, Rudolf Bockelmann, Frieda Leider, Margarete Klose, Max Lorenz and Herbert Janssen. Returning year after year to the same leading rôles, they gave Bayreuth a continuity of authoritative interpretations that it has not enjoyed at any other time in its history. German singers dominated the stage as never before – or since. The festivals also gained because productions could be tried out first on the Berlin and Dresden stages.

Frau Winifred lost Karl Muck, the senior conductor, who had had a hand in every festival since 1901, immediately after her arrival. It remains a matter for conjecture whether he resigned because of her intention to engage Toscanini for the following year (1931) or, as he told Winifred, because he was now seventy-one, had done his duty by Siegfried, and wished to retire. Undeterred, she replaced him by Furt-

wängler, although she soon lost him too (he was back in 1936) because he said he was not prepared to listen to the musical requirements of a non-musician. The year 1931 turned out to be the last Bayreuth appearance of Toscanini, who resigned ostensibly because of a row with Furtwängler over Siegfried Wagner's memorial concert, although the real reason was almost certainly his disapproval of Bayreuth's political colour. A personal appeal from Hitler failed (perhaps not surprisingly) to persuade him to return. For the 1933 and 1934 seasons Winifred succeeded in bringing back Richard Strauss to conduct *Parsifal* – the last time he had conducted there had been for Cosima's *Tannhäuser* in 1894. Tietjen was a competent conductor as well as producer and he was often at the rostrum in these years.

The outbreak of war did not put an end to the festivals, which continued until 1944, although *Parsifal* was dropped after 1939 and there were no new productions. The *Ring* of 1942 was the last occasion when the Bayreuth boards were pawed by the hooves of a real live Grane. The festivals of 1943 and 1944 featured *Meistersinger* alone, which was conducted by Furtwängler and Hermann Abendroth. The war-time audiences were largely workers and troops who were given tickets and special leave to attend.

That the rites and ceremonies of the music-drama had become so closely associated with those of National Socialism was a severe obstacle to an imminent post-war reopening. Perhaps it was a necessary penance that the theatre's sanctity should be violated by its appropriation for variety shows for the occupying American forces. Winifred was declared a major Nazi collaborator by a de-Nazification court in 1947, and although the theatre belonged (as it still does) to her, the Allies were unwilling to allow her to resume control. Various reopening schemes were considered, included handing over the festival to trustees – such names as Albert Schweitzer and Ernest Newman being mentioned – but responsibility for the festival passed eventually to Winifred's sons Wieland and Wolfgang. Neither was unprepared: Wieland had spent the war years at Altenburg, a former court theatre near

XII (*Opposite*) A scene from the Deutsche Oper production of Hans Werner Henze's opera *'Der junge Lord'* (see also plate 49). XIII (*Overleaf*) Giuseppe Quaglio's stage set for the Queen of the Night's appearance in the first (1793) Munich production of *Die Zauberflöte*. The large Quaglio family, hailing from Laino between Lakes Como and Lugano, made a notable contribution to architecture and painting for five generations, spanning the seventeenth to the nineteenth centuries.

77 (*Above*) Wieland Wagner rehearsing the 1963 Bayreuth production of *Die Meistersinger von Nürnberg*.
XIV (*Opposite*) Birgit Nilsson as Brünnhilde in Wieland Wagner's production of *Der Ring*.
Although Cosima would not have felt very much at home with it, Wagner himself may have seen
in this degree of abstraction something for which he was subconsciously seeking.

Leipzig, where he had already produced a *Ring* on a virtually bare stage, while Wolfgang, discharged early from the forces with serious wounds, had been apprenticed to Tietjen at the Berlin State Opera. They reopened in 1951 with a traditional *Meistersinger* (by Rudolf Hartmann), and a *Parsifal* and *Ring* by the thirty-four-year-old Wieland – revolutionary productions whose simplicity scandalized traditionalists, thrilled many others, and left no one indifferent.

It was the *Parsifal* (conducted by Hans Knappertsbusch) which set the style of the new Bayreuth, and to this day it can be seen in substantially the same form (although Wieland, like his grandfather, did not stand still for a minute and his productions were in continual evolution). To a hostile critic, the 1951 *Parsifal* was 'a symphony in gloom, a formless play of patterns and shadows which dispenses with individual dramatic relationships, confines itself exclusively to symbols and thereby becomes wearisome', while Ernest Newman found it 'not only the best *Parsifal* that I have ever seen or heard, but one of the three or four most moving spiritual experiences of my life'. Wieland was less immediately successful with the *Ring* where, understandably enough, he had not yet gone quite so far in his repudiation of realism.

In the following years Wieland's productions and Wolfgang's administrative flair quickly restored Bayreuth's international standing. It was a typical gesture of new Bayreuth to print this extract from Wagner's essay 'Art and Revolution' on the back of the programme book for Wolfgang's centenary *Meistersinger* of 1968 in the usual three languages, German, French and English:

> Whereas the Greek work of art expressed the spirit of a splendid nation, the work of art of the future is intended to express the spirit of free people irrespective of all national boundaries; the national elements in it must be no more than an ornament, an added individual charm, and not a confining boundary.

The genius of new Bayreuth has been its simplification. And the Wagner grandsons were right to simplify their productions, for the classic Wagnerian tableaux had fossilized the operas and created an orthodoxy which was more faithful to Wagner the pedant and visual philistine (for such he self-confessedly was) than to Wagner the innovator, Wagner the musician. The picturesque seduction of the senses by the staging was unfair to the music and to the mythological, psychological and large-scale dramatic construction. By foreswearing visual lollipops and darkening the stage, new Bayreuth focused attention on the music. The stylization of whatever was seen brought out the wider and deeper patterns and structures.

Wieland presented us with the essence, just as Wagner had done, whether hewing out the *Ring* from a complex of Teutonic and Norse mythologies and sagas, or plucking *Tristan* from an equally involved and confused background. Wieland's settings were often reminiscent of natural, geological forms, of the runes cut in rough stone forms by our ancestors. The last setting in this line was the primitive *Urwelt* of his 1965 *Ring*, which relegated problematic dragons to an enveloping outer darkness. It abolished rainbow bridges, manifest Valhallas and everything that stood in the way of a dream world of ambivalent symbols revealed in a dim play of light, orchestrated scarcely less cunningly than the music itself.

In *Tannhäuser* (1964) there was no wayside shrine for Elizabeth's prayers, but an enormous black cross reaching beyond the confines of the proscenium. In *Tristan* (1962) each act was dominated by a phallic representation – whether the prow of the boat, the all-seeing totem of the second act, or the sharp, pierced segment which presided over Tristan's delirious death throes. The cold, eerie greens, airless grey-blues, and the curve of the stage floor suggested the surface of some mysterious, alien moon. In her *Verklärung* (transfiguration) Isolde, in yellow, rose up like a new sun while the light behind her was the moon's final eclipse into eternal night. This *Tristan* featured two of the singers for whom new Bayreuth will always be remembered, Wolfgang Windgassen and Birgit Nilsson, and, as Marke,

78 Wieland Wagner's set for *Siegfried* at Bayreuth; a revolutionary departure from the traditional 'museum' productions the theatre had for long presented.

a distinguished series of basses, Josef Greindl, Hans Hotter, and from Finland, Martti Talvela, one of the finest singers of this younger generation.

In the invention of symbols additional to those specified by Wagner, Wieland was unfailingly resourceful – there was a striking instance in the 1965 *Rheingold* where the hoard, when completely piled up, took the form of a woman's body. But if Wieland disliked a symbol – for example Valhalla and the rainbow bridge, the Wanderer's hat, Tristan's bandages, the door of Hunding's hut flying open – he was apt to pretend that it did not exist, or he overrode it with another – his gods went unmistakably down at the end of *Rheingold*. Clashes occasionally arose between symbols old and new although Wieland was only trying to discriminate between symbols which

matter and those which do not – in Wagner a task perhaps set for all time.

It was tragic that he should die so soon after finding in Pierre Boulez a conductor whose revolutionary approach to the music matched his own approach to staging. In the summer of 1966, while Boulez conducted his first *Parsifal*, Wieland lay critically ill in a Munich hospital and by October he was dead. Boulez did an astonishing job on the *Parsifal* score although we can only speculate as to how Wieland might have rethought his staging in the light of Boulez's 'musical picture cleaning', as it has been aptly described.

Since Wieland's death the double burden of artistic and administrative direction has fallen on his brother's shoulders. As a producer Wolfgang

is more sympathetic towards realism than Wieland was. His 1968 *Meistersinger* had the virtues – and shortcomings – of a traditional-style repertory production. It was disappointing in that one has come to expect rather more than this from Bayreuth. He launched a new *Ring* in 1970 whose scenic idea (also used in his 1960 *Ring*) is a vast flying-saucer-like disc which is seen complete in *Rheingold*, subsequent settings being built from its various segments. Only when the ring is safely back with the Rhine maidens does the disc appear once more complete. This *Ring* was still in rough shape when I saw it in 1970 (the Valkyries wore calf-length pantaloon suits from the Arabian nights), although its basic idea is so good that it will surely improve enormously.

We must hope so; for it would not be unfair to say that rehearsal time has been far from adequate in the last few years and Bayreuth has been living mostly on the extended credit earned for it by Wieland. These have been difficult years for Wolfgang, who for so long has had to live in his brother's shadow. But he has a warm and modest temperament, and is very ready to invite others to produce – as witness August Everding's 1969 *Holländer* (with designs by Joseph Svoboda). This was well received and the 1972 *Tannhäuser* is by Götz Friedrich from the Komische Oper in East Berlin; the designer is Jürgen Rose.

Wagner once said that his stage directions 'must remain puzzles for aesthetic criticism until they have fulfilled their purpose as technically fixed points in a complete dramatic representation, as hints for acting, as stimuli for the creative imagination'. Each generation will rediscover these great, problematical works for itself. We must hope that Bayreuth will continue to uphold the best aspects of its tradition – the thorough preparation of a complete dramatic experience, and responsible experiment in the search for ever better ways of staging the Wagner operas.

PATRICK CARNEGY

79 Josef Svoboda's set for Act II of *Der fliegende Holländer* at the 1969 festival.

SPAIN

El Gran Teatro Liceo
Barcelona

The Catalans, like all Spaniards, have a highly developed, highly individual sense of music. And Spain has a great tradition in the realm of drama. Yet Spanish opera, as such, is a comparatively limited phenomenon. The number of operas by Spanish composers which have found their way into the international repertory could be counted on the fingers of one hand. This, however, did not deter Barcelona from building one of the largest opera houses in Europe in 1847, nor has the city failed to keep it going, through thick and thin, for a century and a quarter, without the benefit of either State or municipal subsidy.

The Liceo is, essentially, a monument – perhaps the most imposing monument – to the emergence of Barcelona as one of the great industrial and mercantile capitals of the world in the mid-nineteenth century. Yet it was not wholly conceived as such. It owes its real origin to a wave of anti-clericalism that swept Catalonia in 1837. Under the impact of this, the Dominican Convent of Montesion (the site is now the headquarters of the Gas Company) was requisitioned as a barracks, and a militia battalion quartered there. The morale of militia men is always the better for a boost, so the commander, Manuel Gilbert, and his officers, set about organizing entertainment. An amateur dramatic society was founded, and the cost of converting part of the convent premises into an auditorium was met by an issue of shares, half of

which were subscribed by the companies in the battalion. In due course, the anti-clerical wave receded, the nuns got their convent back and the battalion was dissolved. But it is easier to dissolve militia than it is to dissolve shareholders, and by now the enterprise had assumed some stature. It was no longer just a garrison show but the Liceo Filarmonico de Montesion. It was producing operas and it had to be compensated for the loss of its premises. The provincial council was prepared to lease a site which had formerly been occupied by a Trinitarian monastery. The situation was promising, but a public appeal for funds to build a theatre failed dismally. Nevertheless, the city was growing; the idea was not without its attraction, and eventually a company was formed to implement it in which the other 'liceistas' participated with new subscribers. The great Catalan industrial dynasties which were in the process of taking root – the Güells, the Serras, the Muntadas – felt they owed themselves an opera house if only to demonstrate that they were what they believed themselves to be, and an architect, Miguel Garrija y Roca, was commissioned to prepare plans. He was succeeded a year later (1846) by José Oriel Mestres, and the new theatre was ready the year after that. Needless to say, the whole project encountered furious opposition. There was already a perfectly good theatre in being where opera was performed,

80 The Catalan artist saw this Barcelona theatre scene through spectacles as little rose coloured as those of his French contemporary Toulouse Lautrec. The drawing is entitled '*El vestibulo del Gran Teatro Liceo*'.

81 (*Above*) 1861: The burnt-out ruins. Destruction was total – and led to the immediate decision to rebuild on an even bigger scale than before. 82 (*Below*) This was how the Liceo auditorium looked before the fire.

quite big enough for a city whose population was still less than two hundred thousand. But the future, it was held, lay not with the 'Italian Opera' tradition, as prevalent there as everywhere else, nor with the Catalan literary revival of the period, the 'Renaixança', but in the forum of world culture. The only time the Liceo became even vicariously involved in politics was when an anarchist threw a couple of bombs during a performance of *Guillaume Tell* in 1893. The one that exploded killed fourteen people and injured about a hundred more.

The opening, on 4 April 1847, was a tremendous affair. 'All Barcelona', as the audience would doubtless have described itself, was there. Before they had a chance to be dazzled by the inside, they were dazzled by the outside: the whole façade was lit by hundreds of wax torches and the audience made its way in to the strains of military music from an army band. They thronged into the stalls and up the great staircase to their boxes. Little girls handed posies to the ladies, broadsheets with poems lauding the occasion to the gentlemen. The completion of this exercise took most of the evening, and would have proved a distraction had the objective been a serious one. But it was not. It was just a gala: the goings-on in the auditorium were no less important than those on the stage. These, by the way, consisted of a three-act play by Ventura de la Vega, a ballet to music by José Jurch and a cantata composed by Mariano Obiols: all of them ephemeral, but all Spanish. The climax of the evening came early on, when, in an atmosphere of hushed and tense expectancy, the curtains of the Royal Box parted to reveal – a bust of the young Queen Isabella II, bathed in light, on a pedestal. In case this in itself should not suffice to induce a frenzy of loyalty, her marble majesty was attended by three (living) young women, as it might have been ladies in waiting, but actually representing the Three Graces. At our present distance in time the whole idea appears slightly macabre. In point of fact, it was perhaps the least controversial pseudo-appearance of Queen Isabella's unfortunate reign. Daughter of the formidable regent, Maria Christina, she was the immediate cause of the Carlist wars which were to rend Spain and eventually cost her her throne.

Of course, things could not go on as they had begun. The wax torches burnt themselves out, the posies withered in the ladies' hot, gloved hands and the Santa Cruz Theatre fought back like anything. The huge size of the Liceo, the cost of filling so vast a stage, made it, from the first, a hazardous enterprise financially. But even when, in April 1861, both stage and auditorium were gutted by fire, the decision was immediately taken to rebuild even more sumptuously than before. The government was asked for a subsidy, but refused it, so the shareholders raised the necessary money among themselves. The Liceo reopened its doors scarcely more than a year later. This is the theatre we see today, decorated in the grandiose style known as Isabelline. In it most of the great singers of the past century have appeared, and many distinguished opera and ballet companies. Even during the Civil War its doors stayed open, though a visiting French ballet company chose for their first night the same night that the Nationalists had chosen for

an air raid. The dancers departed almost as quickly as the planes. The theatre was also much used in these years for the performance of *Zarzuela*, a Spanish variant of musical comedy or *opéra comique*, combining some of the characteristics of both. Here Victoria de los Angeles made her triumphant début in *Le Nozze di Figaro* in 1945. Here, too, in 1961, was the world première of Manuel de Falla's fragmented *Atlantida*. Victoria de los Angeles sang in this as well. The Liceo was at one time the scene of masked balls, which were brilliant affairs. But the taste for them declined round about the turn of the century, and an attempt to revive the practice in the 1920s failed.

The Liceo never set out to be a focal point of Catalan culture. It has always aimed at cosmopolitanism, which seems to have been the right idea. For there can be few, if any, major opera houses that have survived into nearly the last quarter of the twentieth century by the impetus of private enterprise alone. The population of Barcelona is now, incidentally, well over one and a quarter million.

RICHARD COMYNS CARR

83 A token of the affectionate respect in which her native city holds her was due to Victoria de Los Angeles ten years after her triumphant début at the Liceo – ten years in which she had won worldwide acclaim.

AUSTRIA

Die Staatsoper Vienna

Vienna is historically a frontier city. Like Venice, it was a gateway to the East. In 1683 it came perilously close to proving, for the Turks, a gateway to the West: for two months in the summer of that year the siege guns of Mohammed IV's 200,000 strong army battered the outskirts. It is also the meeting place of former great trading routes – from the Baltic, through Silesia and Bohemia to the Adriatic; from the Alps, by way of the Danube, to the Carpathians. On its site the Romans established a fortress against the Germanic tribes; late in the thirteenth century it became the seat of the Habsburg dynasty; in the middle of the fourteenth century its university was founded. In the eighteenth century it was acknowledged one of the chief European centres of civilization and culture. In 1804 it became the capital city of the Austrian empire – and sixty years later, just when the idea of the Court Opera (as it was called until 1918) was being conceived, its decline began. The state of Austria is today sadly diminished; its aristocracy, not so very long ago one of the most exclusive in the world, is largely dispersed; the palaces are public buildings; the great collections either under public ownership or subject to the periodic blows of the auctioneer's hammer.

The State Opera, however, may be reported in fine fettle. Of course it is still subject to a more or less continuous barrage of abuse and denigration, sometimes merited, sometimes just part of the internecine warfare which traditionally pre-

vails. But in opera houses this is not always a sign of ailing health, and when, in 1969, the Vienna State Opera celebrated its centenary, it really did have something to celebrate. Vienna's musical antecedents are of the best. Gluck conducted the imperial opera for ten years, and it was Vienna that saw the first production of his revolutionary *Orfeo ed Eurydice* in 1762. Haydn was born and died there. Mozart composed his greatest operas there, and *Die Zauberflöte* was originally produced at the Theater an der Wien. So was Beethoven's *Fidelio*, and he himself was virtually a citizen of Vienna by adoption.

The Emperor Franz Joseph came to the throne as a result of the rash of revolutions that spread through Europe in 1848. His entire life was spent in trying to conserve the fabric of his empire by granting enough regional autonomy to forestall its total disintegration. As a holding operation this was not unsuccessful, and to the people of Vienna the future looked deceptively bland. Troubled times were followed, as usual, by portents of better ones and the Emperor, still in his thirties, determined on a bold scheme to extend the boundaries of the city, replacing the fortifications which surrounded his own baroque palace and the palaces of the nobility with a fine new boulevard fitting for a *Weltstadt*. This was where the university should be, and the museums, the city hall, the Parliament building and – the opera house. One feature common to all nineteenth-century architecture, whether in the

84 Mozart's *Die Zauberflöte* was first performed at the Theater auf der Wieden (rebuilt six years later as the Theater an der Wien) in 1791, just two months before the composer's death. It has proved one of the most durable works in the entire repertory. This engraving, executed about 1793, by Joseph and Peter Schaffer, is of the scene in Act I between Tamino, Papageno and the Three Ladies.

classical style, the gothic or the renaissance, is that the buildings are unmistakenly nineteenth-century, a fact which lends a not unpleasing unity to as much of this particular project as survived the Second World War. Vienna is now made up of four architecturally quite distinct cities – gothic, eighteenth-century, nineteenth-century, and varying shades of the twentieth century. The winners of the competition to design the new opera house, Eduard van der Nüll and August Siccard von Siccardsburg, chose what they called a modification of 'the principles of the French Renaissance', which turned out to be, of course,

genuine nineteenth-century Viennese. It evoked howls of derision which drove both of them, literally, to their deaths before they could ever see the work complete. This is a sad story which must be briefly told, if only to honour their memory. The two men were architects of repute and integrity. They won the competition quite fairly, from among a total of 35 entrants. But building was a slow business, and van der Nüll was a depressive. In 1858, five years from the laying of the foundation stone (it came to light again in the rubble of the Second World War), and goaded beyond endurance by all the silly jokes at his expense, he went off to the villa of a friend and hanged himself. Siccardsburg, who at the time was convalescing after an operation, promptly had a relapse and died two months later. When the opera house was completed in the following year, there was found to be nothing whatever the matter with it, except that the ceiling of the third tier was too low and the pillars supporting the roof obscured the view from some of the seats in the fourth tier. But the Viennese went on grumbling for nearly a quarter of a century, even though by that time it had achieved a magnificent musical record.

The Emperor attended the opening performance (*Don Giovanni*) without the Empress. The Empress was there a few days later (*La Muette de Portici*) without the Emperor. They were known to be unhappily married and she never concealed her dislike of Vienna and the formality of its court life. Even as late as 1914, when the heir to the throne, the Archduke Franz Ferdinand, and his morganatic wife, the Countess of Hohenburg, were assassinated, *he* was given a state funeral while *she* was buried obscurely, with only a pair of crossed white kid gloves and a fan, the insignia of a lady-in-waiting, to adorn her coffin. The cast-iron framework of 'Society' survived to the end; yet all around it, and even within it, Viennese life was gay and tolerant, as well as intellectually stimulating. The Viennese invariably shrugged off their misfortunes, such as the creation of the dual monarchy of Austria-Hungary (which overnight halved Vienna's importance), the stock market crash of 1873, the suicide of their Crown Prince in 1889, the murder of their expatriate Empress in 1898.

So strong a team of singers had been assembled for that first season that it proved possible to give *Don Giovanni* on the second night as well, with an entirely different cast. But audiences at first were poor, and only began to pick up when Johann Herbeck was appointed director, the same Herbeck who in 1865 had unearthed the manuscript of Schubert's unfinished symphony. His predecessor, Dingelstedt, had in any case just held the post on a temporary basis. The job he really wanted was the directorship of the Burgtheater, which only became vacant when Herbeck was

85 The Vienna Court Opera in its early days, from an etching by Rudolf von Alt. The Stephanskirche, Vienna's gothic cathedral, is seen in the background.

already chief conductor. He scored an initial success by giving Vienna its first *Meistersinger*. Viennese opinion was divided in its feelings about Wagner, but Herbeck's own enthusiasm did much to make the evening a popular success, though the critics were hostile. Perhaps part of the success was due to his cutting the score by one-and-a-half hours. Wagner was furious when he learnt about it. Indeed, his whole relationship with Vienna over a period of years was a kind of running fight, deriving from a row concerning royalties, which was never settled to his entire satisfaction. Herbeck, nevertheless, did very well by him. In the following year, 1871, *Rienzi* was put on, as well as *Der fliegende Holländer* (in a production of Herbeck's own devising).

For all his good work, poor Herbeck only succeeded in holding the job for five years. Two particular circumstances were to blame. First, the economic depression which hit Austria in 1873. Although infinitely worse things were to happen later, this, at the time, was comparable to the Wall Street crash of 1929. The age of prosperity which the building of the Ringstrasse was supposed to symbolize had been ushered in prematurely. Industrial over-expansion and a series of abnormally good harvests were the cause. In 1872, fifty-four new banking houses were established, on the flimsiest basis of speculation, to finance developments in every field, and particularly in the extension of the railways. By 1873, thirty-nine of them had collapsed, and confidence was not really to return before 1892. Against this background the steady progress of the Court Opera, after the initial set-back, will be seen to be the more remarkable. By a stroke of irony, the crash occurred in the middle of a world fair, and all the world was there to witness it. The effect on the box office was predictable. Indeed, the only two theatres which came through at least partially unscathed were the Theater an der Wien and the Carl Theater. These provided a steady diet of Austrian and French operettas respectively.

Empty seats at the Court Opera inevitably attracted the attention of the 'General Intendant' – the functionary who held the purse strings, who was the theatre's link with the First Court Chamberlain, who was in turn the link with the Ministry of Finance. Between them, and with the aid of some backstairs intrigue ably manipulated by Richard Lewy, the first horn player, they toppled Herbeck, who died a couple of years later. The first horn seems to have had an exacerbating effect on the characters of other horn players as well. Richard Strauss's father, first horn at Munich, was a notoriously tiresome and disruptive man.

Because of his success with operettas at the Carl Theater, it was judged that Franz Jauner would be just the man to bring the Court Opera round. Oddly enough this proved right. Doubting his own ability in such a different field, he refused the job twice. But when he *did* yield, in 1875, he made a tremendous success of it, because he was a real man of the theatre – resourceful, resilient, imaginative. The first example he gave of his resourcefulness was to insist that the post of General Intendant be done away with. The next two were to get Verdi to come and conduct his newly written *Requiem* and a couple of performances of *Aida*. Verdi, who had not conducted in Vienna for more than thirty years, was delighted. The Emperor came to the *Requiem* and received him in audience. As Verdi had previously symbolized the spirit of Italian nationalism in its struggle to be free of Austria, it was a distinct compliment. Probably no one, except the mistress to whom he was faithful for life, ever knew the austere, dedicated Franz Josef, quite solitary at the heart of his doomed empire. But he had an instinct for doing the right thing, and though the words he used to express appreciation were invariably the same, whatever the occasion – '*Es ist sehr schön gewesen . . . hat mich sehr gefreut*'[6] – people believed them.

Jauner's next coup was the first performance outside Paris, where it had been received badly, of *Carmen*. Jauner had wanted Bizet to conduct, but he died four months earlier, at the age of thirty-six, ignorant of having composed one of the most enduring works in the whole operatic repertory. From there Jauner went on to Wagner, having shrewdly followed Herbeck's advice and engaged Hans Richter as chief conductor. Richter was a friend of Wagner, and the best contemporary interpreter of his work. The longstanding feud that had separated Wagner from Vienna was ended (for 10,000 guilders, on account of past performances of *Tannhäuser*, *Lohengrin* and *Der fliegende Holländer*, and a 7½ per cent royalty to be paid on future ones), and the composer himself supervised new productions of *Tannhäuser* and *Lohengrin*. 1875 had certainly been a brilliant beginning for Jauner! In the following years the whole of the *Ring* was given, but the crowning all-round triumph of Jauner's term of office was when, in 1879, Franz Josef and the Empress Elisabeth attended together a gala performance which included the final scene of *Die Meistersinger*, in celebration of their silver wedding anniversary. Only a year later, he himself was to be forced out for incurring too big a deficit. It is sad that the career of so brilliant a man should have ended twenty years later in suicide. He had interpreted, he had even helped to form, the cultural climate of Vienna at a certain period. But time passed, a new century dawned, and he sensed that he did not belong to it.

In essence, his achievement was to make the Vienna Court Opera, for half a century and more, one of the leading opera houses, if not *the* leading opera house of the world. Various elements contribute to this provocative assertion: boldness and eclecticism in the choice of works performed; splendid casting and coherence of production – many of the greatest singers have performed there, not merely as guest artists, but as members of the company, season after season; orchestral playing of a quality which is unique in the sense of having a timbre different from that of orchestral playing anywhere else. Of course, it is universally acknowledged that instrumentalists are amongst the most cynical professionals on earth, that given twenty bars rest they will turn to their newspapers, that if the conductor cannot dominate them, they will not scruple to ruin him . . . and nowhere have these characteristics been mulled over with greater satisfaction than in Vienna. Yet there is a golden warmth about the Vienna strings the like of which is scarcely known elsewhere.

They can play so softly that the music would seem almost inaudible, were it not in fact perfectly and exquisitely clear. Their woodwinds are pure. Their brass is bold without being brassy. And over a period of years all these qualities have merged into a tradition.

Another contributory element to Vienna's greatness is the calibre of the conductors who have worked there: Richter, Mahler, Richard Strauss, Karajan . . . it is a formidable list, but no name in it stands out more distinctly than that of Gustav Mahler. This great man was a storm centre during his life and has become a legend since his death: a legend that continues to grow in proportion as his own music, beyond the comprehension of most of his own generation, becomes increasingly well known. His appointment as director in 1897 brought to an end the rule of Wilhelm Jahn, which had lasted for seventeen relatively tranquil years. Jahn had done a great deal to consolidate the brilliant tactical triumphs of his predecessor, Franz Jauner. He worked in perfect harmony with Hans Richter and he widened the range of the repertory, bringing in such works as *Manon*, *Werther*, *The Bartered Bride*, Mascagni's *L'Amico Fritz*, Humperdinck's *Hänsel und Gretel*, as well as a number of others now forgotten. Of Jahn it could almost be said as in the old rhyme about Augustus of Rome: 'Of marble he left what of brick he had found'.

Yet the arrival of Mahler gave a new, galvanic impulse to the whole undertaking. Both Richard Strauss and Egon Wellesz have recorded what an extraordinary effect Mahler had on them when they heard him conduct opera for the first time. Brahms, too, had admired a performance of *Don Giovanni* in Budapest, and a slightly improbable rapport was established between the two men, which proved helpful to Mahler in getting the Vienna appointment, as a counterweight to all the influence Cosima Wagner was able to muster in opposition. He was staunch in maintaining the full Wagner repertory, bringing in two new conductors, Franz Schalk to help with the German works and Bruno Walter with the Italian. When Karl Goldmark, composer of *Die Königin von*

86 Gustav Mahler, two years before his resignation as Director of the Vienna Court Opera.

Saba, said he never listened to Wagner because he was afraid of growing like him, Mahler offered dry encouragement by observing, 'You eat beef without turning into an ox'. He seems to have brought to bear a power of total comprehension on everything he tackled, to have possessed an inner vision of absolute clarity along with the will to convey it to singers and orchestral players alike. He insisted on a double cast for every opera he undertook. No production detail was too small for his attention and whatever he decided was usually final. Almost the only man who ever succeeded in overruling him during the Vienna years was Charpentier, whom he had invited to come to the première of *Louise*. The composer found so much to complain about at rehearsals

that it had to be postponed and Mahler virtually abdicated in his favour. Mahler must have realized instinctively that Charpentier, whose ideas about production were in advance of the time, had much to teach him, because the change was accomplished with perfect good humour on both sides.

Perhaps the peak of his Vienna achievements was reached with the 1903 production of *Tristan und Isolde*, to mark the twentieth anniversary of Wagner's death. He engaged Alfred Roller (most widely remembered now for the original Dresden and Vienna *Rosenkavalier*) to design the sets. Cosima Wagner certainly would not have approved of them. Nor did the more conservative elements in the audience, who henceforth judged Roller to be a bad influence.

Still another element which may have contributed to making the Vienna Opera great is the ferocity of the music critics. Hanslick and Speidel had savaged Wagner for a quarter of a century, Hugo Wolf had savaged Jahn, because he loathed some of the lighter operas that Jahn and the Viennese rather enjoyed ('this opera needs a comprehensive cut, from the first bar to the last', he wrote of one of them). Mahler dismissed all the critics together in a single disparaging phrase – 'our lords and masters'. Yet it was never the blunt instruments of the critics by which directors of the Court Opera were finally struck down. In Mahler's case it was not even a rival's stiletto (though it might well have been); it was rather an alliance of all the people who over the years he had contrived to offend, and there were a great many of them. He called their campaign the 'revolt of mediocrities', but bowed to it. He resigned in 1907, and in farewell to his colleagues said bleakly, 'Instead of something complete and entire, as I had dreamed, I am leaving behind something imperfect and unfinished, as is our human lot.' He also left behind, in a drawer of his desk, all the medals and citations he had been awarded – 'for my successor'.

The years following Mahler's departure were inevitably something of an anti-climax – except that everybody in and around the Court Opera continued feuding with the zest of Scottish chieftains. Weingartner (the successor for whom the medals had been left behind) did as much as he could, by advertance and inadvertance, to dismantle all that was best in Mahler's edifice, but he had over-estimated the weight of the antipathy to Mahler and contrived to make himself fairly unpopular thereby. He did, on the other hand, bring *Pelléas et Mélisande*, d'Albert's *Tiefland* and Puccini's *Tosca* into the repertory: Mahler would never have tolerated this last. And in 1909 came Richard Strauss's *Elektra;* Weingartner himself was probably better pleased by the bad press than by the enthusiastic public response. He was jealous of Strauss for handling, with more originality, the same subject that he had taken for an opera of his own called *Orestes*. When, in the following season, Strauss conducted *Elektra* himself, Weingartner stayed away. By way of contrast, he took a marked interest in Johann Strauss's *Der Zigeunerbaron*. It is a peculiarly Viennese trait that the Court Opera should have often been equally at home to operettas as to serious works. Weingartner enjoyed conducting more than producing, and it was he who fixed the conductor's position in the orchestral pit where it is today in every opera house – at the point where the pit is separated from the stalls, where he can be seen by the audience as well as by the players and singers. Some conductors previously used to place themselves in the middle of the orchestra. In Paris it was customary for a time for them to have the orchestra behind them. Weingartner also liked to see his name on playbills, and so his colleagues Bruno Walter and Franz Schalk soon saw theirs as well.

The climax of the Vienna Opera's pre-war sunset glow came with Richard Strauss's *Der Rosenkavalier*, in 1911. The public was from the first delighted with what has proved the most successful opera of the twentieth century. The press notices were quite otherwise. They have to be read to be believed:

> Waltzes of this kind cannot support the strain of such a steep social ascent as Richard Strauss – who moreover lacks all understanding of the art of Johann Strauss – has conferred upon them.

87 Richard Hanslick, the critic, telling Richard Wagner, the composer, how not to do it. A silhouette by Otto Böhler.

> It is a comedy, in truth highly comical, the way in which Richard Strauss instantly realized that the boom in sexual neuropathology was over. . . .

> We are unable to say that *Rosenkavalier* marks an advance in his creative work, nor do we believe that this 'comedy for music' will retain a place for long in the repertory of the Court Opera.

> Hugo von Hofmannsthal and Richard Strauss, who believed themselves capable of writing a musical comedy, are wholly devoid of humour; all that they offer in their work is cheap, low-class wit.

By a tremendous feat of rearrangement on the part of the director, Hans Gregor, who did not

Lisa. By the beginning of 1916 a new generation of opera-goers was in being – the war profiteers. Most of them cared nothing about music but a great deal about being seen in the right place. Not surprisingly the price of seats rocketed. The old Emperor's death in November 1916 called a halt for mourning, but activities were resumed in the New Year, and his successor, Karl, heir to a bankrupt dynasty, even found time in the course of his two years' reign to appoint a new 'Intendant'. He lasted just long enough to offer the post of director to Richard Strauss. Even the death throes of the old order were not enacted without an element of light relief. In February 1918, Janáček's *Jenufa* had been put on to flatter the disaffected Czechs. In October, to hearten Austria's German allies, the censorship of *Salome* was lifted. To this end Richard Strauss had intervened personally with the Cardinal Arch-bishop of Vienna: it would be pleasing to have a record of their conversation! As an ultimate stroke of irony, the first performance was given 'by Imperial command for the benefit of the Royal Austrian War Widows' and Orphans' Fund'. Jeritza, as Salome, seems to have done her best to make the occasion a success: according to the *Deutsches Volksblatt* she 'displayed all the ferocity of a beast of prey and looked ravishing in an ingenious garment that revealed her charms long before the Dance of the Seven Veils'. But Germany and Austria lost the war, the unhappy Czechs won, for all too brief a period, their independence, and the Emperor Karl died an impoverished exile in Madeira four years later.

Of course, a newly established republican government could not simply take over agreements entered into by their imperial predecessors, and it was only in December 1919 that Richard Strauss was actually confirmed in his appointment as co-director, with Franz Schalk, of the Vienna State Opera – as it had now become – in succession to the Imperial and Royal Court Opera. Strauss was no idealist. Intellectually he was a lightweight and he cheerfully conceded that in *Die Frau ohne Schatten* Hugo von Hofmannsthal's libretto was quite beyond his grasp. There was a good, working relationship between the two

know much about music, but who could recognize when he had a success on his hands, *Der Rosenkavalier* was given thirty-seven performances before the end of that first season.

It was for long accepted (indeed, until the country found its present equilibrium as a kind of second Switzerland) that the situation in Austria, though always critical, was never serious, and this perhaps explains why the war years 1914–18, which saw the final, frightful collapse of the empire, seem to have passed almost un-noticed at the Court Opera. Of course that is an exaggeration, but after a slightly late start (October) to the 1914–15 season, there was an average of four performances a week, which included the presentation of two new works, Pfitzner's *Der arme Heinrich* and Schillings' *Mona*

88 Maria Jeritza was one of the great sopranos of her day and scored a succession of triumphs at the Vienna Opera from 1913 onwards, and at the Metropolitan Opera, New York from 1921. She excelled in such dramatic roles as Tosca, Carmen and Santuzza in *Cavalleria Rusticana*. Indeed, when she swooned at the end of the last named, she was liable to roll down the steps before the church so veristically as to excite fears about her ultimate destination. Here she is seen as Puccini's *Manon Lescaut* in 1918.

men, but no spark of spiritual affinity. Yet this does not mean that Strauss lacked other, compensating gifts. He was a highly articulate composer, with an uncanny facility for exploiting and enhancing dramatic situations by his musical interpretation of them. He was thoroughly professional in everything connected with the creation, production and performance of opera. And he was an able man of business in every aspect of his chosen *métier;* in fact, just the person Vienna needed in a period of extraordinary difficulty. New political régimes are always born in turmoil, and the turmoil is usually accompanied or quickly followed by dreadful suffering. Inflation totally destroyed the comfortable bourgeoisie; the aristocracy was routed; the profiteers squandered their profits and were no more seen. But of course, there was yet another new generation growing up for whom this was normal life – the only life they knew. And because they were Viennese they were hungry for music. Strauss was just the person to ensure that they got what they needed. He fed them a substantial, but not an exclusive diet of his own and Puccini's works. The characteristically Viennese sneer that he hogged the repertory for himself is by no means wholly true. His stated belief was that a composer should have proved himself elsewhere before seeking admission to such a hallowed shrine as the Vienna State Opera. It was no place for experiments, he maintained, but he was preferentially disposed towards Austrian composers. He would even, he added, have 'played Schoenberg and Křenek – since he was not obliged to like everything he played'. But Schalk was not keen on risking money experimentally, and extra subsidies were hard to come by.

During this period the Opera was greatly strengthened by a magnificent team of singers. Jeritza and Lotte Lehmann were at the height of their powers, and the rivalry between their respective groups of supporters reflected something of the feelings they entertained for one another. They even entered the opera house by different doors and when, ultimately, they went to live in America, they still kept the width of the continent between them. But Jeritza did, on at least one occasion, deputize for Lehmann at short notice (in *Il Tabarro*, at a performance with Puccini present) and they did appear together in the original production of *Die Frau ohne Schatten*. Other memorable names are Richard Mayr (who interpreted, and it seems ideally, the rôle of Baron Ochs, as well as that of Barak, in *Die Frau ohne Schatten*), Leo Slezak and Piccaver, of whom it has been said that when he was singing one felt as if one were being stroked. It was not only the two prima donnas, however, who needed separate entrances. The relations between the co-directors, at first fairly cordial, grew cooler season after season and in 1924 Strauss quit, leaving his antagonist to five years of undisputed sovereignty. Although the change was accompanied by all the customary overtones of Viennese venom, it worked out well, for Schalk was a dedicated man and knew his job. He filled out the repertory in places where it was weak – *Boris Godunov*, for instance (to which Chaliapin contributed a major tantrum), and *Turandot*, with alternate casts of exceptional brilliance. The producer was Lothar Wallerstein, who worked constantly at the Vienna State Opera thereafter until 1938. The same year, 1926, is also memorable for Jan Kiepura's performance as Calaf: the Viennese went mad about him. In 1926, too, there took place a production of *La forza del destino*, with the new German libretto translated by Franz Werfel.

It seemed as if the golden sunset of twelve years before had been succeeded by another golden dawn. But in 1928 the swastika appeared on a poster announcing a protest meeting against Ernst Křenek's *Jonny spielt auf*. This opera enjoyed an immense popular success for two or three seasons, after which it was virtually forgotten. At about the same time the quarrel with Strauss as a guest conductor was ended on extremely favourable terms: he was never one to harbour grudges if the terms were favourable. This brought *Intermezzo* and *Die ägyptische Helena* into the repertory. It also brought in Ravel's *L'Enfant et les Sortilèges* and Stravinsky's *Oedipus Rex*: Strauss was fully alive to the operatic potential of both these composers and urged their claims with Schalk. Thus, an extraordinarily wide-ranging repertory was again in

89 Leo Slezak, seen here as Walther von Stolzing in *Die Meistersinger*, sang regularly at the Vienna Court Opera from 1901 to 1911, and during the course of a long career was heard and valued in most of the world's leading opera houses. He studied for a time under Jean de Reszke and profited greatly thereby. A thoroughly serious artist he was also blessed with a strong sense of humour and in 1928 wrote a highly entertaining autobiography. He died in 1946 at the age of 73.

90 (*Above*) The Vienna State Opera in 1920; a caricature by Leo Zasche. Strauss is conducting, Slezak and Jeritza are on stage. But the new, republican audience is clearly under-rehearsed.

being; the standard of production was high and the company perhaps the best that has ever worked in any opera house anywhere. The world fame of the Vienna State Opera was fully deserved. This, for Schalk, had a consequence not altogether unfamiliar to those who do too well: he got the sack. And Clemens Krauss reigned in his stead, though only after a rather awkward hiatus in which the post nearly went to Furtwängler. Schalk died in 1931 and his grateful country thought up a posthumous title for him by way of amends: *Österreichischer Generalmusikdirektor*. It has only been enjoyed (if that is the right word) by one other man since – Karl Böhm.

Clemens Krauss was thirty-six when he took up his appointment – a year younger than Mahler had been. Like Mahler, he was a very dominating personality and knew exactly what he wanted to do. Dictators were coming into fashion and Krauss established a personal dictatorship in the Vienna State Opera more complete than any before. This would assuredly have been his undoing later, had he not chosen other means of undoing himself sooner. Austria was now being dragged, half conscious, towards an abyss even more terrible than that of 1914. Krauss and Strauss were partners in deception – or if not quite that, at any rate complaisant tools in the hands of the Nazis. In December 1934, Krauss defaulted on his contract and made off for Berlin, taking some of the company with him. He became a great favourite with Hitler and prospered exceedingly. Strauss's role was more equivocal. He wrote a letter criticizing the Germans for

xv (*Opposite*) The Vienna production of *Le Nozze di Figaro* in 1960 starred Geraint Evans and Lisa della Casa, and was conducted by Director, Herbert von Karajan.

banning his *Schweigsame Frau* which fell into the hands of the police. But no action was taken against him and he lived out the Second World War unmolested.

Weingartner was brought back to plug the hole left in the Opera, which, considering its size, he did with some success. But he was ousted after a year and was followed by a rather uneasy duumvirate of Kerber (a member of the governing body determined to be director) and Walter. It might have worked out, given time, because Erwin Kerber possessed genuine enthusiasm and was no fool; and Bruno Walter was a man of high calibre. But on 11 March 1938 the swastika flag was raised over Vienna. On the 12th German troops began to arrive. And the Vienna State Opera ceased to be the Vienna State Opera.

It would be too sad to do more than pass over the years in the life of this opera house, so rich in musical and social tradition, between the night of 27 March 1938, when Field Marshal Göring attended a gala performance of *Fidelio* (surely as bizarre a concatenation as can be imagined) and the morning of 12 March 1945, when a stick of bombs put an end to speculation as to who was loyal to whom and who was being protected by whom. Marcel Prawy, in his definitive history, *The Vienna Opera*, has covered this period with extreme delicacy and tact, and he concludes his account with an anecdote that sets everything in perspective:

> Two minutes before the bombs fell a small group in the air-raid shelter were whiling away the time by discussing with a blend of piety and humour what the staff of the Vienna Opera, from the Wagner tenors to the humblest stage-hand and the most junior typist, could arm themselves with if ever they were called upon to defend their beloved Opera House.

> The weapons at the Opera were listed one by one. 'There's everything we could possibly want,' claimed one optimist, 'fifty muzzle-loaded rifles left over from the war against Prussia in 1866, complete with bayonets; a thousand swords; and infantry, cavalry and students' sabres, some of them from Maria-

XVI (*Opposite*) The National Theatre, Prague, seen from across the River Vltava. It is more than just an opera house: it is the very shrine of the Czech people's musical genius.

91 (*Above*) Epitaph on an epoch.
92 (*Below*) Richard Mayr was an outstanding Baron Ochs.

93 Back to the old address. A cartoon depicting the triumphant return of the Company to their gloriously restored home in 1955.

Theresa's day, not to mention the stock of fourteenth and fifteenth century troopers' cuirasses.' Someone else remembered the gilt-trimmed aluminium helmets, inset with precious stones, which had been handed down from Winkelmann to Aagard-Oesvig and Schmedes. Only Slezak and Franz Völker always wore their own (outsize) helmets. 'And all absolutely bullet-proof,' put in a third optimist, 'especially Siegfried's helmets with the genuine goose feathers, and the Valkyrie helmets of best quality straw.'

'Apart from all these we've got the oldest armour in the whole of Vienna, all the para-phernalia worn by the knight in *Puppenfee*, complete with anti-rust devices so that the knight can move his arms and legs at the witching hour of midnight.' 'None of it is any good,' sighed a less optimistic member of the chorus. 'Surely there must be something we could use.' 'Of course there is – the Mexican saddle that Jeritza used to gallop in on in *La Fanciulla del West*'.

Opera performances had been suspended with the declaration of 'total war', but there were some concert performances and recording sessions. It was one of these that was brought to a premature end on that March morning. But not even the

death of the opera house could stifle for long the spirit of opera in Vienna. On 1 May 1945, Josef Krips conducted *Le Nozze di Figaro* at the Volksoper, and on 6 October the re-formed Vienna State Opera opened with *Fidelio* (Josef Krips again conducting) at the Theater an der Wien. It was in a dilapidated state, but for the next ten years it served. How could it not – this, after all, was the house which had seen the first *Zauberflöte*, the first *Fidelio*, where Meyerbeer had conducted, and Johann Strauss and Lehár.

The rebuilding of the Vienna State Opera was entrusted to two distinguished architects, Erich Boltenstern and Otto Prössinger. Their first intention had been to achieve an exact replica, but this was impossible because the original sketches had been lost. The façade and the foyer had miraculously survived – at any rate to an extent which made restoration possible. But the auditorium, the stage and all the backstage area had to be entirely rebuilt. What might have been an uneasy compromise has proved a great success. The auditorium is discreet and elegant, in cream, gold and red. There are new, spacious foyers, which somehow complement, rather than contradict the old one. A sense of the past has been preserved and in the hubbub of departure that follows a fine performance one can almost hear the echo of a courteous, ghostly voice, 'Es ist sehr schön gewesen . . . hat mich sehr gefreut'.

CZECHOSLOVAKIA

The National Theatre Prague

The European tradition of opera is deeply rooted in Prague. As the capital of Bohemia, the city played an important part in the affairs of the Habsburg empire. Under the patronage of an enlightened aristocracy it was a lively centre of Italian opera during the late seventeenth century and the eighteenth century, and from this period there dates a baroque theatre, built by Count F. A. Nostic, which is one of the architectural masterpieces of the style. Here two important Mozart premières took place: the first, *Don Giovanni*, in 1787; the second, *La Clemenza di Tito*, composed for the coronation of the Emperor Leopold II as King of Bohemia, in 1791. With the beginning of the nineteenth century, German influence began to dominate (Prague is, after all, little more than a hundred miles from Dresden), a development in which Carl Maria von Weber played some part. He worked there from 1813 to 1815 and set about 'rehabilitating' the opera, which had lapsed from its high estate of twenty years before. He wanted this 'rehabilitation' to be on German lines, but the Czechs have a particularly strong – indeed, a seemingly indestructible – sense of national identity, and nowhere is this more manifest than in their music. The first genuinely Czech opera, with Czech words, was Frantisek Škroup's *Dráteník* (The Tinkler), produced at Count Nostic's theatre, by that time re-named The Theatre of the Three Estates, and

from then on the need began to be felt for a national theatre in which Czech culture should predominate. This was the genesis of the National Theatre, beautifully situated beside the Vltava river. It is not, like many opera houses of the period, just part of the pattern of nineteenth century urban social development. It is much more. The motto over the proscenium arch, 'From the Nation to the Nation', really means what it says: the house was built with money subscribed by the people themselves.

The idea for it began to take shape in 1850, when a patriotic committee was formed. Twelve years later a provisional theatre (the Kralovske Zemske Ceski Prozatmni Divadlo), with a seating capacity of 900, opened its doors. From 1866 to 1874, Bedřich Smetana was director and chief conductor. Here, in 1866, that best-loved of all Czech operas, *The Bartered Bride*, was heard for the first time. Today, more than a century later, this work retains the full measure of its freshness and vigour; audiences all over the world are still applauding it, and through it, the Czech people.

In 1881 the permanent opera house (Národní Divadlo) was opened with another Smetana première, *Libuše*, but almost immediately afterwards a fire put the building out of use for a further two years. When the ravages of the fire had been made good, there was no question but that the architects, J. Zítek and J. Schulz, had

94 A contemporary production at the National Theatre of Janáček's *From the House of the Dead*, the opera based on Dostoievsky's moving autobiographical work of the same name.

done their work well. It is a dignified building, and the leading Czech artists and sculptors of the day contributed to its adornment. Initially it was supported by a powerful, but private, committee, to whom the director was responsible, although it was Bohemian national property. In 1900 there was a re-organization and the National Theatre Company took over. A new director, Karel Kovařovic, extended the repertory considerably – though it took Janáček's *Jenufa* fourteen years to

cover the odd hundred miles from Brno to the capital, which it reached in 1916. In 1920 the opera house came under direct national administration and in 1945 it was fully nationalized, to form part of a complex of three theatres, the other two being the old Nostic House, now once again re-named, this time the Tyl (used principally for drama), and the Smetana, formerly known as the German Opera House, or Neues Deutsches Landestheater, which had been built in 1883.

96 Act I, scene I from the first Prague production of *Le Nozze di Figaro* in 1786.

95 This is the earliest known picture of Count Nostic's beautiful baroque theatre (now the Tyl Theatre). It is a ticket for a ball.

97 From a tablet commemorating the world première of *Don Giovanni* in Prague on 29 October, 1787. The opera had been completed on the 28th.

98 Carolina Perini, the singer who played Annio in the first performance of Mozart's *La Clemenza di Tito* at the National Theatre in Prague, 1791. This engraving was made in 1793, probably by Giovanni Battista.

UNITED KINGDOM

The Royal Opera House Covent Garden

In England, opera sidled onto the national scene more or less surreptitiously, through the masques, dramatic entertainments part sung, part declaimed, which were an amenity of civilized social intercourse in the late sixteenth century and the seventeenth. They were suitable for private houses and private gardens. They derived from patterns set in Italy and France. At that time there was already as much cultured internationalism among the ruling classes of Europe as there was to be in the eighteenth and nineteenth centuries, or of the wider world, both social and geographical, of the present age.

Yet as late as the end of the seventeenth century one of the most beautiful operas in the world, Purcell's *Dido and Aeneas*, was composed merely for a girls' school, and apart from a few public performances early in the eighteenth century, was not seen on the stage again for 195 years. It reached Ireland in 1895 and New York (and even then only by way of a concert performance), in 1924.

It was only in 1732 that the first Covent Garden Theatre was built, on the site of what is now the Royal Opera House. This new theatre was intended primarily for the performance of plays and the first work to be performed there, at the end of 1732, was Congreve's *The Way of the World*. The first opera, five weeks later, was Gay's *The Beggar's Opera*, which had already proved successful at the near-by Lincoln's Inn Theatre. There were twenty successive performances, which meant that the piece had enjoyed another triumph. Indeed, the bitter, satirical humour of *The Beggar's Opera*, combined with its lyricism and warm-heartedness, made a formula that has proved lastingly valid. It also epitomized some of the contrasting aspects of the period: the higgledy-piggledy intermingling of elegance and squalor; the rude, rumbustious vitality of an England that was great as well as grisly. Would that we could recapture the sounds and smells, the harshnesses and beauties, the whole atmosphere of the epoch! But we can at least see what Covent Garden Piazza, society's newest focal point, looked like, what sort of clothes the people who rubbed shoulders there wore; and we can almost guess what it must have felt like to be a member of the Covent Garden audience: stuffy, cramped, uncomfortable, but obviously exciting.

In these years it was the King's Theatre in the Haymarket that was the home of opera, and there Handel presided as musical director of the Italian Opera. All opera then was Italian opera – except for *The Beggar's Opera*, which set out to parody the whole convention. Handel, indeed, harmed himself by his stubborn refusal to read the portents of *The Beggar's Opera* and persisted for years in a style that was becoming outmoded. His real *forte* proved to be oratorio, and he had a spectacular run of successes at Covent Garden between 1743 and 1747. By that time the fierce musical, social and political in-fighting which characterized his earlier career had somewhat cooled off. It was this

99 Peter Pears as Grimes and Joan Cross as Ellen Orford in the 1947 production of *Peter Grimes* at Covent Garden, the rôles which they had both created in the original, sensational appearance of the opera at Sadler's Wells in 1945. On the first night the macabre eerieness of the last act was enhanced by one of the last great November London fogs, which infiltrated the theatre almost totally.

100 'Riot at Covent Garden Theatre in 1763 in
consequence of the Managers refusing to admit half-
price in the Opera of *Artaxerxes*'

101 Covent Garden Piazza: Inigo
Jones' famous *tour de force* of town
planning. In its day it echoed the
very heartbeat of London life, and
at its north-east corner was the
entrance to the first theatre.

in-fighting which was the cause of his peregrinations from the King's, Haymarket, to the theatre in Lincoln's Inn Fields, to Covent Garden and back to the King's. He had a hated rival in the operatic field, Buononcini. There were also two important castrati, Senesino and Farinelli, who hated one another, and a couple of sopranos, Cuzzoni and Faustini, who hated one another even more. But, towering above these feuds, Handel may be seen as a major figure, as large as, if not larger than life. His music echoes vividly the baroque splendour which is the keynote of the reign of George II. Yet the core of his inspiration seems to have been simplicity of heart. For the last thirty-four years of his life he was a naturalized Englishman, but he spoke the language atrociously till the day of his death.

By the middle of the eighteenth century, opera in England was clearly well into its stride. The first genuinely English opera at Covent Garden, after *The Beggar's Opera*, was Thomas Arne's *Artaxerxes*, in 1762, and its success was nearly its undoing. It had cost so much to put on that the management suspended certain concessions hitherto allowed in the price of seats. The public responded in a thoroughly modern way: it demonstrated; the benches were torn up, the chandeliers broken, the linings of the boxes cut to shreds and the pillars dividing them severely mauled. The next forty-six years were less spectacular, except that in 1789 the King's Theatre in the Haymarket burnt down, and the season then in progress was transferred to Covent Garden, the young soprano Anna Storace (Nancy Storace) appearing there for the first time in Paisiello's *Il Barbiere di Siviglia*.[7] During this period, too (in 1776, to be exact), Elizabeth Billington made her début, at the age of eighteen. Then, in 1808, Covent Garden itself burnt down. This was a disaster entailing the loss of Handel's organ and many important musical scores and documents relating to the history of the theatre (the Covent Garden archives have always been victim either to destruction, or wholesale removal by outgoing and often bankrupt managements). No time was lost in rebuilding, £50,000 being subscribed by the public in shares of £500 each.

The total cost of the new theatre was £300,000, and because of this, prices were raised, again with consequences that we, in our modern way, might have been inclined to foresee as predictable: riots. After a few nights of caterwauling, the old prices were restored and the £500 subscribers could enjoy the amenity of three tiers of 26 boxes, bathed in the light of 40 glass chandeliers which consumed 270 wax candles every evening. Yet in the quarter of a century since the end of the Second World War the price of seats has risen enormously, and no upholstery has been ripped, nor any bottle hurled in protest.

The rebuilt theatre was a well proportioned, very handsome building, designed by Robert Smirke, who was also responsible for the British Museum and the Royal Mint. Its seating capacity was 2,800, and though it was still used as much for plays as for opera, there were increasing signs and portents of operatic glories to come. The most significant of these was the choice of Carl Maria von Weber as musical director, in 1824. Weber was all the rage in London just then – indeed, throughout Europe, and to secure his services

102 Nancy Storace was an English soprano of Italian descent, born in 1766. She created the rôle of Susanna in Mozart's *Le Nozze di Figaro* in Vienna, and sang at Covent Garden from 1801 to 1808.

103 Carl Maria von Weber (1786–1826) was a many-sided musical genius, whose greatest passion was for opera.

was a great coup. In the 1824–5 season *Der Freischütz* was given fifty-two performances at Covent Garden. Weber himself had not yet taken up his post: he was working on his next opera, *Oberon*, commissioned by Covent Garden at the time of his appointment. *Oberon* had a spectacular première on 12 April 1826. The audience gave the composer a standing ovation when he appeared on the conductor's rostrum and even the overture was encored. The scenery and costumes were more splendid than anything seen on this stage before. But, alas, it was a doomed work, killed by its libretto. And the composer was a doomed man. Within thirteen weeks of that great first night he was dead.

Madame Vestris, a grand-daughter of the engraver Francesco Bartolozzi, made her first Covent Garden appearance in *Oberon*. Her contralto voice was 'one of the most musical, easy, rich . . . ever bestowed on a singer', but as an operatic singer she was less than wholly serious, being more at home in ballads like *Cherry Ripe*, which she introduced into her lighter theatrical ventures. Indeed, the cult of the drawing-room ballad which was to persist as an ingredient of middle-class English social life right up to and even, marginally, after the First World War, can be largely traced back to her. Later she became manager of Covent Garden, another rôle in which she was not wholly serious: the financial consequences were disastrous. Throughout the 1820s, 1830s and 1840s, however rich and reassuring the warm light of those 270 wax candles, now supplemented by oil (gas had been installed, but taken out again after it had blown up two men in the basement), the place was always tottering on the brink of ruin. There was extravagance and incompetence in the running of it. The payment of rates and taxes was always in arrears, and changes in social attitudes and the climate of opinion worked – or so the managers averred – against profitability: 'The late hours of dining take away all the upper classes; religious prejudice is very much increased, evangelical feeling . . .' etc., etc. By 1843 the theatre's fortunes had sunk so low that for a time it was used as a lecture hall by the Anti-Corn Law League. It has suffered similar humiliations since. In the First World War it became a furniture repository. Throughout the Second World War it was a dance hall. But the Corn Laws were repealed, the furniture was not bombed and the dancing couples eventually withdrew.

In 1846, however, Giuseppe Persiani, husband of the Fanny Persiani for whom Donizetti had written *Lucia di Lammermoor*, was dreaming wakefully of a real opera house, an 'Italian Opera' house on a scale comparable with the two greatest opera houses in the world – La Scala at Milan and the San Carlo in Naples. He and the rest of the 'old guard' at Her Majesty's Theatre in the Haymarket were in revolt against the difficult conditions prevailing there. Together with a compatriot he acquired the lease of Covent Garden. Late in 1846, within a matter of weeks, the interior was demolished and early in 1847 the first prospectus was published of the Royal Italian Opera, Covent Garden; the season opened on 6 April with Rossini's *Semiramide*. Opulence might have been

XVII An unusual view of the stage and auditorium of the Royal Opera House, Covent Garden, warming up for a performance. The ceiling has been aptly described as 'a piece of Fabergé made for a giant'.

the password for the whole venture. There were now six tiers of boxes, instead of three as formerly – 186 boxes all told, and the lighting was so arranged as to display the occupants to best advantage. Above these tiers were two amphitheatres and a gallery, accommodating 600 people, tightly packed against a sky blue, circular ceiling, with allegorical and floral designs in white and gold, from the centre of which hung a chandelier big enough to obscure the line of sight of about five-sixths of these unprivileged spectators. The singing was opulent, too: Grisi and Persiani, Tamburini, Alboni – all great names; and others, if not great, distinguished. In 1848 Pauline Viardot (Malibran's younger sister) and Jeanne Castellan were added to them. And Queen Victoria paid her first visit to the Royal Italian Opera. Some twelve works were added to the repertory over a couple of years. The standard of performance and orchestral playing was as high as any in Europe. But behind opulence trailed its customary sad familiar, ruin, and not for the first time or last time in operatic history the phrase 'a great artistic success' became more or less synonymous with 'a great financial débâcle'. Then, to the threat of financial ruin (which in the case of opera houses seems in general to be only relative) was added a more tangible, and most horrible disaster. On the night of 4 March 1856, the whole beautiful edifice went up in flames. It was let for a short season at the time to a theatrical impresario who liked to be known as 'the wizard of the north'. To recoup the losses sustained in the course of his ten weeks' season he sought – and was granted, though reluctantly – permission to give on the last night a 'Grand Bal Masqué'. Within half an hour of 'God Save the Queen' being played to bring it to its rowdy end the roof had fallen in. Thirty-six hours later, the Queen herself was surveying the silent ruins, escorted by Frederick Gye, the managing director. Persiani's dream was over.

Gye was a remarkable man, who exercised an effective dictatorship over the fortunes of Covent Garden for a quarter of a century. His qualifications were a good business head, a total commitment to the job and a persuasive, resilient person-

104 (*Above*) Joint manager of Covent Garden with her husband Charles Matthews, from 1839 to 1842, Lucia Elizabeth Vestris was also said to be the possessor of 'one of the most luscious of low voices, great personal beauty, an almost faultless figure, which she adorned with consummate art, and no common stage address'.

105 Queen Victoria and the Prince Consort entertain
Napoleon III and the Empress Eugénie at Covent Garden.

ality. He needed all of them to get the opera house
re-financed and rebuilt within two years. The
Duke of Bedford owned the site, and Gye obtained
from him a new ninety-year lease. He also found
some substantial backers among the opera-
minded section of the aristocracy and the monied
class. Edward Barry was the architect of the new
house, and this is substantially the Covent
Garden we know today. It differs in one important particular from its predecessors. In their case
the stage occupied the northern section and the
audience the southern. Barry put the stage at the
west end and the auditorium at the east, with the
entrance in Bow Street instead of from the
Piazza. On the site of the old entrance was built
the Floral Hall, a concert hall resembling the
Crystal Palace, which, to the fond eye of recollec-
tion, now seems an edifice of great enchantment,
even though by the time living memory begins it
had already fallen from its high cultural estate and

been absorbed into Covent Garden Market.
Edward Barry designed the Floral Hall, too, and
because he dwelt somewhat in the shadow of his
more famous father, these Covent Garden achievements have perhaps been underrated. It was said
of him after his death that he 'aimed at being a
man of his day, neither a Greek nor a Goth.'
Indeed, he was to prove too little of a Goth to
win the competition for designing the Albert
Memorial, and too little of a Greek to succeed in
carrying out his design for the National Gallery
without becoming subject to a lot of numbing
restrictions. But he *did* build a beautiful opera
house.

The first season in the new theatre opened on
15 May 1858, with *Les Huguenots*. Grisi and her
husband Mario sang the two chief rôles. They had
both been known on the London stage for twenty
years and continued to be immensely popular.
They were intelligent singers and their union

106 After the Grand Bal Masqué was over: The Wizard of the North's last fling.

107 The Bow
Street frontage of
the Opera House,
rebuilt by Edward
Barry, following
the fire of 1856.

108 Adelina Patti reigned supreme at Covent Garden from 1861 to 1884. Born in Madrid in 1843, she died, châtelaine of a picturesque Welsh castle, in 1919

somehow enhanced the romantic appeal which had led Heine, in his *Letters from Paris*, much earlier, to describe them as 'the rose and the nightingale – the rose the nightingale among the birds, the nightingale the rose among the flowers.' Grisi came of a distinguished artistic family, Mario of a noble Italian one. His father had been a Piedmontese general, and he himself started off in the army. But the quality of his voice, allied to an extraordinary gracefulness of manner, inevitably lured him on to the operatic stage. They were not, however, to escape time's ravages: she continued singing too long and he continued living too long after her death, and finished in straitened circumstances. On this night of 15 May their troubles were more immediate. The performance started late, the intervals dragged out endlessly and at 12.30 a.m. when the third act

ended, the stage manager called a halt. The audience was not amused.

In the season that followed, opera at Covent Garden was not without formidable competition. At Her Majesty's Theatre, Gye's particular *bête noire*, Lumley by name, did rather more than survive. And a young agent, Mapleson, who furnished both companies with singers had also, on the side, been largely responsible for a season of 'Italian Opera for the People' at Drury Lane, in competition with them. Lumley was the first to give up and Mapleson stepped into his shoes. Then Gye had to call a truce with Mapleson, though not before he had snatched Adelina Patti from under his nose. Patti, aged eighteen, arriving in London in 1861 went first to Mapleson for an audition. He was so enchanted by what he heard that he resolved to finance a season for her himself, leased a theatre (the Lyceum) and hurried off to Paris to collect a company. Patti took advantage of his sudden disappearance to get an audition from Gye. Gye was equally enchanted and signed her on forthwith, although his company for the season was already complete and their names announced. Mapleson returned from Paris with some splendid singers under contract, and the Lyceum all ready to receive them. He lacked only Patti to crown his whole design, but she was by now ensconced just up the street at Covent Garden. She was to continue singing at Covent Garden every successive season until 1884 and thus give her name to an era. She sang in every other great opera house as well, but the peak of her career was when, in 1876, she became the first Covent Garden Aida. This rôle seemed to open up to her hitherto unsuspected resources in dramatic representation, assuring her of a place in history as one of the greatest prima donnas of all time. Something of the unique quality of her voice can still be gleaned from gramophone recordings. She was also an indefatigable concert performer and her rendering of 'Home, Sweet Home' brought tears to innumerable Victorian, Edwardian and even Georgian eyes – she sang it for the last time at a Red Cross concert in the Royal Albert Hall in 1914, when she was seventy-one. She had, with apparent absent-mindedness, interpolated it into

'A light duet'; Melba and Caruso in *Punch*, 1904.

Dudley Hardy.

the last act of *Linda di Chamonix* one evening nearly thirty years earlier, but as by that time her contracts invariably carried a clause that she should be excused rehearsals and another that on all posters her name should appear on a line by itself and in letters 'at least one third larger than those employed for the announcement of any other artiste', her public were presumably content to accept whatever came their way.

At this time there was both beautiful singing and splendid orchestral playing and chorus work under Michael Costa, 'the most exigent of maestri'. The repertory was extensive, and was being added to by the works of Verdi's middle period. Going to the opera was once more a popular as well as a fashionable pursuit. The Queen and the Prince Consort had helped to make it so, for they were genuine enthusiasts. Yet audiences were insensitive

and ill-behaved. People came in late and went out early; they gossiped and fidgeted and visited each other's boxes, quite oblivious of what was happening on the stage. The auditorium lights were still not even dimmed during performance and it was only after special instructions from the Queen that the whole proceedings were not halted and the national anthem played the moment she arrived, whenever it might be. London in the 1850s and 1860s was a great, growing, brash, self-confident place. It is difficult to speculate as to just what the aesthetic responses of the opera audience really were.

One of the final landmarks of the Gye regime was the first Covent Garden *Lohengrin*, in 1875. The amphitheatre and gallery liked it better than the stalls and boxes, and by the time the curtain fell (at a quarter to one) a substantial proportion of

the audience had gone home. But this was more Gye's fault than Wagner's, for it was a poor production. A final achievement that just eluded him was the introduction of electric lighting into the theatre. He had patented a system considerably in advance of his time, but he was accidentally killed while out shooting in 1878, before it could be tried.

There followed a period of relative eclipse. After the death of the Prince Consort in 1859 the Queen, although she continued to subscribe to the Royal Box, never set foot in it again. She commanded singers to Windsor instead. There were, moreover, other musical attactions in London: German opera was becoming popular despite the views of the older critics – the *Ring* cycle was performed for the first time in England at Her Majesty's Theatre in 1882 – and the Carl Rosa Company was showing unexpected competitive strength. In 1884 the Royal Italian Opera Company had to be wound up and Covent Garden closed. In 1885 Mapleson rented it for a short season, with Patti as the star. At the end of it she was presented with a diamond bracelet and conveyed, in a torchlight procession headed by the band of the Metropolitan Police, back to her hotel. In 1886 a Signor Lago, who over a period of years emerged from his chrysalis state as a prompter and became an impresario, raised enough money to mount a season which opened with Donizetti's *Lucrezia Borgia*. Patti did not participate this time: at £500 a performance her fee was judged too high. But the Prince and Princess of Wales, who had assumed the position of chief royal patrons in succession to Queen Victoria and the Prince Consort, were there. Indeed, they used the Royal Box to scotch a family scandal on the night of the Prince's return from India in 1876.

110 Flaxman's frieze was saved from the building of 1808 and incorporated in the façade of the new one, not altogether happily, perhaps because its graceful lateral flow is interrupted by the pillars which support the pediment.

The Prince of Wales (later King Edward VII) was notoriously unmusical,[8] but his wife (Queen Alexandra) despite a latent and increasing deafness, really enjoyed going to the opera. In 1905, she attended all the first three of Emmy Destinn's performances as Cio-Cio-San in *Madama Butterfly*.

Partly, if not almost wholly responsible for this new wave of royal interest was Lady de Grey, the *éminence grise* of Covent Garden during the decades preceding and following the turn of the century. Immensely tall, immensely handsome, with an expression of great sweetness masking her iron will, she was also impeccably aristocratic. There can be no question of Lady de Grey's dedication to opera, nor of the value of her influence at Covent Garden on both sides of the footlights. Her finest hour was the installation of Melba there. This was achieved, surprisingly enough, in the face of what many singers have discovered to be their most

potent foe: apathy. Downright hostility breeds partisanship, and partisanship excitement. Apathy breeds nothing. Melba had made a brilliant début at Brussels as Gilda, in *Rigoletto*, and followed it up with an equally brilliant *Lucia di Lammermoor*. She had wanted her first appearance in London to be as Gilda, but was told that Emma Albani, a beautiful soprano and Frederick Gye's daughter-in-law, had an exclusive claim on that rôle. *Lucia* was second-best, and what was still less good, she sang it in May 1888 to a half-empty house, after a single, inadequate rehearsal. Any aspiring young artist of a fibre less tough, a conviction less absolute of the uniqueness of her gift, would have settled for Brussels and the rest of the world and never come back. Even Melba might have done this had it not been for Lady de Grey's determination to bring her back.

By now Covent Garden was emerging from

the trough of depression which had followed Gye's retirement and death. Augustus Harris, a really great impresario, had taken over and collected a formidable host of singers, including the de Reszke brothers, Jean Lassalle, Zélie de Lussan, Lillian Nordica and Minnie Hauk. The 1888 season was a brilliant one from every point of view – except Melba's. But in 1889 she was back, and singing opposite Jean de Reszke in Gounod's *Roméo et Juliette* (in French). She conquered London in a night, and from then on, London was to be, for her, the capital of the world. Even a short, but glamorous liaison with the pretender to the French throne, the Duke of Orleans, who was eight years her junior, did not seriously upset the pattern. This, apart from her early, disastrous marriage, seems to have been her one brush with deep emotion. Perhaps her voice echoed her state of mind; it was pure and passionless, like a boy's unbroken voice, or an *oboe d'amore*, yet so ravishing in sound, so consummately produced, that it could excite deep emotion in others. That her best rôle of all was Mimi, in *La Bohème*, is easily understandable, despite her ample figure; so also is her rage when Caruso, the compulsive practical joker, once pressed a hot sausage into her tiny, frozen hand.

With Augustus Harris boosting morale backstage, Lady de Grey maintaining discipline in the auditorium and Bernard Shaw (as 'Corno di Bassetto') keeping the critics and everybody else on their toes, the prescription for success seemed complete. And so it was when in 1892 a German season (provided by the Hamburg Opera under their dynamic young conductor Gustav Mahler), increased the substantial repertory of French and Italian works already being sung in their own language. The Royal Italian Opera was at last The Royal Opera. In 1894 came the first performance of a Puccini opera in London, *Manon Lescaut*. It was not a great success: in London it never has been. More important was the first London production of Verdi's *Falstaff*. *The Times*, praising it, added a qualifying sentence: 'It remains to be seen whether the subscribers and the fashionable world in public will care for an opera which, since it contains no dull moments, allows no

opportunities for comfortable conversation during the music'.

Harris, unhappily, died in 1896, and to cope with this loss there was formed a Grand Opera Syndicate, whose members included, not unexpectedly, Lady de Grey, and also her husband and brother-in-law. They remained the ruling class until the outbreak of war in 1914. When Melba returned to Covent Garden in 1919, after the jumble of stored furniture had been moved out, she felt she was 'singing to ghosts'. And so she was. Lord and Lady Ripon (as the de Greys had become) were dead. Queen Alexandra, long since widowed and now stone deaf, had left the social field. The chasm of 1914–18 was spanned only by the person of Sir Thomas Beecham, first sighted as a comet in the operatic sky when he had launched an experimental Covent Garden season in the early spring of 1910, at the age of thirty.

It was possible to dislike Beecham as a man, and many people did. But it was impossible not to admire him as a musician, for he dedicated to the service of music a personality that has been described as a 'combination of supreme talent and willpower'. 'As those who fall in love,' he wrote of himself, 'profess to find their faculties stimulated in every direction and to discover a fresh colour and meaning in all they see and hear, even so had the revelation of the beauty and eloquence of great music a like effect on me.'

The most outstanding feature of that spring season in 1910 had been the first London production of Richard Strauss's *Elektra*. As scenic ultra-realism had then come into vogue, the audience was duly harrowed, both visually and acoustically. Edyth Walker sang the title rôle, and such was the impact of the work that four extra performances had to be given in addition to the five originally scheduled. A second season was planned for the autumn (the 'grand' summer season intervening) and for this Beecham's trump card was *Salome*. The public's appetite had been whetted by censorship troubles, which led to some ludicrous compromises. *Salome* had ten performances in three weeks, and the bookings were possibly stimulated by a headline used for one of the newspaper reviews: 'Beautiful Art Wasted on Vile Subject'.

These two operas had been so sensational that inevitably *Der Rosenkavalier* followed, only a short time after its triumphant launching in Dresden. Before this, Beecham and André Messager had conceived a plan for the former to conduct *Elektra* in Paris, but the occasion disproved the often heard assumption that Art knowns no frontiers. A Saxon chef was not wanted in the kitchens of the Paris Opéra, the French asserted, in one of their periodic bouts of chauvinism, and the project died.[9]

In 1915, Beecham had formed his own opera company, and he subsequently held the lease of Covent Garden for eight months from November 1919. A period of eclipse followed when he was in great financial difficulty. But he was never, as has sometimes been said, declared bankrupt. A receiving order was made against him, but a majority of his creditors opposed bankruptcy: it would have been killing a goose that might yet lay a golden egg. He did, in fact, at this time

111 Sir Thomas Beecham, Bt. was more than a conductor: he was an elemental force in shaping the interpretation of music for four decades of the twentieth century.

become controller of Covent Garden Market, and if that can be termed a wilderness he remained in it till 1932, when he was asked back to the Opera House to conduct a four weeks' season of Wagner.

The early 1920s had been, on the whole, a period of debility and slow convalescence for Covent Garden. But between 1925 and 1927 it recovered a good deal of its old *panache*. There were beautiful clothes and plenty of jewels to be seen in the first two tiers during the 'international' season every summer, and the queue for the gallery was immensely long. A new and capable managing director, Eustace Blois, was in charge and a new generation of singers – English, German, Austrian, Italian, American – had emerged, who commanded fantastic loyalty from the London opera-going public. Wagner had really come into his own and the *Ring* cycle and *Tristan* had many performances. Richard Strauss was now less popular, except for *Der Rosenkavalier*, in which Lotte Lehmann achieved her own individual immortality. Those *Rosenkavalier* performances still evoke a measure of hand-wringing nostalgia among the generation which was just then discovering opera for the first time and, indeed, Lehmann's interpretation of the rôle of the Marschallin was fabulously accomplished.

At the very close of the 1939 season, Beecham rounded on the audience and told them (as he had told them via the press a few days earlier) that they did not deserve opera, and that there never had been and never would be a public for the fine arts. The audience got its own back by tittering – a normal reaction in times of uncertainty. That was the end of another epoch. There was no more opera at Covent Garden until 1946.

The Second World War having ended, Covent Garden's fate was once more in the balance. But the scales fortunately came down on the side of culture rather than – who knows what? The age of private patronage was clearly over. Yet the State had at no time accepted opera as deserving financial support. Indeed, the British have always been suspicious about spending public money on the Arts and no British government has ever created a ministry specifically devoted to the defence and enhancement of cultural values. Pic-

112 (*Above*) The Covent Garden production of *Don Carlos* in 1958 was perhaps the most brilliant seen there since the Second World War. Luchino Visconti produced: He also designed the sets and costumes and directed the lighting. Carlo Maria Giulini was the conductor and the cast included Gré Brouwenstein, Fedora Barbieri, Jon Vickers, Tito Gobbi and Boris Christoff. It set the seal on Sir David Webster's success as General Administrator.

ture galleries and museums have been helped by the Treasury, with degrees of generosity varying from time to time; but until the end of the Second World War there had never been a broad national policy regarding the Arts as a whole. In the context of our present study one thing alone was historically clear: if the people wanted opera they had to pay for it themselves, which, as we have seen, they had contrived to do for a couple of hundred years. Now they could no longer afford to, but still they wanted it. The British rather fancy themselves as pragmatists, and by 1946 they had evolved a design which supported this approach – the Arts Council of Great Britain. This was an independent buffer body, charged with the task of wheedling money out of the Treasury and disbursing it, at discretion, among the whole range of cultural activities which, it was claimed, enriched the life of the nation but could never be self-supporting in a commercial sense. The Arts Council ensured that there would be no 'artistic dictation' by the State of the kind which has in many countries enforced a sterile academicism; also, that minority enterprises could be encouraged in a way that might mean political suicide if authorized directly by a minister responsible to Parliament. But a member of the Government was designated to do battle for the Arts.

By and large it has succeeded well, and in the case of Covent Garden particularly well. In the years since the war this great theatre has survived all hazards to become the home of a ballet company and an opera company that are not only nationally, but internationally famous. The British were highly gratified when, seventy-six years after *The Times* had wondered whether an opera which allowed no opportunities for comfortable conversation could ever really succeed, the Covent Garden Company, playing *Falstaff* in Italian, with a predominantly home-grown cast, earned thirty curtain calls in Berlin and as many again in Munich.

The ballet company (then known after its old theatre, 'Sadler's Wells') had only to expand to the measure and beauty of its new home. The opera company had to be started from scratch, and there were inevitably some falterings by the way. Its first asset was a good chorus, because there is a strong tradition of choral singing both in Wales and in the north of England. Soloists were harder to come by. Seven years can be a long time in an opera singer's life (the new company started in 1946), but there were still some links with the pre-war past. Eva Turner and Edith Coates were two of them. Both had sung in Beecham's 1939 season and Eva Turner was still a magnificent Turandot in 1948. In the 1947–8 season there were fourteen performances of *Peter Grimes*, with Joan Cross in the rôle of Ellen Orford, which Britten had written for her. She also produced the Company's first *Rosenkavalier*, and in 1953 had another fine rôle as Queen Elizabeth I in Britten's *Gloriana*, an opera which, on its first performance at the time of Queen Elizabeth II's coronation, was savaged by the press. The so-called 'age of the producer' was now dawning and it was necessary to experiment. Some of the experiments were far from happy, but the general administrator, David Webster (equivalent of the old managing director) kept his head, and went on keeping it for the whole twenty-five years of his tenure of office. In the last few of these his own diplomatic skills benefited from an invaluable alliance with the artistic awareness and demoniac driving force of Georg Solti as musical director. The fortunate conjunction of these two personalities has done much to raise the Royal Opera House to its present eminence, though the process was well under way before Solti's arrival. Successes were consolidated; failures recognized and quietly discarded; an opera school was started, and it now seems proved that the opportunity to sing breeds singers; works by five living British composers have been brought into the repertory; the seating capacity of the house has been increased and its amenities improved – at any rate as far as the audiences are concerned. The auditorium, the foyer and the crush bar look fresh and beautiful. The orchestral and backstage facilities remain deplorable. It is perhaps another aspect of British pragmatism that there always seems to be a working knowledge of just how much people will put up with. Artists, evidently, will put up with quite a lot.

113 (*Opposite*) *The Knot Garden* is Sir Michael Tippett's most recent opera (1970) and his most controversial. The composer also wrote the libretto. It was brilliantly produced by Peter Hall and conducted by Colin Davis.

Glyndebourne

Eccentrics are born, but they are also made – self-made. Eccentrics who discover their potential young, tend to devote years to enhancing it, which may lead them into novel activities. None but a genuine eccentric like John Christie would have conceived the idea of building a small opera house in a fold of the Sussex downs, attached to his home; and then, after doing so, running it with undeniable success for a number of years, ably assisted by his beautiful and gifted wife (herself a singer, Audrey Mildmay), some of the most distinguished musical personalities of our time, and a succession of pug dogs. It would have seemed natural enough to Prince Nicholas Esterházy, who had done much the same thing himself on a more lavish scale; but Hungary in the eighteenth century was one thing and Sussex in 1934 quite another. Christie was surprised at doubts as to whether his expected patrons might not respond happily to the idea of leaving London in full evening dress at 3 o'clock in the afternoon, and travelling fifty miles by train or car. The expected patrons were themselves in turn even more surprised when they found themselves doing just that.[10]

Dedicated eccentrics are sometimes also endowed with a streak of genius, or, to put it at its lowest, of 'flair' – which is in itself no mean attribute. In John Christie's case, this quality, whatever it was, became manifest in the speed with which he adjusted his aspirations, always disciplined by good musical taste and aesthetic sensibility, to the size and true possibilities of his theatre, and in his persuading Fritz Busch, musical director at Dresden, to come and be musical director at Glyndebourne. Of course, in 1934, the flocks and herds which grazed round the Glyndebourne opera house must have looked distinctly less menacing to a serious artist than the Nazis who raged round Dresden. Busch had in fact left Germany in 1933, and in the (northern hemisphere) summer of that year, had conducted a season of German opera at El Colón: Glyndebourne was not the only opera house open to him in the free world. But Christie persuaded him that it was the best, and he in turn persuaded Carl Ebert to join him as producer. Originally an actor by profession, Ebert's interest had gravitated towards opera. In 1931 he had been appointed general administrator of the Charlottenburg (Städtische) Oper, Berlin, and had worked harmoniously with Busch when the latter came to Charlottenburg as a guest conductor. He thought the whole Glyndebourne project crazy and said so. But he came, and the partnership was to prove one of the most creative of our time. Christie backed his team with enthusiasm. Even when the second season showed a £10,000 deficit he did not wince. He did much better; he engaged Rudolf Bing as general manager. Next year the deficit was down to £4,000.

Busch was a perfectionist. He demanded, and got, twenty-four three-hour orchestral rehearsals for his opening opera, *Le Nozze di Figaro* (it was a

14 A seeming anachronism enfolded in the Sussex Downs: the opera house which has been grafted on to the ancient manor house at Glyndebourne.

rule that all operas should be sung in the original language of the libretto). In that first season, *Figaro* and *Così fan tutte* were given six times each, at the end of May and in early June. They were beautifully cast and meticulously prepared, and as an added inducement to attend, prospective patrons were graciously informed that not only was there a good restaurant and an admirable wine cellar, but that they 'may consume their own refreshments in the Dining Hall, and in this case may, if they wish, be waited on by their own servants.'

Even if the number who took advantage of this amenity was limited, people came. And they came again, in 1935, when *Die Entführung aus dem Serail* joined the repertory, and again and again in the following four years, when *Die Zauberflöte*, *Don Giovanni*, *Macbeth* and *Don Pasquale* were also brought in. The sets for *Macbeth* were designed by Caspar Neher, and were brilliantly conceived. In 1939 there were thirty-eight performances, and distinguished musical visitors converged from all over the world to behold this new wonder that had arisen in an allegedly unmusical nation. On a particular occasion two of them elected, rather unfortunately, to converge on the same evening – Toscanini and Furtwängler. They had quarrelled bitterly over Bayreuth. Toscanini had left no one in doubt about his opinions of Hitler, Frau Winifred Wagner and Nazi Germany generally. Furtwängler had left everybody in doubt about everything except the obsessive intensity of his love for music. But Christie had taken more explosive situations than this in his stride, and the 640 acres of Glyndebourne proved broad enough to accommodate both maestri.

It seemed in this arcadian summer of 1939 as if warm days would never cease. Yet cease they did, and Christie's next miracle was to ensure that they did not cease for ever. After vicissitudes, initiatives, ruses and expedients which reveal him as a kind of latter-day Odysseus, and which are another story in themselves, Glyndebourne, under its own steam, started up again *at* Glyndebourne in 1947. Rudolf Bing was soon lost to the New York Met., but Ebert resumed as artistic director. Then, in 1951, Busch died. He was replaced as chief conductor, and in no way unworthily, by Vittorio Gui. But he was in truth irreplaceable. His association with Ebert had been a rare planetary conjunction in the operatic firmament, and those who witnessed or participated in those pre-war years have always surreptitiously felt they should be entitled to sport a commemorative star or ribbon along with their other orders and decorations.

England was now enduring the rigours of austerity, and Christie's original objective: 'good opera at high prices rather than bad opera at low prices', had lost something of its pioneer freshness, especially as it was still being given in Sussex, well out of range of the nascent Covent Garden audience. Yet Glyndebourne was notably endowed with friends who were neither poor nor stupid. The stage was enlarged, the seating capacity of the house increased. Within quite a short time a Festival Society and an Arts Trust had both been set up, and between them they have enabled the summer season to continue year in, year out, for what is, at the moment of writing, a span of nearly twenty years. It was easy to widen the repertory to take in Rossini and more Donizetti; less easy, and certainly less obvious, to produce such a novelty as Stravinsky's *The Rake's Progress* – yet the production (first seen when the company gave it at the Edinburgh Festival) was brilliantly successful. Again it was less easy, and in this case less acceptable, to give the world première, in its original language, of Henze's *Elegy for Young Lovers*. The story is told that one day during rehearsal John Christie came and slumped down in a stall next to a tow-haired, weather-beaten looking man. When there was an interval he asked him what he did.

'I wrote the libretto', answered W. H. Auden.

'Oh,' said Christie, 'you shouldn't have done that.' And silence between them was resumed.

This was in 1961. A happier occasion for the founder had been in 1959 when, after many doubts and questionings, it was decided to stage *Der Rosenkavalier*. It seemed much too big a work for such a house, even with a slightly reduced (but by no means mutilated) orchestra. As producer, Carl Ebert made the most, with his extraordinarily subtle theatrical sense, of the intimacies

115 Carl Ebert's 1958 production of *The Rake's Progress* was one of Glyndebourne's greatest achievements up to the present. Paul Sacher came from Basle to conduct; Osbert Lancaster designed the sets, and in Act II, Scene 2, Hugues Cuénod gave a sparkling performance as the auctioneer.

of the piece. The presentation of the rose scene did not lack splendour, but it also had a quality of innocence and pathos that sometimes goes for nothing in a larger house. Oliver Messel's sets were elegant. Leopold Ludwig exercised a finely calculated control over his orchestra. Elizabeth Söderström was a captivating Octavian and Régine Crespin's Feldmarschallin realized all the sadness in this saddest of rôles.

If one comes to think of it, Glyndebourne has perhaps changed less than most places under the impact of the past three decades. Patrons are no longer waited upon by their own servants as they consume their own refreshments in the dining room. They tend rather to share their sandwiches with their dogs, who have come too, and stayed in the car, because there are no servants to care for them. Picnics are still eaten in the grounds and the eaters are still themselves a meal for midges. In the case of men, 'black tie' is condoned, though as the phrase itself now covers so wide a range of style and colour as to be meaningless, the results are sometimes rather picturesque. One evening a member of the audience failed at the beginning of the supper interval to retrieve from the lakeside irises a bottle of champagne he had laid down before the performance, and went to the bottom after it. He surfaced like Ondine, and as his girl friend's handkerchief was too small to help, he was advised to go and consult 'wardrobe'. This he did, and ten minutes later was once more looking quite indistinguishable from any other member of the audience.

Glyndebourne is no longer wholly arcadian. Or perhaps to the young it is? Who knows? But it is certainly not Disneyland. How long will it go on? Who knows? There seems no reason why it should not continue indefinitely. Even if standards are slipping, they are slipping no faster than Venice or the leaning tower of Pisa. And if, in some productions, they have fallen below the high excellence John Christie and Audrey Mildmay demanded, the reason is that artists, even young artists, are no longer available for the extended period of rehearsal which was part of the original concept.

It cannot be said that Glyndebourne has initiated a new style of production or performance. One or two points stand out clearly, however. The Busch-Ebert epoch achieved a quality, a degree of integration, rare at any time or in any place. But the lesson they taught has never been quite forgotten. Within the framework of its physical limitations the Glyndebourne repertory has maintained a spirit of eclecticism rare in any opera house. It has been brilliantly served by two English designers of high distinction – Oliver Messel and Osbert Lancaster. And most recently, with the introduction of Cavalli's *L'Ormindo* and *La Callisto*, both arranged by Raymond Leppard, whose arrangement of Monteverdi's *L'Incoronazione di Poppea* was immensely successful in 1963, it has brought new life to the whole field of seventeenth-century Italian opera.

The Maltings Snape

The Aldeburgh festival was started in 1947. That news of its birth should have been greeted with incredulity is understandable. No more unlikely venue for a music festival could be imagined. Aldeburgh was just a small fishing town on the Suffolk coast, to the perimeter of which admirals, generals and civil servants were liable to retire when their careers ended. There was a shingle beach, bracing air, good safe sailing in the estuary of the River Alde, an agreeable golf course – and virtually no facilities whatever for the performance of music. Opera could be given only in 'The Jubilee Hall', a small, ill-ventilated edifice within sound of the sea, seating about three hundred people. Despite these apparent disabilities, within twenty years the Aldeburgh festival had become a magnet for some of the greatest musicians in the world, and for audiences far larger than could be accommodated. The question had long been debated as to where and how a concert hall-cum-opera house might be built, big enough to seat seven or eight hundred people and with a stage on which opera could be properly presented. The answer was provided when the Malt House at Snape, a tiny hamlet in the neighbourhood, became available. This is part of a large complex of buildings erected in the middle of the nineteenth century for the storage and conversion of grain at the point where the River Alde, before winding through five miles or so of marshland to its mouth in the North Sea, becomes navigable to barges and small boats. The place has an aura of stillness and beauty that is rare. It must be the most 'remote' opera house in the world.

The Association of Architects and Engineers (Ove Arup, Derek Sugden and their colleagues) who undertook the transformation, were quite clear about what they wanted to do. 'We thought it very important', Mr Sugden has written, 'that this building should be designed either as a concert hall or as an opera house. Many post-war auditoria have failed because they have tried to fulfil too many functions and have not succeeded in fulfilling any one properly. It was agreed that The Maltings should be a concert hall, and, although opera lighting was to be provided, it was felt that the single auditorium space would create its own type of opera production. As the design developed this became clearer, and the introduction of any temporary proscenium within the auditorium would have been quite wrong.'

It would indeed. The homogeneity of the interior, emphasized by the plainness of its brick walls, the lightness and purely functional construction of the roof are startling. Here is something quite new, yet mellow with inherited tradition. It is a step into the future.

The task was accomplished in just over a year and The Maltings was opened by Queen Elizabeth II on 2 June 1967. Its acoustics proved to be incomparably good. During that festival the English Opera Group gave three performances of Britten's *A Midsummer Night's Dream*, in a new production by Colin Graham, with costumes and

116 *The Building of the House*. This is the title of the choral overture which Britten composed for the opening of the Maltings. 'It was certainly inspired', he said, 'by the excitement of the planning and building'.

117 The Maltings, Snape, where marshes and the gentle Suffolk countryside begins, and great music is heard with increasing frequency. Benjamin Britten once lived in a converted windmill nearby.

scenery designed by Emanuele Luzzati, Rudolf Schwarz conducting. There was also a concert performance of Purcell's *The Fairy Queen*, in a version devised by Peter Pears and edited by Benjamin Britten and Imogen Holst.

In 1968 the Sadler's Wells Opera Company brought their production of Britten's *Gloriana* to The Maltings during the Aldeburgh festival. There was also a concert production of Handel's *Hercules*. This second season confirmed what the

first season had seemed to prove – that even without a proscenium arch The Maltings was no less viable for operatic performances than for concerts and recitals. *Gloriana* looked and sounded splendid.

Thereafter disaster struck. Late on the opening night of the 1969 festival (there had been a concert in the afternoon) fire broke out, and by morning only the blackened walls were left standing. The planned production of *Idomeneo*

had to be transferred to a gothic church fifteen miles away, where it was given under seemingly impossible conditions. But even before a month was out, plans were being laid for the rebuilding of The Maltings, and exactly twelve months later it had been completed. *Idomeneo* was seen there, also *The Rape of Lucretia*. And in September 1970, quite outside the context of the festival, a short season of opera was given which attracted audiences from far and wide, filling the house almost to capacity: no mean achievement, considering its remoteness. And it was no mean achievement that the rebuilding should have been made possible in large measure by public support, though the Arts Council of Great Britain and the big charitable foundations were also very generous.

It may be mentioned that the population of Aldeburgh does not consist exclusively of fishermen and retired admirals and civil servants. Benjamin Britten and Peter Pears live there too.

SWEDEN

The Theatre Drottningholm

Few monarchs are passionately interested in opera and the theatre. Few are assassinated. Even fewer can have met their death in an opera house. Gustavus III of Sweden is the exception. Not only did he preside over the destinies of the beautiful little theatre at Drottningholm, a royal palace in a splendid park just eight miles from Stockholm, in its late eighteenth century heyday, but he was assassinated at a masked ball given at the Stockholm opera house. What is more, his tragic fate has served as the subject of two operas, one by Auber and one by Verdi. The Verdi *Un Ballo in Maschera* is the better known. Scribe wrote Auber's libretto (the work was first performed in 1833); Somma adapted it for Verdi. But in the mid-nineteenth century, the death of kings was a subject slightly too near the knuckle for comfort. An attempt had just been made on the life of Napoleon III, and the cause of Victor Emmanuel as prospective king of a united Italy was running high. Verdi's opera was composed for the San Carlo in Naples, for the carnival of 1858, but with Bourbon destinies at an uncomfortably low ebb in the capital city of the Two Sicilies (Garibaldi's invasion of the island was only a couple of years away) the theme of regicide struck the censors as unfortunate. A compromise was arrived at by shifting the whole plot to Boston and making Gustavus III a British governor, the Count of Warwick. Even so, it was Rome, not Naples, that saw the first performance, the following year: no one would dream of assassinating the Pope.

The first Drottningholm theatre was built in 1744 as a betrothal present to Princess Louisa Ulrica, a sister of Frederick the Great, by her bridegroom, the Crown Prince of Sweden, who succeeded to the throne as Adolf Fredrik in 1751. The new queen shared many of her brother's characteristics, including a strong predilection for the arts. She also had a taste for learning and founded the Swedish Academy of Science, one of the original members of which was the famous naturalist Linnaeus. Like her brother, too, she was under the spell of French culture. The court of Versailles seems to have impressed the Brandenburgers as being in every way admirable. It was natural, therefore, that the first use of the theatre should have been for contemporary French plays. But 'the Italian Opera' was then also in vogue throughout Europe and it was not long before an Italian troupe, under its director Francesco Uttini, was established at Drottningholm. He was himself a composer, who set to music Metastasio's libretti, *La Galatea*, *L'Isola disabitata*, *Il Re pastore*, *L'Eroe cinese*, *L'Adriana*. These were performed every summer between 1754 and 1757, on the namedays and birthdays of the King and Queen.

In deference, one might almost say, to usual opera house practice, there was soon a fire. It occurred during the course of a performance and was announced by a member of the audience who rushed on to the stage and was for a moment thought to be a member of the cast giving a new dramatic twist to the action. Everybody escaped

118 The park at Drottningholm is a perfect setting for such an architectural gem as the little Theatre.

199

119 (*Above*) The assassination of Gustav III, engraved by J. E. Rehn.

120 (*Below*) Curtain for Gluck's *Orfeo ed Eurydice* by A. W. Küfner.

with their lives, however, and the court circular was able to record next day that there had been 'no mishap except that the theatre was destroyed'.

Again in deference to the usual practice, its rebuilding was immediately determined upon. The architect commissioned was Carl Fredrik Adelcrantz and apart from the foyer, which was added in 1791, it is his conception, an architectural gem of the highest quality, that one sees realized today. The first royal visit to the new building took place in the summer of 1765, and for the next eleven years French classical drama dominated the repertory. In 1771 Adolf Fredrik was succeeded by his son Gustavus III, who six years later took over the theatre from his mother. For the first time a director of opera, Gustav Johann Ehrenswärd, was appointed. He held the post until 1776 and was succeeded by Adolf Fredrik Barneker (1776–80), Karl Reinhold Fasser (1780–86) and Anton Moritz Arnefelt (1786–92). Grétry's *Zémire et Azor*, Monsigny's *Arsène* and Piccinni's *Roland* were all staged in the course of these few years. A company of 150 artists and technicians was built up. Detailed records still exist which even state just what quantities of wine its various members were entitled to. With the King's assassination – he died in March 1792, a fortnight after the fatal masked ball – all this activity ground to a halt, and the theatre is only known to have been used for a few dramatic performances in 1854, and again in 1858, for a performance by a troupe of French Zouaves, touring Europe after the Crimean War, whose presence in Sweden chanced to coincide with the birth of a new Crown Prince, later to become the tennis-playing Gustaf V.

Apart from these brief flickers a sleep descended on the little court theatre as profound, as unstirring as that imposed by the wicked fairy Carabosse on Princess Aurora and her castle. And its rediscovery, in 1921, was just as romantic as the awakening of the Sleeping Beauty. For it had not been destroyed or adapted to other purposes. It had been quite literally forgotten about except as a royal lumber room, a place for putting the kind of things which, once out of sight, were quickly out of mind. The eerie experience of

121 The auditorium at Drottningholm seen from the stage. The objects in
the foreground are eighteenth-century billows which, when the appropriate handles
are turned in the wings, roll menacingly and convincingly.

bringing it all to light fell to Agne Beijer, an assistant in the royal library, who went there with a couple of officials from the National Gallery to look for a painting which was known to be in store somewhere or other. They found their painting, under three feet of dust. They also found thirty complete sets of scenery and all the stage machinery designed by Donato Stopani in 1766, quite intact and wanting nothing but new ropes to make it operable: The theatre was reopened in August 1922 and has been in continuing summer use ever since, with regular opera performances from 1946 onwards. To be invited to play there

is one of the greatest joys that can befall a foreign company, and to be a member of the audience is no lesser joy, for even though the seats are rather uncomfortable, one has not the illusion, but the very assurance, of recapturing the charm, the beauty, the elegance of an eighteenth-century private theatre belonging to an urbane and sophisticated court.

But that, of course, is not the whole truth. The eighteenth century was in fact no more idyllic than any other century. Behind the rococo façade, for all its measured proportions, political passions ran strongly and in conflicting tides. Sweden had

122 The original machinery in the fly loft at Drottningholm.

long since ceased to be a great power in her own right, but she was still a factor in the politics of the Great Powers, and both France and Russia desired her as ally against each other. Adolf Fredrik was a cypher in his kingdom, which was governed in a more or less democratic way by a parliament consisting of two parties, nicknamed the 'Hats' and the 'Caps'. When Queen Louisa Ulrica tried to stage a monarchical revolution it nearly cost the King his throne. Gustavus III, however, was a much more positive person. He was on friendly terms with Louis XV and it was, indeed, from Paris that he was summoned to assume the throne, and when his attempts to mediate between the parties failed and the country was in imminent danger of becoming absorbed into Russia's 'northern system', he in turn had recourse to a monarchical revolution – and succeeded (it was to commemorate the 150th anniversary of this event that 19 August 1922 was chosen for the reopening of the Drottningholm Theatre). A hostile aristocracy opposed his policy and mocked his passion for the arts. But he was popular and daring, and his assassination at the masked ball was the measure of his opponents' quality and – alas – their power.

123 An example of eighteenth-century stage techniques: a ship riding the waves.

The Royal Opera Stockholm

Gustavus III's musical ambitions far exceeded the confines of the Drottningholm Theatre. He was responsible for the founding of the Royal Opera in Stockholm, which was inaugurated in 1773 with Uttini's *Thétis och Pelée*, for which the King himself had drafted the libretto and which was given thirty-seven successful performances between 1773 and 1776. In the same year Gluck's *Orfeo ed Euridice* (first produced Vienna, 1762) was also given, in advance of its Paris première. The music of Gluck appealed both to the King – especially after he had tasted the serene beauties of the Italian landscape – and to his people. The old Bollhus, a former tennis court, which had been used for these early performances, was superseded in 1782 by a real opera house, designed by Carl Fredrik Adelcrantz and held to be, at the time, one of the most beautiful in Europe. It was to serve for just a century before being replaced by the present building.

Despite the gathering dust at Drottningholm, operatic activity was continuous in the capital throughout the nineteenth century, though Gustavus IV conceived an understandable aversion to the new house, as the scene of his father's murder, and would even have liked to pull it down. Indeed, when war against Finland broke out in 1808, it was immediately requisitioned as a military hospital (it cannot have been a very comfortable one), but the King was deposed a year later and his successor, Charles XIII, restored it to its proper function. This it continued to serve until 1891, when it was replaced by the present building on the same site. The first house had opened with a highly spectacular work, *Cora och Alonzo* (music by Johann Gottlieb Naumann, libretto by G. G. Adlerbeth, from a novel, *Les Incas*, by Marmontel). It included an earthquake scene, with 'crashing temples and mountains belching fire', but it was not memorable musically. More important was another work by the same composer, with a libretto which King Gustavus III had helped write, *Gustaf Vasa*. This was first produced in 1786 and remained in the repertory for years. The music was reminiscent of Gluck, the scenery, by a very fine designer, Jean-Louis Desprez, was again striking, in the manner of Géricault or Delacroix. Madame de Staël saw it in the course of her travels and pronounced favourably. The French influence was to predominate at the Stockholm Opera throughout the greater part of the nineteenth century, but German works and German production ideas began to infiltrate before the end. Carl Fredrik Lundqvist recalls in his memoirs the deep, silent emotion with which *Lohengrin* was greeted in 1874. All the same, the Swedes went on preferring Meyerbeer to Wagner for quite a while longer. The *Ring* cycle was not heard until 1907, *Tristan und Isolde* 1909 and *Parsifal* 1917. In that first *Lohengrin*, Lundqvist sang the herald. Later he was to be highly praised for his Telramund. He must, from all accounts, have been an outstanding artist. Sir Thomas Beecham, as a boy, was tremendously impressed by him, though he only saw him once (and, indeed, accompanied him on the piano during a transatlantic crossing), when owing to a glandular defect he had become a great mountain of a man, far too fat for opera. Another notable Swedish singer, of an earlier generation, was Christoffer Karsten, a tenor-baritone with a voice of 'unusual range and great beauty'. He had a long career. He made his début in 1776 and sang his last operatic rôle in 1821. And he gave a recital even four years after that.

It is through singers that Sweden has made her greatest contribution to opera. The nineteenth century was a golden age. So, for that matter, is the twentieth. Think of some of them: in addition to Karsten and Lundqvist there were Elisabeth Frösslind, Henriette Widerberg, Jenny Lind, Louise Michaeli, Matilda Geelhar (a remarkable coloratura), Fritz Arlberg, Arvid Ödmann, Christine Nilsson; and in our own time, to name only some, Mathilda Jungstedt, Jussi Björling, Birgit Nilsson, Kerstin Thorborg, Set Svanholm, Nicolai Gedda, Kerstin Meyer, Elisabeth Söderström . . . But lists, as lists, are boring, and this one could be extended almost indefinitely.

Jenny Lind made her début at the Royal Opera, Stockholm (she was a native of the city, born in 1820) as Agathe, in *Der Freischütz*, at the age of seventeen. Three years later she went to Paris and studied under Manuel Garcia. She was in Stockholm again for the coronation of Oscar I in 1844. The King was musical (as Crown Prince he had actually directed opera, tried his hand as a librettist and he also composed). His coronation was celebrated with three gala performances – Gluck's *Armide*, and Bellini's *La Sonnambula* and *Norma*. For Jenny Lind there followed now a dazzling European career (although she declined to sing in France or Italy – the former she judged too wicked and the latter too popish), until she abandoned the stage in 1849. Hers must have been one of the purest soprano voices of all time, but stage appearances subjected it to some strain, and she was really happier on the concert platform.

Although generations of Stockholmers justified the vision and enthusiasm of its founder and attended the opera regularly throughout the long winter season, it suffered, like all such institutions, a number of financial vicissitudes, each one of

124 The very first home of opera in Stockholm – a converted tennis court adjacent to the royal palace.

which looked terrifying when it cropped up, and each one of which was duly resolved. The most intractable of all occurred towards the end of the nineteenth century and continued ferociously even while the old building was being pulled down and the new one erected. Indeed, so intent were the protagonists, so bitter the parliamentary debates, so violent the press, that the actual architectural upheaval seems to have taken quite a subsidiary place.

The opera had always been in receipt of a State subsidy, which more or less coped with those recurring crises. But in 1888 things were looking particularly black and the Riksdag, by a narrow majority of seventeen votes, decided to withhold the subsidy altogether, including, for good measure, the subsidy to the Dramatic Theatre as well. Arguments which are nowhere more familiar than in Great Britain, were adduced: why should the taxpayer be called upon to support a minority interest? Were there not more urgent priorities for the employment of State resources? How important was culture anyway? If a few

people wanted to hear Meyerbeer, or Mozart or Wagner, was it not fair that they should pay for the enjoyment of their esoteric tastes themselves?

A kind of interim answer was found by Conrad Nordqvist, chief conductor, who undertook to manage the Opera as a private enterprise. Then the personnel of the company and of the opera house were brought in to share the revenue – as was the practice in Paris. But none of this proved really workable and Nordqvist resigned within a couple of years. Axel Burén was appointed to succeed him as director, and during that period the State subvention was restored. The present building was completed in 1898, and after seven years in the wilderness (the 'wilderness' being the Swedish Theatre, which actually served its purpose quite well), the company moved into its new house with an appropriate gala performance. The wilderness years had not been entirely barren. In the course of them *La Gioconda* (1892), *The Bartered Bride* (1894), *Hänsel und Gretel* (1895), *Manon* (1896) and *Falstaff* (1896) were all brought into the repertory. *Carmen* had been introduced

125 and 126 These are two of a series of watercolour sketches of Jenny Lind done by Princess Eugénie, only daughter of the Swedish King Oscar I; one shows Donizetti's *La Fille du Régiment* the other his *Lucia di Lammermoor.*

in 1878, *Aida* in 1880 and *Otello* came in 1890.

After the First World War Armas Järnefelt, as chief conductor, brought together a fresh, fine ensemble of singers. He himself was a remarkable personality – a magnet in the cultural life of Stockholm. But, as always in Swedish operatic history, many of the stars were attracted abroad, and a proportion stayed there. Järnefelt worked well with the producer Harald André, and between them they introduced a new spirit of eclecticism. It was no longer a matter of French or Swedish 'dominance'. The Stockholm Opera was open to new ideas, from wherever they might stem. Scenery and production again came into their own – though not with volcanic eruptions or desperate shipwrecks as their *tours de force*. The bold use of colour, lighting and semi-abstract design gave the Royal Stockholm Opera a lead over the rest of the world that the rest of the world was curiously slow to follow. Nothing is more revealing of the internationalism, the ferment of original ideas that prevailed in Sweden in the 1920s, than a visit to the Stockholm Museum

of Modern Art. Incidentally, the first Stockholm production of *Un Ballo in Maschera* was in 1927. Despite the lapse of time, there must have been some eerie overtones to that particular première.

Yet, it must be admitted, Swedish operas have proved distinctively less exportable than Swedish opera singers. The old Gustavian works have passed, understandably, out of the repertory. *Värmlänningarna*, which has had more than a thousand performances in Stockholm since 1846 and is still given every Christmas, is not even listed in Löewenberg's *Annals of Opera*; nor is *Lycksalighetens ö*; nor Lars Erik Larsson's *Prinsessan av Cypern*. Even the staying power of Karl-Birger Blomdahl's *Aniara*, which was acclaimed tumultuously in 1959 and had fifty sold-out performances during the course of a single year, seems doubtful.[11] But it is, in fact, hardly surprising that there are not more. Out of all the vast number of operas that are composed, how few survive even in their own country, how thin a trickle find their way across national frontiers! In the case of Sweden, the thing to marvel at is that broad

127 (*Above*) Karl-Birger
Blomdahl's *Aniara*, the 'space-
ship' opera, proved a great
sensation in the 1958–9 season.
The company subsequently
brought it to the Edinburgh
Festival. 128 (*Right*) Armas
Järnefelt was an artist at living –
sportsman, connoisseur,
composer, conductor. He brought
new life to Stockholm opera in
the years following World War
One. He was a brother-in-law of
Sibelius.

stream of golden voices which for a century and a half has enriched the whole world.

The present Stockholm opera house does not dominate the capital to the same extent as other great houses do – Paris, for instance, or Vienna. There are only two really dominating older buildings in Stockholm: the enormous square royal palace, a splendid example of Italian Renaissance design, which was the work of the younger Nicodemus Tessin, and the town hall, begun only thirteen years after the opera house was completed, in an idiom that at the time was considered 'advanced' and that can only be broadly described as 'Scandinavian'. The name of Ragner Östberg, who conceived it, is better remembered than that of Anderberg, who designed the opera house, or of Jungstedt, who did the paintings which flank its main staircase, or of Andrén, who did the ceiling paintings of the auditorium, or of Carl Larsson, who painted the medallions and most of the frescoes in the foyer. The opera house is a handsome, well proportioned, dignified building, but not a breathtaking one. And it occupies a splendid site, the façade looking on to the Gustavus Adolphus Square, in the fashionable heart of the city. It is, indeed, part of the city's heart, whether seen through dappled summer trees or the strange half light of winter, silenced by snow.

Because I knew him a little and admired him, I cannot end this note without paying tribute to Set Svanholm. Born in 1904, he started teaching at the Stockholm Conservatory in 1929, and made his stage début, in *I Pagliacci*, shortly afterwards. In 1936 he changed from baritone to tenor rôles and his Siegfried was one of the best there have ever been. In the 1940s and early 1950s he was world famous and only retired to become general administrator of the Stockholm Opera, a post for which his knowledge of opera and his organizing abilities made him doubly well equipped. He died, all too young, in 1964.

129 Set Svanholm played all the great Wagnerian tenor roles – Lohengrin, Walther von Stolzing, Siegfried – before he gave up his singing career to become General Administrator of the Stockholm Royal Opera.

UNION OF SOVIET
SOCIALIST REPUBLICS

The Bolshoi Theatre Moscow
The Kirov Theatre Leningrad

To reach the auditorium I had to pass through the stage entrance . . . past immense machines for changing the scenery . . . in the gloom and dust I saw workmen busily engaged . . . amid various poles and rings and scattered scenery, decorations and curtains, stood and moved dozens, if not hundreds, of painted and dressed-up men, in costumes fitting tight to their thighs and calves, also women, as usual, as nearly naked as might be. . . . On the stage a procession of Indians who had brought home a bride was being represented. . . . They all came from one place and walked round and round again . . . first the Indians with halberds came on too late; then at the right time, but crowded together at the exit. . . . The procession was introduced by a recitative, by a man dressed up like some variety of Turk, who, opening his mouth in a curious way, sang, 'Home I bring the bri-i-i-de'. . . . that no one on earth can be moved by such performances . . . all this is beyond the possibility of doubt. . . . It would be difficult to find a more repulsive sight. . . . Whom *can* it please. . . ?

The writer is Tolstoy, but I have been unable to determine which opera was being rehearsed when some unsuspecting 'Intendant' admitted him, flattered, no doubt, by the great man's curiosity. Certainly, in the second half of the nineteenth

century there was a vogue for elaborate stage productions, with striking scenic effects and the excuse to bring on lots of animals. But Tolstoy was quite wrong in his conclusions. Ever since the eighteenth century, Russians of all social strata and of every epoch have taken a deep delight in opera; they possess, in Leningrad and Moscow, two of the finest opera houses in the world, and these have been subject to perhaps a greater degree of care by the State, both before and since the revolution, than similar institutions anywhere else. The obverse of this medal is a degree of control which may inhibit free artistic development; but one of the endemic characteristics of opera throughout the world and throughout its history has been a running fight with censorship in some form or other. The fact remains that today's visitor to either of these beautiful theatres, whether he goes to see ballet or opera, experiences a sense of enveloping warmth within their doors that derives as much from the responsiveness of the audience as from the architectural dignity of the staircases, foyers and auditoria. In the case of the Kirov, the emphasis is rather on grace and elegance; in that of the Bolshoi on massive proportions and rich gilding. The great size of the Bolshoi, like that of St Peter's, Rome, only impinges gradually on one's awareness. It explains why a standard production of some work from the Western repertory, such as for instance *Rigoletto*,

212

130 Act III, Scene 2 from the 1931 production of Tchaikovsky's *The Queen of Spades* at the Bolshoi. The designer was V. V. Dimitriev.

131 The Kirov Theatre, Leningrad, formerly the Maryinsky.

headed the Leningrad Communist Party in the 1920s. During the appalling wartime siege of Leningrad it suffered considerably, but has now been brilliantly restored and the backstage facilities enlarged and improved.

The tradition of opera in St Petersburg goes back more than a century from 1860. In 1734 the Empress Anna, seven years before her death, had imported an Italian operatic troupe under the leadership of one Francesco Araja, whose *La forza dell'amore e dell'odio* was the first opera ever to be heard on Russian soil. If Peter the Great is rightly held to be the creator of modern Russia, it was that extraordinary woman, Catherine II (next but one in succession to Anna) who set the seal of westernization on St Petersburg; opera was one of the elegant refinements that the aristocracy came to relish. The very first 'native' Russian opera, *Aniuta*, by Evstigney Ipatovich Fomin, was written during her reign, and another work *Amerikansti*, one of his last, shortly after her death: the title suggests future preoccupations casting very long shadows! Neither of these however, is to be confused with the 'nationalist' school, which came to birth in 1836, with Glinka's *A Life for the Tsar*. The première took place in a newly rebuilt St Petersburg theatre, the Bolshoi, which stood close to the site of the present Kirov, and it was a great social affair. The

may look rather thinly spread out over the width and depth of the stage (with *Aida* it is a different matter – there the possibilities of the stage can be exploited to the full, without it ever appearing cluttered). It also explains why, when the Bolshoi Ballet first visited Covent Garden, every leap carried them well into the wings until they had, so to speak, had time to adjust their sights.

In writing of Russia it seems arbitrary and partial to deal with opera houses in the context of opera only, rather than of opera and ballet combined, because for very many years Russian ballet had a unique position in the world, and as an 'export-culture' made a far greater impact on the West than did Russian opera. There have been many outstanding Russian dancers and choreographers whose genius has contributed notably to that aura which, however impalpable, is unmistakably apparent to even the most casual observer of the Kirov or the Bolshoi.

The Kirov Theatre as we know it today opened its doors on 2 October 1860. Until 1919 it was called the Maryinsky (or Imperial Theatre). Then it was renamed the State Academical Theatre of Opera and Ballet, which rather cumbersome title it retained until 1935, when it was given its present name in tribute to Sergei Kirov, who had

administration of the Imperial Theatres had been opposed to its production at all, and even when this opposition was withdrawn, Glinka was made to disclaim, in advance, the payment of any fee. Trouble with the censor was feared, but Glinka received strong backing from Prince Youssupov, and Tsar Nicholas I consented to attend a rehearsal. This was the very accolade of censorship ('*I will be your censor*', that same terrifying monarch had once informed Pushkin blandly). The work proved immensely popular, and it became the practice, right up to the time of the revolution, to open every season with *A Life for the Tsar* both at St Petersburg and Moscow. *Ruslan y Lyudmila*, which followed it at the St Petersburg Bolshoi in 1842, did not prove quite so popular (the full score was not published until 1878), but it is important as the first opera inspired by a text of Pushkin's. In 1847 Berlioz conducted his choral symphony *Roméo et Juliette* both there and in Moscow, and scored a success of which he stood badly in need. He was delighted at the amount of time put at his disposal for rehearsal – less delighted, however, by the discomforts of sleigh travel in winter: he had arrived bruised and exhausted, but he carried good letters of introduction and was made much of by the aristocracy. An Italian opera company founded in 1843 competed with the Russians at the Bolshoi for three years, then moved to Moscow. But the real stronghold of Russian

133 The Bolshoi-Petrovsky Theatre, on what is now Sverdlov Square.

nationalist opera became the Teatro-Cirk, built in 1847 by Cavos. This theatre was destroyed by fire in 1859, and Cavos forthwith set to work on the Maryinsky. Its first musical director was the father of the composer Anatol Liadov, and he pursued an energetic policy – though the Maryinsky did not replace the Bolshoi as the imperial opera and ballet theatre until 1885. The commissioning of an opera from Verdi (*La Forza del Destino* – 1862) was a bold step, and annoyed the nationalist composers a good deal. Verdi himself supervised the production, though he was not there for the opening night. When the size of his fee became known, there were demonstrations of native fury. Quite apart from these, the work got a rather cool reception. It had been postponed owing to the illness of one of the cast, and Verdi was unable to stay for it. Giuseppina Strepponi (who had had vast quantities of pasta, cheese and wine sent on in advance) found time to comment during the course of their stay that a Russian winter was a very different problem for the sleigh drivers waiting outside the theatre than for the audience inside it.

The comparative failure of *Forza* may well have been due as much to the lugubriousness of the plot as to xenophobia on the part of the St Petersburg

132 A scene from V. Murandeli's opera *October*, produced at the Bolshoi in 1964, with Galina Vishnevskaya and V. Nechipailo in the leading rôles.

public. Indeed, it has never been quite clearly established how far the 'nationalist' mystique was a genuine upwelling of the soul of the Russian people or how far it was self-induced by a small group of composers who thought that their native gifts were being sacrificed to a snobbish penchant for the Western European repertory. One has only to note the triumphant re-engagements year after year of Pauline Viardot, and the warmth with which she was invariably received in St Petersburg and Moscow to guess that there existed a real public for the Western repertory and not just a fashionable one. This is a fascinating subject and would repay much closer study.

Alexei Verstovsky, like Glinka, a pupil of John Field, was the composer of an opera, *Askold's Tomb*, which was produced in Moscow in 1835. This relied for much of its inventiveness on gypsy tunes and street songs – but it did not stop him from becoming manager of the Imperial Opera at Moscow, a post he held up to the time of his death in 1862. Dargomizhsky, a good amateur pianist and a civil servant until Glinka interested him in opera, got his *Russalka* accepted by the Bolshoi at St Petersburg in 1856. But it proved too un-italianate to please the public taste. His truly nationalist opera, *The Stone Guest*, was still unfinished at the time of his death in 1869. Rimsky-Korsakov took over the manuscript and it was put on in 1872, only to get the same response.

In 1863 a remarkable figure made his first appearance at the Maryinsky, where he was to remain for almost as long as the theatre kept its name – Eduard Nápravník. The exceptionally gifted Czech-born son of a village schoolmaster, he had become director of Prince Youssupov's private orchestra at the age of twenty-two. Liadov snapped him up as his assistant a couple of years later, and he was given an official appointment as organist of the Imperial Theatres. In 1867 he became second conductor at the Maryinsky, and succeeded Liadov as chief conductor in 1869. There he remained until his death in 1916. It may be surmised that over this long period procedures tended to become ossified, but as in the administration of all opera houses, the chief conductor was not the only pebble on the beach. There was,

now and then, a shake-up from above. For instance, when Alexander III came to the throne in 1881, and reversed all the liberal tendencies of his father (not surprisingly, perhaps, since Alexander II had been assassinated), he expressed a marked partiality for Russian opera, and particularly for the operas of Tchaikovsky and Rimsky-Korsakov, a preference which was quickly reflected in the repertories of the Maryinsky in St Petersburg and the Bolshoi in Moscow. When Prince Volkonsky became director of the Imperial Theatres in 1899 and Vladimir Telyakovsky administrative director in Moscow, everybody knew where was the real seat of power. Colonel Telyakovsky, a retired cavalry officer, was a man of refined musical taste and remarkably enlightened ideas. It was he who had Chaliapin recalled to the Maryinsky, where he had abandoned his contract in a huff at lack of official appreciation. On leaving the Maryinsky, Chaliapin scored a big success with the Moscow Private Opera (a company formed and financed by a remarkable sculptor-lawyer-millionaire industrialist, Saava Ivanovich Mamontov) in 1896, and was with them for two years.

There have been many great singers in Russian operatic history, from Menshikova and Melnikov in the 1870s and 1880s to Vishnevskaya and Rezhetin today. But Chaliapin was more than a singer: he was a force of nature. Although brought up in wretched poverty, in 1890, at the age of seventeen, he contrived to shake the dust of the Kazan back streets off his heels and attach himself, although completely untrained, to a provincial touring company. His rapid strides there enabled him to secure a year with a good teacher, called Ussatov, in Tiflis. Then he presented himself to be auditioned by Nápravník at the Maryinsky. He was accepted into the Company of the Imperial Theatres, and Nápravník even fancied he heard in him a possible successor to Melnikov. His first big rôle, however (that of the Miller in *Russalka*), at a morning performance, turned out less well than had been hoped, and a kind of mutual disenchantment set in between him and Nápravník The latter saw him, for all his latent talents, as a very young man, of very humble origin (he had, after all, had more than thirty years in which to forget his own age when he arrived on Prince Youssupov's doorstep, and his own background). Chaliapin fretted under the irritations of bureaucracy and red tape. He hated the uniformed administrative staff – representatives of 'the system' – and believed they despised artists both as artists and as human beings. The vital formative years with the Moscow Private Opera drew him into the circle of the liberal intelligentsia, and the study he made of Russian history when preparing the rôle of Boris Godunov penetrated deeply into his awareness. He seized an opportunity to consult the historian Klynchevsky, who fascinated him by talking as if he had known the great characters of the past personally. In particular, Klynchevsky emphasized Godunov's quick-thinking mind, his efforts to bring some kind of enlightenment to his country. With this background knowledge, Chaliapin found it extremely galling to have to perform a work that had been savagely cut by the censor. Likewise, when studying the rôle of Ivan the Terrible in Rimsky-Korsakov's *The Maid of Pskov*, he had been particularly impressed by a painting of Vasnetzov's. He also studied paintings by Schwarz and Repin, and the sculpture of Antonkelsky. He not only learnt different parts; he learnt whole operas – he felt his way into them and identified himself with them until, because he was such a great actor as well as a great singer, he came to dominate them. Gorky, after their first meeting (in 1900) summed him up as 'a simple fellow, enormous and clumsy, with a roughly hewn, intelligent face'. A great deal was going on behind that intelligent face and the political attitude which emerged did not pass unnoticed. Telyakovsky has recorded in his journal that for many years Chaliapin's friendship with Maxim Gorky prevented him being ap-

134 A scene from Glinka's *Ruslan y Lyudmila* at the Maryinsky in 1871. This was a period when lavish productions were greatly relished.

135 Apart from one rude interruption, Chaliapin and Gorky were close friends for much of their adult lives. They were born in neighbouring streets in the poorest quarter of Kazan, though they did not meet until 1900, when Chaliapin was already 27. Gorky died in 1936, Chaliapin two years later. This photograph was taken in 1902 or 1903.

136 and 137 Chaliapin was a self-taught master of
make-up. Here are his first sketch for Rossini's
Don Basilio (1912) and – the finished product (1913).

138 Water colour sketch by I. V. Bilibin for Act IV of the 1937 Kirov production of Rimsky-Korsakov's *Tale of Tsar Saltan.*

pointed 'soloist of His Imperial Majesty'. Indeed, that same Imperial Majesty (Nicholas II), finding his name on a Bolshoi programme in 1905, demanded that 'this hooligan be chased out of the Imperial Theatres': he had been one of the signatories of a letter to the press from a group of leading artists, which stated that:

'when there is neither freedom of thought nor conscience in a country, when there is no freedom of speech or press, when all creative activity is stifled and hampered, the title of free artist becomes a mockery. We are not free artists, but merely the victims of abnormal social and legalistic institutions, deprived of the rights of ordinary Russian citizens'.

In the first decade of the twentieth century he sang every major rôle in the repertories of the Bolshoi and the Maryinsky. Russian opera was now playing a much bigger part, and included some minor pieces, since largely forgotten, such as Cui's *Angelo*, Tchaikovsky's *Oprichnik*, and

Serov's *The Power of Evil*. These had scarcely been heard in the twenty-five or thirty years since their premières. They were not, of course, as popular as what had now become the 'standard' works – *Boris Godunov, Prince Igor, Eugene Onegin* or *The Queen of Spades* – works that lent themselves to grand, spectacular productions, for which the vogue persisted. Perhaps spectacle was needed more than ever, now, because underneath the opulent surface of life there were rumblings of the revolution to come, and the war with Japan had been a major catastrophe. Rimsky-Korsakov's *The Golden Cockerel*, produced in 1909, was a daring commentary on the event which would never have escaped censorship in the days when the imperial power was still playing from strength and not from weakness. The Maryinsky and Bolshoi audiences, right up to 1914, remained as glittering as any in the world: probably more glittering, because Russian men were still much preoccupied with uniforms and decorations, even those whose political sympathies were liberal.

There was an occasion at the Maryinsky in 1911 when the medals must have rattled audibly. The chorus had chosen a night when the Emperor was to be present at a performance of *Boris Godunov* to make an ingenious appeal for greater freedom without jeopardizing themselves too much. In the second scene of the prologue, the coronation scene, at the point where the Tsar receives the plaudits of the people, Chaliapin came on stage just in time to see the people turn their backs on him, as Tsar Boris, and flop down on their knees with arms outstretched towards Tsar Nicholas in the royal box. Overcome with surprise, and yielding spontaneously to the histrionic possibilities of the situation, he flopped down, too, with arms outstretched in the same gesture. It must have enhanced the strength of the appeal immeasurably, but it ruined his relations with Gorky and the rest of his left-wing friends for a long time to come. Two years later he sought to make amends by declining to take part in a concert to celebrate the tercentenary of the Romanov dynasty, and in 1915 he managed, with some skill, to avoid singing Susanin in a charity performance of *A Life for the Tsar*. After the revolution he was declared 'First People's Artist of the Russian Soviet Federation of Socialist Republics'. In 1922 he left Russia for good, following a trial period abroad from which he returned and was allowed to collect his belongings. At a press conference in New York he answered the inevitable question whether the conditions of artistic life in Russia were better or worse as a result of the revolution, with a flood of volubility and many gestures and changes of facial expression. His bewildered listeners looked at the interpreter, who summed up succinctly: 'He says they are about the same'.

Another musician who went abroad at the time of the revolution, and who had yet to make his name, was Prokofiev. But he returned home and stayed home, and on his shoulders was to descend the mantle of many famous predecessors in the fields of both ballet and opera. In due course he was to find on the stage of the Bolshoi and of the Kirov a marvellous frame for his works; among the singers and dancers of the two theatres, magnificent exponents of their respective arts; and from their audiences that degree of appreciation and gratitude which the Russian, more perhaps than the creative artist of any other nation, seems to need from his fellow countryman if the spark is to be kept alive. What would Tolstoy say if today, invited to attend a rehearsal, he were to find himself in the splendid auditorium of the Bolshoi, watching a production being prepared by that many-sided genius, Mstislav Rostropovich, of Prokofiev's opera score – *War and Peace*?

UNITED STATES OFAMERICA

The Metropolitan Opera New York

The history of opera in America did not start with the Met., nor will it end there. No opera house in the world ever had a more diversified range of fairy godparents, nor perhaps has any opera house ever witnessed the conjunction of so many major planets in the operatic firmament. The auditorium, too, has in its time sparkled with enough diamonds to dim the Milky Way, and the institution as a whole has faithfully mirrored the changing facets of New York life in a manner which, to people who love the place, is at once nostalgic, funny, evocative and encouraging.

It is strange to think that one of the fairy godparents – he is really a great-godparent – was Lorenzo da Ponte, the librettist of *Le Nozze di Figaro*, *Don Giovanni* and *Così fan tutte*; a man who could have told us just what Mozart looked like, what his voice sounded like, what he was like to work with; who had known (and passably followed the unexemplary life pattern of) that splendid eighteenth century roué Casanova. It is strange that this slightly shady adventurer, who in his time made both Venice and Vienna – neither of them lacking in tolerance – too hot for him, should have died a respected pedagogue, with all the honour appertaining to extreme old age, in the young United States; even stranger that he should have qualified for this apotheosis by way of keeping a general store in Elizabethtown, New Jersey, and a liquor distillery in Sunbury, Penn-sylvania. His very name, which incidentally was only his own at one remove, marks him out as a bridge, in music, between the eighteenth century and the nineteenth, between the old world and the new.

Another fairy godparent of the Met., to go to the opposite end of the scale, was Otto Kahn. He was born in Mannheim, in 1867, and died in New York in 1934. The son of a banker, he initially made his career in banking, first in Germany, then England, then in the United States. But he came of a musical family; as a boy he had learnt to play the piano and the 'cello, and his passion for music never left him. He started his career at the age of fifteen as an office boy filling inkwells in a small Karlsruhe banking house. He finished it as Maecenas to the Metropolitan Opera, New York, at a moment when the rôle of a Maecenas was anything but easy. He was one of those public benefactors of private means (a breed in which America has been fortunate) without whose combination of zeal and practical acumen the old Met. would probably never have survived to make its historic move to Lincoln Center in 1966.

Opera in New York moved gradually up town before it came to rest, for a long spell, at 39th Street. Opera of a kind (including *The Beggar's Opera*) had been performed there even before the War of Independence, but the real beginnings, as far as this book is concerned, are with the Park

139 Enrico Caruso as Pagliacci: the 1903–4 season at the Met. introduced to American audiences for the first time the Italian tenor who was to sing on every opening night (with one exception) for the next seventeen years.

Theater, the Richmond Hill Theater and the Italian Opera House. It was at the Park Theater, in November 1825, that Manuel Garcia's company made their début. The piece was Rossini's *Il Barbiere di Siviglia*. Garcia himself played Almaviva and his daughter, Maria Felicita, afterwards to become world famous as 'La Malibran', Rosina. Their season was so successful that it continued until September 1826. Da Ponte was the moving spirit behind a season at the Richmond Hill Theater in 1832–3, and in the opening of the Italian Opera House on Church and Leonard Streets in 1833. This was the first New York theatre to be built specifically for the performance of opera, but it only endured as such for two seasons. His idea had been basically sound, and the signs were there, but the time was not yet ripe. And he himself had only six more years to live. Next came Palmo's Opera House on Chambers Street. Fernando Palmo was a restaurant proprietor who could find no other means of slaking his thirst for opera than by remodelling his premises into a theatre. That lasted from 1844 to 1848 and it was there, in 1845, that German opera was heard for the first time in New York. In November 1847 the new Astor Place Opera House opened with *Ernani*. Support for five years was guaranteed by a group of 150 prominent citizens, but at the end of that term it closed. Then, in 1854, came the immediate forerunner of the Met. – the Academy of Music, at 14th Street and Irving Place. It was to serve as the city's operatic centre for the next thirty years, a period in which those social patterns by which the century is best remembered took shape and habits crystallized. One of the most interesting strands in the design was the emergence of a plutocracy ranging itself alongside the aristocracy of privilege asserted by the old families who were the descendants of the early Dutch and British settlers. They formed a tightly knit, entrenched class, the more sure of themselves for having successfully survived the Revolution, the more determined, for the same reason, to be identified and be seen to be identified with the prevailing values of European culture. One of these values, of course, was opera, and to occupy a box at the Academy of Music

was not only a source of enjoyment but also a social affirmation. For some, the latter consideration carried more weight than the former.

With the rapid increase of wealth during the third quarter of the century there came increasing pressure on the limited number of boxes available at the Academy. Indeed a box was, in effect, an admission card to the charmed circle of those who had 'arrived'. This social fact, in itself no more than an anthropological footnote, was the prime, if not the only begetter, of the Met. When it was found (in 1880) that the number of boxes at the Academy could not be increased by more than twenty-six,

140 The Academy of Music was destined to lose the battle against the Met. in which, from the first it was heavily out-gunned. This print shows the arrival of a lady at the Academy opening in 1873.

the only way out of the dilemma was to build another opera house. Money being by then available in vast quantities (three years earlier, William H. Vanderbilt, one of the supporters of the project, had inherited $90 million from his father), this presented no great difficulty. On 8 April 1880, the Metropolitan Opera-house Company, Ltd. was incorporated, and three-and-a-half years later, on 22 October 1883, the curtain rose on Gounod's *Faust*, with Christine Nilsson in the rôle of the beautiful Marguerite. On the same evening the Academy was giving *La Sonnambula*, with Etelka Gerster. Some distracted patrons

are alleged to have gravitated twenty-five blocks from one opera house to the other during the course of the evening, and a few to have taken in the horse show as well, since that was also fashionable. If they did, things were at least made easier by the fact that the performance at the Met. started half an hour late and did not end until close on one o'clock.

It is a pity that for so much of its life, attention at the old Met. was focused on the wrong side of the footlights – on the auditorium rather than the stage – for this has tended to distort the real dedication and achievements of patrons such as Otto

METROPOLITAN
OPERA HOUSE.

MR. HENRY E. ABBEY, - - - - - - - Director·
Acting Manager, - - - - - - MR. MAURICE GRAU.

MONDAY EVENING, OCTOBER 22, 1883,

INAUGURAL NIGHT

AND

First Night of the Subscription,

WHEN GOUNOD'S OPERA OF

"FAUST."

Will be presented with the following Cast :

FAUST, - - - - - - Sig. ITALO CAMPANINI
MEPHISTOPHELES, - - - - Sig. FRANCO NOVARA
VALENTINO, - - - - Sig. GIUSEPPE DEL PUENTE
WAGNER, - - - - - - - Sig. CONTINI
SIEBEL, - - - - - - Mme. SOFIA SCALCHI
MARTA, - - - - - - Mlle. LOUISE LABLACHE
(Who has kindly consented to assume the part at short notice. Her first appearance.)
AND
MARGHERITA, - - - - Mme. CHRISTINE NILSSON

Musical Director and Conductor, · Sig. VIANESI

WEBER PIANO USED.

Mason & Hamlin's Organ Used.

All the above Operas performed at this House can be had in every form, Vocal and Instrumental at G. SCHIRMER, No. 35 Union Square, Importer and Publisher of Music.

The Scenery by Messrs. Fox, Schaeffer, Maeder, and Thompson.
The Costumes are entirely new, and were manufactured at Venice by D. Ascoli
The Appointments by Mr. Bradwell.
Machinists, Messrs. Lundy & Gifford.

NIGHTLY PRICES OF ADMISSION :

Boxes, holding six (6) seats................................ $50
Orchestra Stalls.. 6
Balcony Stalls... 3
Family Circle (reserved).................................. 2
Admission to Family Circle................................ 1

Seats and Boxes can be secured at the Box Office of the Metropolitan Opera House, which will remain open daily from 8 A. M. to 5 P. M.

Doors open at 7.15.   Performances at 8 precisely

Gunerius Gabrielson & Son, Florists to the Metropolitan Opera House.

Opera Glasses on Hire in the Lobby.

L. F. Mazette, Caterer.
Parties desiring Ices can be supplied by the Waiter, in Corridor.

Business Manager - - - - - - Mr. W. W. TILLOTSON.
Treasurer - - - - - - - Mr. CHAS. H. MATHEWS.

Kahn and Mrs August Belmont as well as to diminish the stature of some of the great performances with which the history of the repertory is studded. Perhaps it would have been better if New Yorkers had taken their opera not less seriously, but more lightheartedly, as did the people of New Orleans. There, opera had been part of the way of life since 1840, when Julie Çalvé had appeared at the Théâtre d'Orléans with a French Company brought over by her husband, Charles Boudousquié. In 1859 the three existing theatres, the Saint Pierre, the Sainte Philippe and the Théâtre d'Orléans, were replaced by the French Opera House. Here, until it was burnt down in 1919, never to be rebuilt, the tradition of important first performances in America, inherited from the Orléans, was zestfully continued. In 1843 the Théâtre d'Orléans had staged the first American production of *La Favorite*, in 1844 of *La Juive*, and in 1850 of *Le Prophète*. The French Opera House opened with *Guillaume Tell*. Gounod's *Le Tribut de Zamora* was seen there in 1888; Lalo's *Le Roi d'Ys* in 1890; Massenet's *Hérodiade* in 1892, Saint-Saëns's *Samson et Dalila* in 1893; Berlioz's *Benvenuto Cellini* in 1897; Gounod's *La Reine de Saba* in 1889. It is indeed a record of achievement. The people of New Orleans rejoiced in it, but they took it as part and parcel of their French heritage. There were *loges grillés* for the bereaved and a so-called *loge des lions* for the unattached smart young men. So reluctant were subscribers to miss a performance to which they had been looking forward that on one occasion a subsequently famous Creole beauty narrowly escaped being born in the theatre: 'I'm afraid', said Madame Blanque, turning to her husband half way through a performance of *Faust*, 'I shan't be able to stay for the ballet . . .'

The pattern of events at the Met. was more erratic. For that inaugural season of 1883–4 the directors had leased the house to an impresario, Henry E. Abbey, who had collected an international cast of high quality and been given a free hand with the choice of repertory. The chief conductor was Covent Garden's Vianesi, while fifty members of the orchestra were drawn from Venice, and another thirteen from Leipzig, five

from London, fifteen from Naples, and one from Brussels. The works performed included *Lucia di Lammermoor, I Puritani, La Sonnambula, Rigoletto, Don Giovanni, Il Barbiere di Siviglia, Die Zauberflöte* and *La Gioconda*. There were 61 performances. The season lasted until April, after which the company went on tour (58 more performances). And at the end of it all a staggering deficit of $600,000 had been achieved. This was partly due to the large fees which it had taken to break the Academy's monopoly of singers, but partly, also, to Abbey's conviction that nothing but the best would do for those three tiers of well-heeled box holders. This led to every costume, even down to shoes and stockings, being ordered from Worth of Paris. The directors were therefore called upon for the full implementation of their guarantee of $60,000. It did not go a long way towards helping Abbey, who cautiously said he would only undertake another season if the losses on it were fully guaranteed, whatever they might be. Equally cautiously, the directors declined his proposition.

The consequence of the initial débâcle was seven years of opera sung entirely in German. It was educative. It inculcated a taste for German opera which might otherwise have only taken root very slowly. And there was a growing influx of German immigrants who helped fill the less expensive seats. But it was not quite what the box holders had bargained for. Wagner in German was fair enough, but Rossini, Meyerbeer, Bizet, Verdi, all in German, in due course took their toll, though the ensemble was of a high standard and the general level of production permeated with German thoroughness. The initial agent in the formulation and execution of this policy was Leopold Damrosch, conducting the Symphony Society orchestra. But he died almost immediately, and to succeed him was appointed Anton Seidl, a conductor of great ability and strong will, whose teutonism was unimpeachable: he had actually worked at Bayreuth. A landmark in the life of the new régime was the first production of *Die Meistersinger* in 1886. It was a calculated risk, which did credit to the Met. as a serious institution. *Die Walküre* followed next season, then *Tristan und Isolde.* Financial deficits were still the order of the day, but the prospects of the Met. were much brightened by the capitulation of Colonel James Mapleson as impresario at the Academy. He could not, he was forced to admit, 'fight Wall Street'. Even so, Wall Street, too, had to make its compromise: the third tier of boxes was eliminated in 1884, a so-called 'dress-circle' taking its place.

By 1887–8 even the two remaining tiers of box holders were beginning to feel restive under a surfeit of Wagner, and attempts were made to lighten their burden by the introduction of Halévy's *La Juive* and Spontini's *Fernando Cortez* – but still in German. Here were the seeds of a dilemma that germinated three seasons later. Early in 1891 it was announced that in 1891–2, opera in German would cease, and French and Italian take over. Seidl went out in a blaze of Wagnerian glory. Out of 35 performances given in the final weeks of the season, 29 were of operas by Wagner, and the era terminated with a triumphant *Meistersinger*. Thereafter Abbey, chastened by experience and wiser with time, was back in control of an international cast with Vianesi once again in the pit.

All went well until, on a hot Saturday morning in 1892 the theatre was gutted by fire. Josiah Cleveland Cady, the architect of the Metropolitan Opera House, had been grieved that his achievement was not greeted with more rapture. He had won the commission quite fairly, in an open competition, and he was by no means the first of his profession to venture, without previous experience, into the uncharted waters of sight lines and sound waves. In a letter to the *New York Times* he drew attention to the care and thought he had lavished on the project. This included a substantial use of iron and metal in the construction, rather than inflammable wood. Indeed, so complex were his specifications that for some of the work the contractor had to equip a special mill. To make assurance doubly sure a sprinkler system, fed from a tank on the roof, protected the stage. The opera was as uninflammable as the *Titanic* was to be unsinkable. But in 1892 the water tank on the roof had been emptied (against frost) and not re-filled, and the 4,000 sectional iron

142 Twilight of a day in New York's history. It was accepted that the 39th Street opera house had served its turn, but the mere sight of it evoked nostalgia to the last.

143 Geraldine Farrar in 1900: One of the greatest singers America has produced. After an initial success in Berlin she joined the Met. in 1906 and remained with the Company as principal soprano until her retirement in 1922.

144 (*Opposite*) The opening of the Metropolitan in 1883 was heralded by the *Daily Graphic* on 23 October with detailed drawings of its newly revealed splendours.

supports below the stage had been largely supplanted, as a matter of convenience, by timbers. The insurance policy alone remained unchanged, so that the fire, when it *did* come, proved a particularly expensive one. All thought of an 1892–3 season had to be abandoned and the stockholders of the Metropolitan Opera-house Company determined to recoup their losses by selling the site. It was bought by a new corporation, called the Metropolitan Opera and Real Estate Company, about half of whose 35 stockholders had belonged to the old company. They were presumably the individuals who best combined the love of opera with a flair for real estate.

Rebuilding began in April 1893, and the new auditorium was to remain substantially unchanged for the whole subsequent lifetime of the building. It had its disadvantages and its infelicities (Chaliapin hated it), but it *did* acquire the aura, the patina, which entitled it to the accolade 'great'. 'We have no such structure in Italy. It is indeed a noble house,' said Giulio Gatti-Casazza when, fresh from La Scala, he took over as director in 1908 – even though, as he tells in his memoirs, he voiced a number of reservations to Otto Kahn, who optimistically promised him a new building within two or three years.

The threshold of that era of great singing for which the Met. is best remembered had been reached before the fire with the return of Henry Abbey, but it was not really crossed until the new auditorium had been completed. From then until 1908 Abbey, as lessee of the theatre, worked in close collaboration with Maurice Grau, the manager. Grau was a man of considerable operatic ability tempered by unpredictability and in time he came to assume a dominant position. The names of Emma Eames, Jean and Eduard de Reszke, Lasalle, Plançon, Calvé, Melba, Lilli Lehmann, dominated the cast lists. *Otello* was seen with Tamagno in the rôle he had created under Verdi's eye, and *Falstaff* with Victor Maurel. Another landmark was the first appearance of the de Reszke brothers in a German-language *Tristan und Isolde*, with Lillian Nordica as Isolde and Anton Seidl conducting. There were five performances

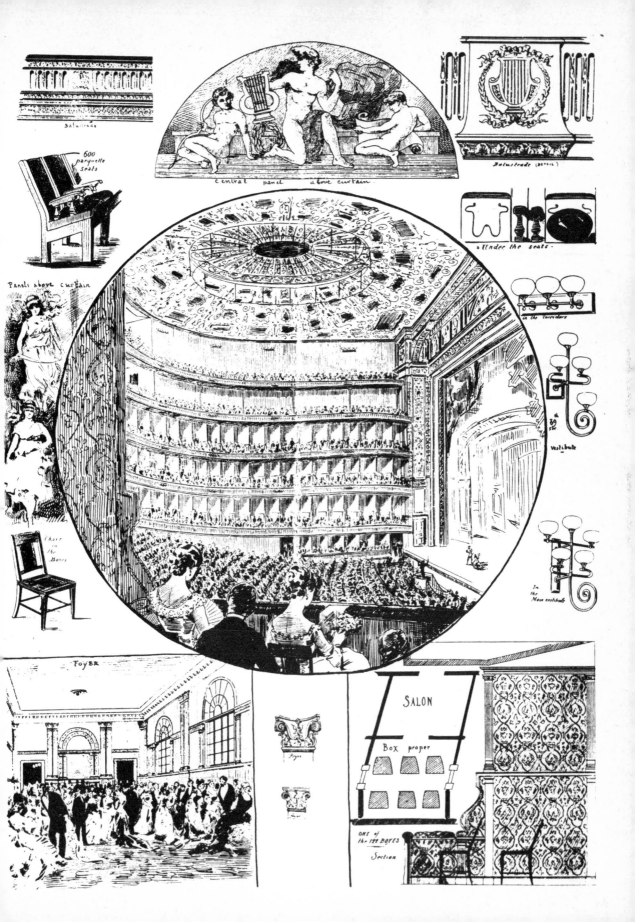

Balustrade.

600 parquette seats

central panel above curtain.

Balustrade (DETAIL)

Under the seats.

Panels above curtain

in the Corridors

35 th St. Vestibule

In the Main vestibule

Chair in the Boxes

FOYER

Foyer

SALON

Box proper

ONE of the 122 BOXES

Section

145 The Old Guard go into action for almost the last
time. First night arrivals in the early 1940s.

of this during the 1895–6 season, and it was in the following season that Melba made her ill-advised bid for the rôle of Brünnhilde in *Siegfried*.

Poor health forced Grau's retirement in 1903. A succession was smoothly effected, for the fortunes of the Metropolitan Opera were riding high. It was said at this time that $100,000 had been offered – and refused – for one of the *parterre* boxes that were reserved for the stockholders on subscription nights. The mantle of Grau descended on the shoulders of Heinrich Conried, who formed the Company that was to give opera at the Met. for the next twenty-four years. It was Conried who engaged Caruso. It was Conried who defied Cosima Wagner by putting on *Parsifal*. Rather oddly, he chose Christmas Eve for its première, just as, no less oddly, he chose a Sunday morning for the dress rehearsal of *Salome*. Again, it was Conried who staged *Die Fledermaus* with an all-star cast, and it was Conried who had to cope with the first strike, when the entire chorus of 140 walked out, save for two men and six women, just before a matinée performance of *Faust*, which was considerably truncated in consequence. But the trades union movement among musicians was still far from militant: there were too many recent immigrants from Europe among them for that. Conried also had to face the threat posed by Oscar Hammerstein's Manhattan Opera House. Hammerstein made his entry like a bull coming into the ring. Within less than four years he had acquired a nuisance value of $1,200,000. It was largely the worry of Hammerstein's competition that undermined Conried's health and led to his premature replacement in 1908. Not even fifty-one appearances by Caruso in a single season, or Gustav Mahler conducting *Tristan und Isolde*, could slay the dragon of the Manhattan Opera House; nor yet the first appearances of Geraldine Farrar and Chaliapin.

In dropping Conried, it was also necessary to drop his name from the title of the company, which accordingly was known from then on as the Metropolitan Opera Company instead of the Conried Metropolitan Opera Company. This provided the opportunity for a measure of reorganiza-tion, the most significant feature of which was that

146 The opening night of Puccini's *La Fanciulla del West*, which had its world première at the Met. in 1910, starring Caruso, and Emmy Destinn, with Pasquale Amato as the Sheriff.

henceforth profits should go to the establishment of a pension fund or to 'other permanent uses for advancement of the Company as an artistic institution'. Just as it was largely due to Otto Kahn that the engagement of Toscanini and Gatti-Casazza came about, so it was he and William K. Vanderbilt who together bought out the Conried company, paying $50,000 each. By then Kahn was one of the leading bankers of New York and he is said to have contributed $350,000 from his own resources to make good losses incurred between 1908 and 1910, as well as the $1,200,000 it took to buy off Hammerstein. 'I must atone for my wealth,' was the phrase he used to explain these actions.

The reign of Toscanini opened with a new production of *Aida* in which Emmy Destinn sang the title rôle for the first time, opposite Caruso. It was perhaps one of the most brilliant occasions ever experienced at the Met., even though the full force of Toscanini's remarkable personality did not at once become apparent. The press concurred in recognizing him as a re-creator. Only later was it seen that 'the age of the conductor' had dawned. Working at the Met., because of the fame it conferred, encouraged unduly in some artists that self-awareness which is a necessary element of a singer's armament. Toscanini, of course, held that the whole is greater than the sum of the parts and that the presentation of the whole was the conductor's responsibility. When, in rehearsal with him for the first time, a certain prima donna took liberties with her rôle, he pushed ahead:

'Avanti, avanti, signorina.'
'Maestro, Lei deve dirigere come io canto, io sono una stella.'
'Signorina, le stelle sono sul firmamento. Qui siamo tutti artisti, buoni o cattivi. Lei è uno cattivo artista.'[12]

By 1914 disenchantment had set in and Toscanini announced that he would not accept a renewal of his contract when it became due the following year. As he had threatened this before, he was not taken too seriously. When, however, half way through the 1914–15 season the directors decided to retrench, this may have proved the watershed

147 Rosa Ponselle's rich, dramatic soprano was one of the best loved voices of the early twentieth century. Born Rosa Ponzillo, of Neapolitan-American parents, she made her début at the Met. (discovered by Caruso) in 1918.

148 (*Opposite*) The interior of the old Metropolitan.

149 (*Above*) The same view of the company's new home in Lincoln Center.

150 Visible, if not wholly convincing, evidence that Maestro Toscanini was deterred from renewing his contract in 1915 solely because he had become 'a burning bush of patriotism'. He never went back to the Met. but another brilliant phase in his career opened when he became Director of La Scala, Milan, in 1922.

of his discontent. In the summer he went to Europe as usual. But he did not return, though the fictional hope of his doing so sooner or later was maintained until late into the fall. 'The Maestro is a burning bush of patriotism,' said the press representative of the Metropolitan Opera, Italy by then having entered the war. This was perhaps true, though a photograph of him in civilian dress, conducting a uniformed military band, provided only moderately persuasive evidence. He had, in fact, firmly declined to accept the policy of retrenchment, although it was fully justified in the circumstances. Salaries had been grossly inflated during the era of competition with the Manhattan Opera House ('I am told that my influence in the operatic field has lifted the other institution to a less jocular position than it has held for the past several years,' Oscar Hammerstein once remarked in his pride); war in Europe had increased the availability of singers; the suspension of opera in Chicago and Boston ended 'exchange' arrangements with those companies and so left the Met. more than fully staffed for its own needs. Toscanini tried to get Gatti-Casazza to resign with him, but he refused, and the two men were not on speaking terms for the next seventeen years.

The impact of the war was felt emotionally when Enrique Granados and his wife were torpedoed and drowned on their voyage back to Spain after the première of his *Goyescas* – the first time Spanish had been sung at the Met. and the first Spanish work ever to be performed there. America's own entry into the war on Good Friday, 1917, was marked, incongruously enough, by a German language performance of *Parsifal*. The German repertory continued as planned until the end of the season, but after that there was no more Wagner until 1920, when *Parsifal* came back – in English.

The post-war years were prosperous in New York, and this prosperity was reflected at the Met. in a way which glossed over the failure to replace Toscanini by anybody of comparable calibre as a driving, co-ordinating, central artistic force. He was, indeed, irreplaceable, and standards began to slip. How should this be perceived, though, in an

151 Geraint Evans playing Leporello to Elizabeth Schwarzkopf's Donna Elvira in *Don Giovanni* at the Met. in 1966; it was one of Schwarzkopf's last stage appearances.

atmosphere of hectic social competition wholly unrelated to artistic values? The *parterre* boxes of the stockholders still retained their diamond sparkle, and in a single season the owner of one of these rented it 47 times out of 115 subscription performances for a total of $9,525, which meant a net profit of more than $5,000.

To opera goers, the loss of Caruso seemed more important than the loss of Toscanini. Over the space of twenty years he had become part of the very fabric of the opera house. In the eighteen seasons starting with that of 1902–3 there were 104 performances of *I Pagliacci*. Caruso was in 76 of them. Between 1902 and 1918 he sang Radames 64 times, out of a total of 110 performances. His last appearance at the Met. was on Christmas Eve, 1920, in *La Juive*. It was his 607th. The following August he was dead. Caruso was one of the greatest opera singers the world has ever known, and one of the least self-interested. At the height

of his career he declined the maximum fee offered him by the Met. on the grounds that it would impose on him an obligation he might not always feel capable of discharging: his counter-proposal was a figure little more than half. Yet on the counterfoil of every cheque he was paid, he noted his own appraisal of the performance it represented: these ranged from *buona in generale* to – very occasionally – *meravigliosa*.

As the decade wore on the need of a new site for the opera house, and the inadequacies of the old building, became increasingly apparent. Otto Kahn had not for one moment forgotten his promise to Gatti-Casazza in 1908, but it was not until the post-war boom years that it seemed to come within range of realization. In 1925 he personally acquired a site on 57th Street, between 8th and 9th Avenues, and early in 1926 made a substantial loan to enable building to begin. This got a less than rapturous welcome from devotees

152 George Gershwin and the cast of *Porgy and Bess* after the New York opening in 1935.

of the old house, particularly the hard core of the *parterre* box holders, who lacked Otto Kahn's wider vision as well as his genuine interest in opera. The project ran aground, as did one or two subsequent ones. Then came the financial crash of 1929, and though further plans were canvassed, Otto Kahn died in 1934 without the adoption of any of them in sight. Indeed, when the distinguished musicologist Irving Kolodin published his history of the Metropolitan Opera in 1939, he observed gloomily that the prospect of removal was more remote than at any time before. As things turned out, the new Metropolitan Opera House at Lincoln Center opened its doors in 1966.

From 1923 until the end of the decade the season lasted twenty-four weeks. With the depression it was reduced to sixteen, then to fourteen. These were hard and troubled years, both without and within the organization, though little sign of the troubles within came to the notice of the public, except the dismissal of Gigli, one of the tenors on whom the burden of replacing Caruso had fallen most heavily, in circumstances of extreme acrimony. The real crisis came at the beginning of 1933. It was announced that after a twenty years' record of self support, the Met. could not undertake another season without a sizeable financial guarantee. A 'Save the Metropolitan' appeal was launched, with a good deal of *éclat* and a fine sprinkling of singers and financiers among its sponsors. Edward Johnson, the distinguished Canadian tenor, soon to become general manager (Gatti-Casazza retired in 1934 and his successor, Herbert Witherspoon, died before his appointment could take effect), made the opening speech, followed two evenings later by Lily Pons. With substantial grants from the Juilliard Foundation ($50,000) and the Carnegie Corporation ($25,000), it was announced in May that a 1933–4 season *would* take place. And so it did. But the essential vulnerability of the Met. as an operatic institution had been revealed, and a pipeline to the resources of the Juilliard Foundation had been laid which was to prove invaluable in later years. Meanwhile, the formula of great names – Flagstad, Lehmann, Martinelli, to mention only three – and indifferent productions, was adhered to. Excite-ment was only engendered by such peripheral happenings as Gertrud Wettergren knocking off the hats of half-a-dozen soldiers in *Carmen* and Marjorie Lawrence actually leaving the stage on Grane's back. The outstanding Wagnerian team of Flagstad and Lauritz Melchior were the greatest moneyspinners of the season. Edward Johnson persisted, but in July 1939 the Metropolitan Opera and Real Estate Company announced its intention of proposing to its stockholders the sale of the house to the Metropolitan Opera Association. The love affair between New York 'society' and the Met. was over. In fact, 'New York society' was itself no more than a name.

A sum of $1,057,000 was raised from 166,000 donors to enable the Association to complete the transaction, which was done in 1940, and one of the first consequences was the conversion of the grand tier boxes into innocuous, ordinary, balcony seats. This meant that there remained but a single

153 Lawrence Tibbett sang the title role in *Emperor Jones* in 1933, the first world première to be broadcast from the Metropolitan stage.

tier of boxes, with accommodation for 280 seats, as against 732 when the house had first opened. And a new gold curtain was hung as a boost to morale. Edward Johnson faced the difficulties of the decade with good sense and judgement born of his experience as a singer. There was no anti-German discrimination after America entered the war – though perhaps if there had been any Japanese operas in the repertory they would have fared less well. In the 1940–41 season, works were performed by all the composers whose names were inscribed on the proscenium arch – Beethoven, Gluck, Gounod, Mozart, Verdi and Wagner. There were losses in the first years, despite the missionary efforts of the Metropolitan Opera Guild and the continuing success of the Saturday afternoon broadcasts. A further appeal for funds produced $300,000 in 1943, and another in 1949 produced $250,000. Trouble with the trades unions nearly wrecked the 1948–9 season, but it was reprieved at the last moment. This was regarded as a great and dreadful novelty at the time, but since then, it has become a more or less common-place occurrence, and Rudolf Bing, Edward Johnson's successor, was afforded every oppor-tunity to acquire an expertise in labour relations during his twenty years of office. Indeed, the greatly improved physical conditions under which everybody works at Lincoln Center, the Met.'s new home since 1966, seems to have exacerbated wage disputes rather than to have lessened them. It is a far cry from the time when Lilli Lehmann, in her memoirs, could note almost with an air of faint surprise that 'the orchestra had to be paid extra for work on Sundays'.

The move to the house at Lincoln Center marked the climax of Bing's managerial achieve-ment. It was supremely well planned and carried through with remarkable smoothness. The season opened with a new opera (*Antony and Cleopatra*, by Samuel Barber), and there were four new pro-ductions in a space of eight days. At 39th Street, with its limited, inconvenient, antiquated back-stage facilities such a feat would have been impos-sible. But Bing will be remembered as more than an organizer and a negotiator. It was during his years at the Met. that the age of the conductor

gave way to the age of the producer and the designer, and he himself played a distinct part in bringing this change about. If, in the long term, it comes to be seen as the replacement of one stereotype by another, that is no cause for com-plaint. The work of the Met. during the past twenty years has had an overall coherence that it never possessed before.

There had been a number of sporadic attempts to escape from the confines of 39th Street. Otto Kahn had made his promise to Gatti-Casazza in 1908 and thought he had got near to honouring it in 1925. That project fell through, and he tried again in 1932. An alternative proposed site was the Rockefeller Center; another, during the late 1940s, was near where the United Nations building now stands. There were more besides, and the matter was not finally settled until clearance of the Lincoln Center site began in 1958. This time the fairy god-father was John D. Rockefeller III but despite all the gratitude owing to him and to the Juilliard Foundation for making a reality of half a century's dreams, waves of nostalgia began to lap the old, doomed building. Like every parting, it was a kind of small death, and some New Yorkers even

154 Protesting graffiti covered the hoardings which concealed the death throes of the doomed building.

had the uncomfortable feeling that they were conniving at a judicial murder.

The architect of the new building, Wallace K. Harriman, was determined to avoid the pitfalls which had left Josiah Cleveland Cady a disappointed man; and he was determined to try and meet the needs of a new age, to interpret to the best of his ability the tastes and aspirations of contemporary opera-goers – how vastly different from those of the 1880s. Acoustics and sight lines were not left to chance, but referred to science, with the happy consequence that today one can see and hear marvellously from everywhere in the house. There is, indeed, a circle of boxes, and small withdrawing rooms behind them, but so discreet, so unobtrusive, that even Mrs Bradley Martin would have felt anonymous if seated in one of them.[13] The cult of personality on the part of any section of the audience has been effectively obviated by covering every available inch of wall and ceiling space with gold leaf, giving a lustre beneath which all men are equal. And for good measure there are some brilliantly conceived chandeliers, rather like snowflakes seen through a giant magnifying glass, which were presented by

the Austrian Government. These are suspended in mid-air until shortly before the lights dim, when they unanimously rise to the roof and so do not get in anybody's way. It might be argued that the actual architectural design and ornamentation of the auditorium is of an austere simplicity which does not quite accord with such a plethora of light and colour, and it might be questioned whether the abstract emblem over the centre of the proscenium is an enhancement or an error of judgement. However, these are matters of taste, not major considerations. What *is* important is that the orchestra pit is big enough, that the artists' dressing-rooms are agreeable and conveniently positioned in relation to the stage (and are not dependent on air conditioning, but have windows that actually open!), that scenery can be easily and expeditiously shifted, that the lighting console is a marvel, and that audiences can arrive and depart in the greatest of comfort.

It has sometimes been said that during its lifetime of close on ninety years the Metropolitan Opera has given insufficient encouragement to American singers and American composers. This is not true. It has been traditional to offer the best voices the world could provide, but from the time of Emma Eames, Lillian Nordica and Louise Homer, American artists have never been discriminated against *because* they were American. Many native-born luminaries like Rosa Ponselle, Lawrence Tibbett, Richard Tucker, Risë Stevens and Anna Moffo have added their lustre to the continuing brilliance of the House. And with Marian Anderson's superb performance as Ulrica in the *Ballo in Maschera* of the 1955–6 season the first Negro solo singer at the Met. created a precedent which many outstanding black American artists have since followed, among them Leontyne Price, Mattiwilda Dobbs, Martina Arroyo and Grace Bumbry. The net has been cast wide: even Grace Moore had her chance, before the true vehicle for her talent was discovered to be better suited to the sound film.

The list of native operas which have been attempted may make depressing reading, but it is reasonably long.

The Civic Opera House Chicago The War Memorial Opera House San Francisco

The Chicago Civic Opera House is no thing of beauty, as the illustration shows. But just as the city of Chicago itself cannot be ignored, in any national American context, neither can its opera, in the context of American opera houses. Here we may consider opera in Chicago as a kind of pendant to opera at the Met., because the Chicago Grand Opera Company, formed at the end of 1909, was the direct outcome of the Hammerstein/Kahn struggle which had ended in that year with Hammerstein, richer by $1,200,000, closing down his Manhattan Opera House. The whole episode was what we should now call a 'package deal'. The Met. could not afford Hammerstein's continuing competition in New York. At the same time, it aspired to extend its activities to other cities and saw Chicago as 'an opening wedge in the great West'. Three of the backers of the new Grand Opera – W.K. Vanderbilt, Otto Kahn and Clarence Mackay – were directors of the Met. The other eleven were all from Chicago, and included Samuel Insull, Charles G. Dawes and Julius Rosenwald. Early in 1910, Hammerstein offered to sell to the Met. his opera house in Philadelphia. This proved the key to the transaction. The Chicago-Philadelphia Grand Opera Company acquired all Hammerstein's rights and took over the contracts of many of his artists. Hammerstein undertook to produce no opera in New York, Philadelphia, Boston or Chicago for the next ten years. Andreas Dippel was released from an uncomfortable position at the Met. as 'associate director' with Gatti-Casazza, and took over at Chicago, with Cleofonte Campanini as chief conductor. Three years later Dippel resigned, leaving the field clear to Campanini, and the New York stockholders disposed of their interest. The home of the Chicago Company was the Auditorium, opened in 1892, with a display of the particular brand of ostentatious opulence which was part of the city's hallmark (the other side of the coin, of course, was the wretchedness of the immigrant population employed in the stockyards).

In 1915 the Company went bankrupt and was promptly re-formed under the name of the Chicago Opera Association, with Campanini still at the helm. He died in 1919, and from 1922 to 1923 the singer Mary Garden was in charge, coining for herself the title of 'Director'. She managed to achieve a quite staggering loss, even for the taste of the Chicago plutocracy, who through this period contributed an annual guarantee fund of $100,000. Yet the work of the Company was of a sufficiently high quality to make the Met. recognize it as something of a menace whenever they gave a season in New York. A slightly bizarre fact is that Prokofiev's opera *The Love of the Three Oranges* had its world première in Chicago in 1921, and they included it in the repertory of their final New York season, the composer himself conducting.

155 (*Opposite above*) Mary Garden, the Scottish-born soprano singer who created the rôle of Debussy's Mélisande. She became a member of the Chicago Opera Company in 1910 and for one seaon (1921–22) its manager. She is seen here in Carmen costume.
155a (*Opposite below*) The interior of the Chicago Civic Opera House.

Two dominating personalities in Chicago during the 1920s were Al Capone and Samuel Insull. The former concentrated on the organization of vice and racketeering, the latter on public utilities: transport, lighting, heating, and so on. He had backed the Opera from its earliest days, as we have seen, and in 1924 he took the chairmanship. Once again the Company changed its name and became the Chicago Civic Opera. He built it a new home in a skyscraper block. It occupied the first six floors, and he calculated that thirty-eight out of the thirty-nine remaining floors would provide enough in office rents to cover the annual deficit. The top floor he kept for himself. It was called 'Insull's throne', or 'Insull's armchair'. There was a spectacular opening night, with eight squads of detectives to protect the patrons and their jewels. The Wall Street crash had occurred six days earlier, but it did not topple the Insull throne until 1932, when Mr Insull's affairs took him to Paris, and from there on to Greece, which by a fortunate chance had no extradition treaty with America . . .

And that was that. But only for the time being. Chicago is nothing if not resilient. Its appetite for

opera is demonstrably voracious, and the bigger
the bankruptcy, the greater the challenge. By 1933
a new company – The Chicago Grand Opera
Company – was in being, and opened a spectacular five weeks' season with Jeritza playing Tosca.
Soon after that came *Turandot*, with Rosa Raisa,
who had created the rôle at La Scala in 1926. A
whole series of seasons, diminishing sharply in
brilliance as the war progressed, finally ground to
an indigent halt in 1946. For the next eight years
there were only sporadic attempts at opera, the
first of which foundered before it ever reached the
footlights, and has no claim on history but the
melancholy, if unique one, of having left Maria
Callas stranded. In 1954, however, a remarkable
woman, Carol Fox, got things going again with
yet another new company, the Lyric Theater of
Chicago, and brought off a number of spectacular
coups, such as signing up both Callas and Tebaldi
for the same season. These were exciting years
musically, and the rather unpleasant social overtones that had been part and parcel of Chicago in
the past, gradually became muted, if not entirely
stilled. Something of the gilt has worn off the
venture now, but Insull's throne has not collapsed,
and for all its un-Italian atmosphere, the opera
house remains host to what might be almost
described as an Italian company in exile, with a
faithful, if less bejewelled clientèle.

There remains only a footnote to the whole
subject: Chicago opera provided the occasion for
Orson Welles's first appearance on any stage – as
Madama Butterfly's unfortunate offspring.

San Francisco must be the only city in the world that has an opera house for its war memorial. This is not to be taken as a symptom of light-mindedness among the San Franciscans. It is a sober building, forming part of a civic complex. It seats 3,285 people, with standing room for 700. The capacity of the orchestral pit is 75, though the space for that number of players is in fact a little confined. It was opened in 1932, after being ten years in the building. It has a record of achievement which is outstanding and which has its origin in the foundation of the San Francisco Opera Association in 1922.

The two men who have raised it to its present eminence are Gaetano Merola and Kurt Adler, formerly his assistant and now his successor. Merola died in 1953 at the age of seventy-four. The climate in which he started was certainly favourable. San Francisco had a long tradition of zest for opera. As far back as 1854 there were eleven theatres in which opera was performed. At the old Civic Opera House alone there had been 800 performances in the 1860s and 1,000 in the 1880s. A press description of the opera audience in 1872 has all the ring of truth – and universality – about it:

> In the stalls . . . the Germans and Italians who know their opera; in the dress circle the élite, resplendent in silks, laces and diamonds, the splendour of which latter emulates the glories of the great chandelier when in full blaze . . . interspersed are the solid people. . . . In the pit the Dutchmen. . . . Up in the galleries the red-shirted, black-bearded [Italian] fishermen.

Patti appeared with Mapleson's company in 1884 and enjoyed the kind of reception to which she was accustomed. She was there again in 1889, when her performance as Gounod's 'Juliette' moved one critic to describe her voice as 'soft, yet vibrant and far-reaching, voluptuous, yet chaste – as if somehow a rose might be a throat'. On the night of 18 April 1906, Caruso, with the company from the Met., was singing superbly in *Carmen* just five hours before the infamous earthquake. In 1926 the Chicago company, under Mary Garden's directorship, came to San Francisco, and in a two-week season at the Auditorium sang to a total audience of eighty-five thousand. Already in 1912 the idea of a new opera house in the civic centre had been mooted, and now the acoustical inadequacy of the Auditorium lent impetus to the project.

Of the opening on 15 October 1932, the press triumphantly proclaimed, 'Our city has at last . . . the only municipally owned opera house in America . . . probably the finest opera house in the world' (the qualifying 'probably' was certainly no less than prudent). The first work to be performed was *Tosca*, with Claudia Muzio, Dino Borgioli and Alfredo Gandolfi leading the cast. In the same season Lily Pons got ten curtain calls for her Lucia and a matinée performance had to be relayed to the Auditorium and the City Hall Plaza, so great was the demand to hear her. Perhaps Merola's two greatest contributions were his fearlessness in engaging highly paid singers and the determination with which he enlarged the repertory. In 1935 he gave a complete *Ring* cycle, with a cast that included Flagstad, Rethberg and Schorr. For this the orchestral pit was too small and part of the orchestra had to be accommodated under the stage. Bodanzky conducted, and was not entirely happy. Afterwards he called down the vials of San Franciscan wrath on his head by describing the audience as 'unsophisticated'. On Merola's death, Adler was at once appointed artistic director. Then, in 1956 he was promoted to musical director as well, and in 1957 to general director. He has been responsible for the American débuts of Leonie Rysanek, Birgit Nilsson, Oralia Dominguez and Boris Christoff. In 1955 he put on Walton's *Troilus and Cressida*, with Leinsdorf conducting, in 1957 Poulenc's *Dialogues des Carmélites*, in 1959 the American première of *Die Frau ohne Schatten*, in 1960 *Wozzeck*, with Geraint Evans singing the title rôle – one of his greatest achievements – for the first time. There were thirty-two-and-a-half hours of rehearsal for this production. The normal length of season is five or six weeks, in the early autumn, so that San Francisco does not clash with New York in bidding for singers.

156 (*Opposite above*) The American première of *Die Frau ohne Schatten* at San Francisco in 1959, with Sebastian Feiersinger, Mino Yahia, Marianne Schech, Irene Dalis and Mark Elyn. The conductor was Leopold Ludwig.

156a (*Opposite below*) The War Memorial Opera House, San Francisco.

ARGENTINA

El Teatro Colón
Buenos Aires

Buenos Aires was already a self-reliant and growing city when the Spanish colonial régime collapsed in 1810. Theatre had existed there for some years, and one of the symbols of confidence in an independent future which followed the revolution of 25 May was the establishment of an opera house. This was achieved despite a civil war which only ended with the birth of the Argentine Republic in 1816. In Argentina, as elsewhere, the operatic currency of the day was the Italian repertory, and all through the troubled years in which the Spaniards were still contesting their suzerainty over vast South American territories, an indefatigable musician, Juan Antonio Picasarri – pianist, singer and orchestral conductor – was paving the way for the introduction of that repertory. But Santiago Massoni, Italian orchestral conductor, and the Spanish tenor Mariano Pablo Rosquellas were really the parents of opera in Buenos Aires, and their first-born was *Il Barbiere di Siviglia*, performed in 1825, followed until 1830 by eight Rossini operas and works by Mozart (*Don Giovanni*), Zingarelli, Puccitta, Dalayrac and Mercadante.

From 1830 to 1848, during the dictatorial government of Juan Manuel de Rosas, there were no complete opera performances in Buenos Aires, but by the 1850s Italian and French companies were giving as many as thirty premières in one season, and in 1854 there were thirty-four. The people of Buenos Aires were more hungry for this art form than for any other. Their city was on the way to becoming a world capital, and a world capital in the nineteenth century demanded an opera house in which world-class singers would not be ashamed to appear.

So it came about that the first Teatro Colón, with a seating capacity of 2,500, was completed in 1856 and opened the following year. The work chosen for the inaugural evening was *La Traviata*. Violetta was sung by Sofia Lorini and Alfredo by Enrico Tamberlick. Tamberlick, then thirty-seven, was approaching the height of his powers. He had made his début in Naples in 1841 and was currently under contract to the Royal Italian Opera in London, remaining a member of that company until 1864. But he was, however distinguished, only a visitor to Buenos Aires. Another tenor, who perhaps made a more lasting impression, was Luis Lelmi. He came from Rio de Janeiro, in 1859, also as a visitor – and stayed eleven years. It may be seen from this that the Italian company was now well established. Indeed, in 1860–1 it undertook a tour of the provinces and of Uruguay, visiting places hitherto right off the operatic map. The greatest season of the first Teatro Colón was that of 1888, when Adelina Patti and Francesco Tamagno both appeared. This was just a year after Tamagno had created the rôle of Otello at La Scala, Milan. And *Otello* was the work with which

157 The circle at the old, or, as it was called, 'primitive' Colón in 1862.

158 Playbill for the opening performance at the present Colón in 1908.

GRAN APERTURA
DEL
TEATRO DE COLON.

COMPAÑIA DEL SEÑOR LORINI.

HOY SABADO 25 DE ABRIL.

La ópera del célebre maestro Verdi, en tres actos.—

La Traviata.

El rol de VIOLETA por la SRA. LORINI.
El de ALFREDO por el SR. TAMBERLICK.

A las siete y media en punto.

Nota. La Boletería se abrirá hoy á las 12 del día.

the *primitivo* Colón ended its life, for such was the proved passion of the citizens for opera that it had already outlived its usefulness. Demolition began immediately, the important site being destined for the new headquarters of the Banco de la Nación Argentina.

The foundation stone of a new opera house was laid in 1889, with appropriate ceremony and a hymn specially composed for the occasion by Marino Mancinelli. Nineteen years were to elapse before the new Colón opened its doors and during this period the cultural centre shifted to the Teatro de la Opera. For Buenos Aires to have been deprived of opera altogether would have been unthinkable. There were many delays and many changes of plan, as was only to be expected with so grand a project, in a city whose population (three quarters of a million before the end of the century) was expanding year by year. The general

conception was agreed from the first: the building was to be Renaissance in style and the opera houses of Vienna, Paris, Munich and Frankfurt were to be studied for every lesson they could teach. The architect chosen was Tamburini, to be assisted by his pupil Victor Meano. Even from the moment they were named, the two men were subjected to a barrage of criticism. The building of an opera house, like the conduct of foreign policy, is a subject in which many people judge themselves expert and there were – as also in the case of foreign policy – many vested interests to be weighed against each other. In 1900 it was still not too late for the plans to be entirely revised. Then, in 1904, there was a wholly gratuitous and tragic further set-back: Meano was murdered. Following his master Tamburini, he was the most gifted architect practising in Argentina, and he was working at the same time on another giant

159 Erich Kleiber and the Colón orchestra after a rehearsal in 1926.

160 The 1931 production of *Il Barbiere di Siviglia*. A characteristically distinguished international cast including (from left to right) Galeffi, Pinza, Schipa, Pons and Baccazoni.

project: the Palace of Congress. It was a stunning blow. Yet the man who succeeded him left his own distinctive mark on Buenos Aires perhaps more memorably than Meano might have done. His name was Julio Dormal. Belgian by birth, he had studied architecture in Paris and engineering at Liège. He went to Argentina in 1869, when he was twenty-three. His first commission was to build a meat extract factory in Puerto Ruiz and thereafter he made rapid strides. It was he who conceived the idea of the new, fashionable suburb of Palermo, built on a reclaimed swamp, who designed the Jockey Club Hippodrome at San Isidro, and it was he who gave to the newly emerging capital of the Republic – by now growing enormously wealthy – something of that aura of Paris which it retains to this day. Rio de Janeiro may be more spectacular, more lurid, but Buenos

Aires, immensely cosmopolitan, is exciting and varied in just the same way that Paris is: a marvellous place to be young in, a marvellous place to be rich in, a marvellous place to have friends in. Of course, Dormal's architecture is but one contributory factor to this. But because of his association it is worth emphasizing here.

The opening of the new house on 25 May 1908, was as much an occasion for national rejoicing as the closure of the old in 1888 had been for nostalgia. Even the National Anthem was encored. The work was *Aida*, with Crestani as Aida, Verger as Amneris, Bassi as Radames, Bellantoni as Amonasro and Arimondi as Ramfis. Luigi Mancinelli conducted. It was not the greatest of international casts, but it was a distinguished one. And in any case, the real star on this occasion was the house itself. The Colón is the last and greatest of the

161 Maria Callas as Puccini's cruel Princess Turandot in 1949.

opera houses built in the European tradition of the eighteenth and nineteenth centuries. Rich, sumptuous, luxurious: these are the adjectives that spring to mind, and to that first night audience it must have appeared an achievement of breathtaking splendour. The seating capacity is 2,500 – in comfort. But when crammed from stalls to gallery it will take 4,000. There is even a circle of wrought-iron grilled boxes below the level of the stalls, from which in an earlier social climate ladies in mourning could see without being seen. The auditorium appears at once huge and intimate, and the acoustics are perfect. All the backstage facilities are of the same scale and quality. These are the reasons why, from 1908 onwards, it has proved irresistibly attractive to singers, conductors, producers and designers. Provided the performance is good it is irresistible to audiences as well. The Buenos Aires audience is discriminating and will not put up with the second-rate. At the same time, it is capable of generous enthusiasm. And it is a young audience. The cheapest seats are within any youngster's reach, and it is the measure of their response which helps to make or mar a performance. The expensive seats have never proved too expensive for the well-to-do and cultured. But if the production is bad they stay away.

In that first season of 1908 there were 77 performances of 17 operas. Boito's *Mefistofele*, with Chaliapin, had the largest number (seven), Thomas's *Hamlet*, *Tristan und Isolde*, *Il Barbiere di Siviglia*, *La Gioconda* and *Il Trovatore* six each. Mozart has never become popular. The season finished in mid-September. This remained the pattern for many years, though now it both opens in mid-April and finishes in early November. Operas were sung in Italian. From 1909 onwards it was customary to give some orchestral concerts during the season. Ballet was introduced in 1913 and now plays an important (but subsidiary) part in the life of the theatre. In 1913 the famous Diaghilev Company astonished the New World just as they had astonished the Old. For the first sixteen years the Colón was operated by concessionaires, not always the best medium for achieving a consistently high artistic level. Even in that first season some productions were distinctly better than others, while in the second season the emphasis could be placed the other way round: some were distinctly worse. Lack of adequate rehearsal was the prevailing lament. But in 1912 Toscanini prepared fifteen out of the seventeen works produced, the two exceptions being Massenet's *Werther* and Gounod's *Roméo et Juliette*. Six years earlier he had made operatic history in Buenos Aires by abandoning a performance of *La Traviata* at the Teatro de la Opera half-way through, rather than yield to the demands of the audience for an encore.

In 1913, the veteran conductor Luigi Mancinelli, who was still held in enormous esteem, conducted *Lohengrin*, *La Sonnambula*, *Un Ballo in Maschera*, *Salome*, *Il Barbiere di Siviglia*, *Oberon*, *Götterdämmerung* and *Die Meistersinger*, while in 1914, Tullio Serafin conducted at the Colón for the first time. The season's repertory that year included the first performance at the Colón of *Parsifal*, though it had been heard the year before at the Teatro Coliseo. In 1916 the first performances in the French language were given, with Saint-Saëns conducting his own *Samson et Dalila*. In response to popular feeling and diplomatic tightrope-walking the performance of German works, even in Italian, was forbidden in 1918 and 1919, though with the illogicality typical of such affairs, there was no similar proscription of German symphonic works: the artistic conscience always functions rather arbitrarily under the stress of war! But by 1922 sanity had been restored and the *Ring* tetralogy, and also *Parsifal*, were given in their own language, under the baton of Weingartner.

1923 and 1924 marked the peak of the first phase of the Colón's history. They were truly international seasons of a high order, and in 1924 *Boris Godunov*, *The Queen of Spades* and *Prince Igor* were all added to the repertory in the Russian language. During this first period, moreover, fourteen operas by Argentinian composers had been presented. But the epoch was not to end without one of those excursions into the ridiculous common to all opera houses. In 1923 the administration declared that *Elektra* was too short to constitute value for money in the case of those members of the audience who were subscription ticket holders. The composer declined to agree, left Buenos Aires, and three performances were given with three unlikely prologues in turn – *Ilse*, *I Compagnacci*, and the prologue to *Mefistofele*. Strauss himself conducted the three other performances, without the addition of the *hors d'oeuvres*, which have proved less than immortal.

From 1925 onwards, the Colón enjoyed a permanent status: its opera company, ballet company, chorus and two orchestras (some four hundred performers in all) became regular, continuing organizations, as they remain today, and responsibility for the whole undertaking was transferred to the municipality, working through an administrative commission. In 1931 this commission, as an intermediate body, was dispensed with and from then on the artistic directorate was appointed by, and responsible to, the municipality. The theatre's fortunes have inevitably varied according to the prevailing political circumstances, economic circumstances, and the mutual compatibility or incompatibility of those immediately charged with the conduct of its artistic affairs. Compatibility of temperament can produce great results in an opera house. Political or financial pressures from outside inevitably impoverish standards. But the Colón's history, taken all in all, has been a brilliant one. Some of the most illustrious composers, conductors and singers of the past sixty years have tasted its hospitality, and none is better remembered than Sir Thomas Beecham, in what was to be his last season in any opera house (it was also the 50th anniversary of the theatre's opening), who conducted an outstanding series of performances that included *Otello*, *Carmen*, *Samson et Dalila*, *Fidelio* and *Die Zauberflöte*. The Colón has experienced everything and it is surely not imaginary to say that the sheer beauty of the house itself, its warmth, its dignity, its splendid trappings, have enabled it to survive bad times and enhance good ones.

AUSTRALIA

The Opera House Sydney

Here is an opera house whose history dates back to 1954, but which has not as yet witnessed the production of a single opera. That is scheduled for 1973. Nineteen years may seem a long time to wait, but they have been years packed with drama – most of it the drama of municipal politics. Conceived by the Danish architect Jørn Utzorn, a fair element in the Sydney Opera House's inspiration is clearly the desire to astonish. This it has certainly done, because neither Sydney nor anywhere else has seen anything quite like it before. How far its agglomeration of shell-like roofs will add to or detract from anything that goes on underneath them is still a matter of conjecture. The only certainties are that the building has cost a great deal more money than was ever intended to be spent on it and has excited a degree of controversy rare even in the world of opera.

It is more than an opera house alone. It is a complex of buildings which include the opera theatre (capacity: 1,500), a drama theatre (capacity: 600), a cinema, which can also be used for the performance of chamber music (capacity: 450), and a concert hall (capacity: 2,800). And there is a large area set aside for exhibitions as well as a room for recitals or receptions which will take about 150 people.

The situation is superb: a peninsula close to the famous Sydney Harbour bridge, called Bennelong Point, after an aboriginal couple who lived in a cottage there nearly two centuries ago. A fort was built on it in 1817, the guns of which were happily only ever called upon to fire ceremonial salutes. For the half-century before the opera house idea took shape, this fort had been rather ignominiously adapted for use as a tramway depot. How infinitely preferable an opera house! And how appropriate considering the worth of Australia's contribution to the Arts!

162 and 163 (*Opposite above and below left*) Sydney Opera House.
164 (*Opposite below right*) Peter Sculthorpe, whose commissioned work *Rites of Passage* (for which he is his own librettist) will open the Sydney Opera House in 1973. Sculthorpe, like such painters as Sidney Nolan and Russell Drysdale, seems to possess an intense awareness of Australia's pre-history and ethnology.

Notes

1 Beautiful Italy,
   At last I greet you, at last I greet you . . .
   Ah! 'Tis heaven that has made you,
   Beautiful Italy, here on earth.

2 A lamp with a tubular wick, invented by the Swiss physician and chemist Aimé Argand (1755–1803).

3 That delicious Viennese whipped cream confection.

4 His real name was Nicolas but he changed it for the more 'glamourous' one of Victor.

5 Thy wonder, thy name, thine image itself O Louis, Bordeaux with utmost pride, at once salutes them all.

6 It was very nice . . . I enjoyed it very much.

7 In 1786 she had created the rôle of Susanna in Mozart's *Le Nozze di Figaro* at the Imperial Theatre, Vienna.

8 Beecham avers that the singing of Gilibert brought tears to his eyes. It would be interesting to know the occasion of this improbable and doubtless traumatic experience.

9 Yet eventually, as conductor of the London Philharmonic Orchestra, Beecham was to be made a Commandor of the Legion of Honour, on a brilliant occasion in that very place, shortly before the outbreak of the Second World War.

10 He had had longer than they to get used to the idea, which first began to take shape in 1928 with concerts in the organ room. Wagner was at that time his ruling musical passion, and a performance in the organ room of Act III, scene i, of *Die Meistersinger* put ideas into his head. It is curious that the opera house (leading out of the organ room) which was opened six years later, has proved too small for any opera by Wagner ever to be performed there.

11 There are, however, two other recent operas which have been heard elsewhere: *Drömmen om Thérèse* and *Resan*, both by Lars-Johan Werle.

12 'Faster, faster, signorina.'
   'Maestro, you ought to conduct at the speed I sing. I'm a star.'
   'Signorina, the stars are in the heavens. Here we are all artists, good or bad. You're a bad artist.'

13 At a *Rienzi* performance in 1886 this lady had been reported as wearing black '. . . and her enormous diamond star – which, I understand, weights more than Bradley Martin himself – flashed rays of light across the house.'

Index